4 Gardens IN ONE

THE ROYAL BOTANIC GARDEN
EDINBURGH

4 Gardens IN ONE

THE ROYAL BOTANIC GARDEN EDINBURGH

DENI BOWN

EDITED BY

ALAN P BENNELL AND NORMA M GREGORY

For PJ, with all my love.
"These beautiful days must enrich all my life.
They do not exist as mere pictures ... but they
saturate themselves into every part of the body
and live always."
(John Muir: *My First Summer in the Sierra*)

Deni Bown has been a gardener and botanist all her life, starting with a childhood fascination for her grandfather's lilies and tulips, and a passion for wild flowers. After a varied career in horticulture - running an organic smallholding, growing orchids and working to establish Hollington Herbs - she took to the camera and word processor, specialising in botany, gardening and natural history. Her other books include *Aroids - Plants of the Arum Family* (Century Hutchinson/Timber Press, 1988); *Fine Herbs, a plantsman's herbal* (Unwin Hyman, 1989); *Alba - the Book of White Flowers* (Unwin Hyman/Timber Press, 1989); and *Westonbirt Arboretum* (Julian Holland Publishing, 1990). She was a prizewinner in the BBC Wildlife Photographer of the Year Competition in 1986 and her photographs appear in a wide range of magazines and books.
Deni works as a freelance writer and photographer from her home in Milton Keynes.

Frontispiece
The Royal Botanic Garden Edinburgh is most famous as a world centre for rhododendrons.
This Himalayan species, *Rhododendron cinnabarinum* subsp. *cinnabarinum*,
is one of the loveliest and is grown to perfection at Younger Botanic Garden.

© Crown copyright 1992
First published 1992
ISBN 1 872291 08 2

Designed by Graham Galloway
HMSO Graphic Design Edinburgh

Origination by Centre Graphics Limited Livingston

Printed in the UK for HMSO by (10111) Dd 0287511 C10 11/92

CONTENTS

ACKNOWLEDGEMENTS

Over the 18 months of writing and taking the photographs for *4 Gardens in One*, I relied on the co-operation of members of staff in all walks of Botanic Garden life. I would therefore like to thank everyone who helped in whatever way - above all David Ingram, the Regius Keeper, whose enthusiastic support is keenly appreciated.

Firstly, I should acknowledge that the idea for this book, and initial development, came from Julian Holland, publisher of my earlier book on Westonbirt Arboretum.

Inevitably, certain members of the Royal Botanic Garden's staff deserve special mention for going well beyond the bounds of duty in their willingness to assist. First and foremost, thanks to Alan Bennell, Head of the Public Services Department, and Norma Gregory, Publications Manager, who masterminded all meetings and sustained the close communication, eye for detail, and overview that is needed for such a project. In addition, they accommodated me with the caring and generosity of friends. (And thanks also to Frances Bennell and Steve Gregory, for adding their warm welcomes to those of their spouses.) Thanks too to the scientific staff, who were patient in guiding me through the intricacies of their research programmes; and the librarians, who were always attentive in providing archival material promptly. The photographic side of the book made even larger demands, as I had to cover a great deal of ground, literally and metaphorically, often in changeable weather, and with never enough time. The Curator, Assistant Curators and their staff were unfailingly diligent in helping me get to know such large and complex gardens, and locate specific subjects - with an especial mention for Ian Sinclair, Garden Supervisor at the Younger Botanic Garden, whose passion for the place and the plants echoes so much of the Garden's history.

ILLUSTRATIONS

With the exception of those listed below, all the photographs in this book were taken by the author. The Royal Botanic Garden's own photographic collection was used extensively in chapters one and two. The Garden's photographers who have contributed to this book are Sidney Clarke and Debbie White and their predecessors Ross Eudall and Ken Grant.

RBGE: 2, 3, 6, 8 top, 9 bottom left, 9 bottom right, 10, 11, 12 ,13, 14, 15, 16 top left, 18, 19, 20, 21, 24 bottom, 25, 27, 28, 29, 33, 34, 35, 36, 37, 38, 39, 40, 41, 44 top, 47, 48, 49, 53, 54, 55, 56, 57, 61, 62, 63, 64, 90, 112 left, 119 right, 128 right, 129, 151 top, 153, 154 right, 155 left, 170, 177, 181 top left, 186 left, 193, 194; George Argent: 45 top; Col A N Balfour: 179 top; Brinsley Burbidge: 18; Ian Darwin Edwards: 66, 69; Martin Gardner: 32; Sir Nigel and Lady Henderson: 154, 155 left; David Long: 31, 42, 51; Phil Lusby: 44, 68; Ron McBeath: 30, 45 bottom; David Mann: 52; Tony Miller: 13 left, 43; National Library of Scotland: 4; Photoair of Peterborough: 128 right, 177; Jimmy Ratter: 65; Maureen Warwick: 41 right; Younger Family Archive: 129, 151 top.

The colour relief maps of all four gardens (pages 200-207) were prepared by David Mason ARIAS.

FOREWORD

The Royal Botanic Garden Edinburgh is a scientific institution dedicated to the study of plants and fungi. And its work is vitally important, for plants and fungi are of fundamental significance to the daily lives of every one of us, as primary sources of food and medicines, as essential components of all natural communities and as sources of great beauty and colour in an often ugly world.

Botanic gardens like this one, as major centres for the study of plants and fungi, thus have a major role to play in the years ahead - in research, in conservation and in education in its widest sense. The rich and varied collections of living plants in the glasshouses and gardens at Inverleith, Benmore, Dawyck and Logan, of preserved plants and fungi in the Herbarium and of books in the Library are at the heart of the Garden's activities. They have the status of 'biological standards' and, together with the deep knowledge and skills of the staff, provide a unique resource for the Garden's work.

This book tells the story of that work, a story stretching back for more than three hundred years. During that time the Garden has adapted its role many times to meet the changing needs of society, and it is in a period of such change even now. As plant science increasingly focuses on cellular and sub-cellular processes, there is at present a greater need than at any other time in the history of the Garden for the knowledge and skills of those here and in other botanic gardens around the world who know and understand the biology of whole plants and fungi - how they grow and the details of their classification, evolution, ecology and conservation. Without such resources all efforts to harness the new technologies of cell biology to extend the frontiers of scientific knowledge and to improve the world's food supply will be impoverished. Moreover, with the increasing power of the human species to modify or destroy the natural world, with irrevocable consequences that will affect us all, this and other botanic gardens can provide the information and understanding that must underpin all efforts to debate and try to solve the key botanical issues of our time: the conservation of the world's resources of habitats and germplasm, the control of environmental pollution and the release of genetically engineered species into agriculture and the feeding of the growing populations of the planet. During the coming decades the work of botanic gardens, including the Royal Botanic Garden Edinburgh, thus has the potential to affect the quality of life for everyone well into the 21st century. What a responsibility - and what an exciting challenge for us all.

This book about the Royal Botanic Garden Edinburgh results from the dedicated and sensitive research and writing of Deni Bown. Above all, however, it is a tribute to all of the Staff and Students of the Garden, past and present, whose story it relates. I hope that, like me, you will enjoy reading it, for it is not only the stuff of a great history, but is a pointer to an exciting and vital future.

DAVID INGRAM
Regius Keeper

The Royal Botanic Garden Edinburgh began in the 17th century on a plot of ground no bigger than a tennis court. The original garden was founded by two doctors, Andrew Balfour and Robert Sibbald, in the days when botany was part and parcel of medicine. Both graduated at Scottish universities, then studied on the Continent. They met in Edinburgh in the late 1660s and soon joined forces to reform the medical profession, whose members lagged woefully behind their European counterparts in terms of scientific learning and skills. To this end, Sibbald leased a piece of land in 1670 for the cultivation of medicinal herbs so that the study of plants could be introduced into the medical students' curriculum.

The embryo botanic garden (or physic garden as it was then called because of its use by physicians) was situated in St Anne's Yards, Holyrood. Within six years it outgrew its bounds and a second plot was acquired, this time adjoining Trinity Hospital. Further expansion took place in 1684 to include Trinity College Kirkyard, but both sites eventually proved inadequate and in 1763 they were abandoned in favour of a 5-acre site at Leith Walk. This in turn was outgrown and between 1820 and 1823 the garden was moved yet again to its present site at Inverleith.

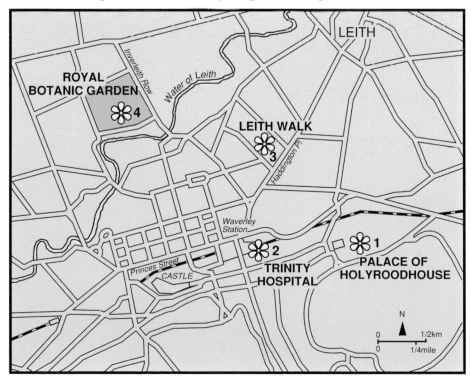

Opposite. The magnificent Temperate Palm House opened in 1858 is the tallest in Britain.

Throughout its history, the Garden has occupied several sites within Scotland's capital city.

Robert Sibbald.

Below left. A plate from Sibbald's *Scotia Illustrata* (1684). The plant in the upper right hand corner is the eponymous *Sibbaldia procumbens*.

Below right. An early plan showing the site of the first Botanic Garden at Holyrood.

Major expansion continued into the 20th century with the development of additional gardens: the Younger Botanic Garden Benmore, near Dunoon, Argyll, in 1929; Logan Botanic Garden, Wigtownshire, in 1969; and Dawyck Botanic Garden, southwest of Peebles, in 1978.

The Beginnings (1670)

There are only three botanic gardens in Great Britain which date back to the 17th century: Oxford (1621), Edinburgh (1670) and the Chelsea Physic Garden (1673). (Kew, the country's only other Royal Botanic Garden, began in 1759.) Edinburgh is, however, second to none in its history of dramatic changes and continued growth. The story of the Royal Botanic Garden Edinburgh is, from its beginnings to the present day, one which is as much about people as it is about plants and places. Indeed, the directions taken over the centuries, in terms of both collections and locations, closely reflect the particular interests of those associated with the Gardens. The Director, with the title of Regius Keeper indicating that this is a Crown appointment, has always exerted the greatest influence, although the curators (heads of garden staff), who were directly responsible for the living collections, have had considerable impact too. Plant collectors have also played a significant role, from early explorers who covered vast and often unexplored regions of the globe, to colonial expatriates and 20th-century scientists with more specific areas of study. And lastly, there is the general public and society as a whole, whose needs are served through the Royal Botanic Garden's fourfold purpose concerning the world of plants: research, conservation, education and amenity.

The founding fathers, Balfour and Sibbald, were eminent physicians. Andrew Balfour (1630-94) was the first doctor in Scotland to dissect the human body. He was a man of great learning and his library of over 3000 volumes and his collection of scientific artefacts - which included everything from fossils to surgical instruments - were among the finest in the kingdom. Robert Sibbald (1641-1715) graduated from Edinburgh University when only 18 and went on to become its first Professor of Medicine. He was appointed royal physician, geographer and natural historian to Charles II, who commissioned him to produce *Scotia Illustrata* - an account of the geography, archaeology and flora of Scotland. Both Balfour and Sibbald were knighted in 1682 for their outstanding contributions to science and society.

The original garden in St Anne's Yards, which measured 40ft (c. 12m) square, was

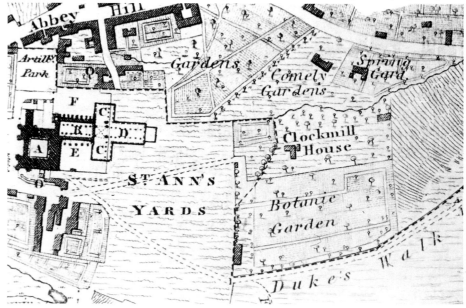

largely stocked with plants obtained from Patrick Murray, Laird of Livingston in West Lothian. This young aristocrat had a passion for natural history and the resources to indulge it. He travelled widely and amassed a collection of nearly 1000 plants which were subsequently handed over to Balfour to form the nucleus of Edinburgh's botanic garden.

James Sutherland: the first Regius Keeper (1699-1715)

The day-to-day task of maintaining the Garden was given to James Sutherland, 'a youth, who, by his owne industry, had attained great knowledge of the plants' and who, for almost 40 years, contributed greatly to the development of the garden. Under Sutherland's care the original garden flourished to such an extent that in 1675 the Town Council leased him a second garden attached to Trinity Hospital. It was significantly larger than the first, measuring some 300ft (91.5m) by 190ft (58m) - totalling approximately one acre - and was bisected by the drainage channel of the Nor' Loch (a marsh to the north of 17th-century Edinburgh, now occupied by Princes Street Gardens). Both sides were divided into plots. They included systematic beds (that is, plants arranged in families, genera and species according to a system of classification), ornamental flower beds, medicinal plants in alphabetical order, aquatic plants, and a small arboretum and nursery. The city wall ran along one side, supporting shrubs and climbers, together with frames for rare specimens. In all, the Trinity Hospital garden housed about 2000 plants and in 1684 was extended to include Trinity College Kirkyard.

In addition to managing the two botanic gardens at St Anne's Yard and at Trinity Hospital, Sutherland also planted the Town College garden, mostly with herbs, and took over the running of the private Royal Garden at Holyrood Palace in which he grew a variety of herbs, vegetables and 'fine exetick forraign plants', such as melons and citrus fruits. Arguably it was this curatorship of the Royal Garden that first established the title Regius Keeper.

In 1689 disaster struck when the dam between the Nor' Loch and its drainage channel was breached as a strategic move during the siege of Edinburgh Castle and the Trinity garden was severely damaged by flooding. The residue - a thick layer of mud and waste from the city's drains - took a whole season to clear and a great many plants were lost. There was a further setback in 1699 when sheep broke through the dilapidated walls and ate most of the plants, whereafter Sutherland turned away

Above. An 18th century engraving of Edinburgh. Trinity Hospital, the second of the Botanic Garden's sites is in the foreground.

Below left. This plaque commemorating the Botanic Garden is on the site of the former Trinity Hospital, now within Waverley Station.

Below right. Hortus Medicus Edinburgensis, the first listing of all the plants grown in the Botanic Garden, was produced by James Sutherland in 1683. The aim of this catalogue was to encourage the "Interchange of Plants, which They can spare and I want, with others which They want and I can spare".

NEAR THIS SPOT FROM 1675 TO 1763
WAS THE EDINBURGH PHYSIC GARDEN,
ORIGINALLY FOUNDED AT HOLYROOD IN 1670
BY
SIR ROBERT SIBBALD AND SIR ANDREW BALFOUR, TWO OF
THE FOUNDERS OF THE ROYAL COLLEGE OF PHYSICIANS OF EDINBURGH.
THE GARDEN, UNDER THE CONTROL OF JAMES SUTHERLAND
THE FIRST REGIUS PROFESSOR OF BOTANY IN THE UNIVERSITY,
WAS THE DIRECT PREDECESSOR OF THE PRESENT
ROYAL BOTANIC GARDEN.

THIS PLAQUE WAS ERECTED IN 1978
BY
THE ROYAL COLLEGE OF PHYSICIANS OF EDINBURGH,
THE UNIVERSITY OF EDINBURGH AND THE
ROYAL BOTANIC GARDEN.

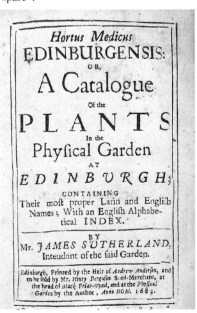

Hortus Medicus
EDINBURGENSIS:
OR,
A Catalogue
Of the
PLANTS
In the
Physical Garden
AT
EDINBURGH;
CONTAINING
Their most proper Latin and English
Names; With an English Alphabe-
tical INDEX.
BY
Mr. JAMES SUTHERLAND,
Intendant of the said Garden.

Edinburgh, Printed by the Heir of *Andrew Anderson*, and
to be sold by Mr. *Henry Ferguson* Seed-Merchant, at
the head of *Black Friar-Wynd*, and at the *Physical*
Garden by the Author, *Anno DOM.* 1683.

Above. The Garden's first Royal Warrant. James Sutherland's fame spread far and wide, and in 1699 he was appointed King's Botanist by William III.

Right. The text of the 1699 Royal Warrant.

William etc. Forasmuch as wee considering yt Mr James Sutherland has bein att great paines to sett up a physick Garden att Edinburgh and yt he hath for some tyme taught wt. good success ye knowledge of plants and has also brought into good order the garden about our palace of holyroodhouse and wee being willing in consideration yrof and for his further encouragmt. yrin to bestow a mark on him of our royall favor therfore witt yee us to have given granted and disponed Lyke as be these prnts we give grant and dispone to thesd, Mr James Sutherland a yearly pension of fiftie pound ster: dureing our pleasure only to pd to him out of the first and readiest of our rents revenues customs and casualities whatever our said Kingdome and yt att twa terms in the year Whit: and Martinmas be equall proportions Begining the first terms payt. att Whitsunday next to come and so furth to continue yearly and termly dureing ye space forsd Comanding hereby ye Lords Commissrs. of our Thesry and all receevers and collectors of our rents revenues customs and casualities qtever present or for the time being to readily answer and pay the forsd pension att ye terms above mentioned to ye sd Mr James quheranent these prnts shall be to all qcerned a sufficient warrant Given at our Court att Kensingtonune ye twelf Janry 1699 and of our reigne the tent year

from botany to his other passion, numismatics. In 1706 at the age of 67, after several reprimands from the authorities over his lack of attendance, Sutherland resigned from his post as Professor of Botany at the University - though he nominally retained those of Regius Keeper and King's Botanist. Despite this less than glorious departure, James Sutherland is remembered as the man who put the Royal Botanic Garden Edinburgh firmly on the map, initiating high standards of cultivation, education and international co-operation which were to become hallmarks of the institution. The genus *Sutherlandia*, a group of South African shrubs belonging to the pea family (Leguminosae) is named after him.

Sutherland's successors

In his academic appointment as Professor of Botany, Sutherland was succeeded in 1706 by Charles Preston (who in turn was followed by his brother, George) whereas his royal appointments only expired on the death of Queen Anne in 1714. So it was that when George I began his reign, Sutherland was replaced as King's Botanist by William Arthur. This period therefore saw a division in the teaching of botany between the Royal Botanic Garden and the University: a rivalry that continued until 1738 when the posts were again held by one man.

William Arthur must go down in history as the least successful of all the Royal Botanic Garden's Regius Keepers. A fervent Jacobite, his knowledge of botany is unrecorded. His chief claim to fame, which merits a mention in Sir Walter Scott's *Tales of a Grandfather*, was his involvement in an abortive plot to take Edinburgh Castle as part of the 1715 rebellion, after which he fled to Rome.

Though certainly more diligent in their duties than Arthur, the Preston brothers achieved little during their terms of office. Charles Preston was a well-to-do physician who had studied botany under James Sutherland. He was obviously highly regarded - the eminent botanist Robert Brown naming the genus *Prestonia* after him. However, he had little interest in the gardens, which became neglected, and he died in 1711 to be succeeded as Professor of Botany by his brother George.

George Preston worked as an apothecary, selling spices, sugar, tea, coffee, cocoa and 'drugs from the Indies' before taking up botany. Though little is known about his teaching capacity, he had a genuine interest in his post as Intendant of the Botanic Garden. (He was not, it should be noted, Regius Keeper or King's Botanist as these appointments were still held by Sutherland.) Having persuaded the Town Council to increase its financial support, he set about improving the drainage and repairing the walls. His greatest achievement was the construction in 1713 of the Botanic Garden's first glasshouse which measured 34ft (10.35m) by 16ft (4.9m). In a letter to James Petiver, an avid collector of natural history objects, he wrote that 'if you have any exotick or rare seeds to send ...... I am more capable to preserve them than my predecessors were by reason I have built a Greenhouse and provyded all other materials for preserving and cultivating plants.'

Unfortunately, George Preston's enthusiasm waned over the years and both his reputation and the state of the Garden deteriorated. He finally resigned in 1738.

Charles Alston: a new era (1716-60)

Charles Alston was made Regius Keeper in 1716 following the abrupt departure of William Arthur. When in 1738 he took over the Professorship of Botany from George Preston, he introduced courses in all branches of medicine. In addition, in his established role as Regius Keeper and King's Botanist, he taught botany to much higher standards, lecturing on materia medica (the study of drugs) in the winter, and botany in the Botanic Garden during the summer months.

The year 1738 is significant in the Royal Botanic Garden's history: from then until

Sutherlandia frutescens. This genus was named in honour of James Sutherland.

Above. Kay's cartoon depicts John Hope greeting one of his gardeners.

Below. The monument to Linnaeus, designed by famous Scottish architect Robert Adam, was erected by John Hope and can be seen behind the main glasshouse range.

1956, the University and Botanic Garden posts were held concurrently by the same person, forging strong links between the Garden's living and herbarium collections, and the University's role of research and teaching.

The city's Botanic Gardens at Trinity Hospital and St Anne's Yard, together with the Royal Garden at Holyrood, also thrived under Alston. He ensured that they were well maintained and expressed concern at the amount of pollution to which they were exposed. Indeed, he wanted to start a new garden on a better site but was unsuccessful in obtaining the necessary funds. Over the years he concentrated on the Trinity Hospital garden for teaching purposes and most of the improvements and additions were made there.

Charles Alston died in 1760 at the age of 75, after 44 years of service in which he realised his ambition of turning Edinburgh into one of Europe's finest centres of botanical learning. There were no dramatic changes but gradual and definite improvements were made.

John Hope and the move to Leith Walk

Although Charles Alston undoubtedly raised standards, it was his successor, John Hope, who presided over the next major changes in the Royal Botanic Garden's history.

John Hope began as a medical student at Edinburgh University, and through Alston's teaching became so keen that he temporarily abandoned medicine in order to study botany in Paris. Unlike the conservative Alston, John Hope became a great admirer of Linnaeus, the Swedish naturalist who revolutionised the system of naming and classifying living organisms. He was also excited by the scientific advances in botanical knowledge that took place throughout his lifetime. Improvements in microscopes and experimental techniques were revealing plants as complex living organisms, with the result that anatomy and physiology took their place in the curriculum beside the old disciplines of classification and materia medica.

When Hope succeeded Alston, his concern was to reflect the new knowledge in the teaching structure of the Botanic Garden and University. With the growing importance of botany as a science in its own right, rather than as an adjunct of medicine, the teaching of materia medica was established under a separate professorship. This encouraged Hope to continue his predecessor's attempts to find a single, larger and less central site for the Botanic Garden. To his lasting credit, he not only achieved this but succeeded in obtaining a modest, though permanent, endowment from the Crown for its upkeep, which greatly improved the prospects for botanical education and set a precedent for the Crown-funding that continues to this day.

The new site was to the west of Leith Walk and was considerably larger than the total area provided by the previous locations at Trinity Hospital, St Anne's Yard and the Royal Garden at Holyrood. It covered 5 acres (2.25ha) and benefited from the relatively clean air of the suburbs. Hope marked the boundaries with willow stakes, many of which took root and grew into mature trees during the 60 or so years of the garden's existence. Plants from the three gardens were moved to Leith Walk in 1763 and a new era began for Edinburgh's Royal Botanic Garden.

The new garden featured an innovative glasshouse range 140ft (42.5m) long, consisting of a hothouse at each end, linked by a passage to a cooler central house. It was an outstanding success, sustaining economic plants such as tea, coffee and bananas, and enabling tropical trees and shrubs to reach impressive proportions for the first time in cultivation.

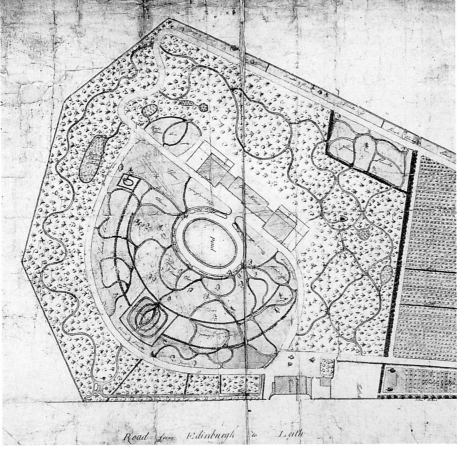

Top. The Leith Walk garden in its suburban setting from an early 19th century engraving. *Bottom.* The 1777 map of the Leith Walk garden shows the glasshouse, pond, woodland areas and most strikingly, on the right, the large acreage devoted to rhubarb, which was grown for medicinal purposes.

Daniel Rutherford.

An excellent teacher and a brilliant botanist with a wide range of interests, John Hope encouraged students to explore and record the Scottish flora, and awarded a gold medal annually for the best herbarium (collection of pressed plants). To his credit, his students made a number of new discoveries, including alpine speedwell (*Veronica alpina*) and pipewort (*Eriocaulon septangulare*). His lecture notes describe many of his own experiments, such as those testing the effects of light and gravity on plants, which were a century ahead of any published findings on these phenomena.

John Hope died in 1786 at the age of 61, having contributed greatly to the Botanic Garden, especially through the learning and methodology he passed on to his students.

Daniel Rutherford and his six Principal Gardeners (1786-1819)

John Hope was succeeded by Daniel Rutherford, the uncle of Sir Walter Scott and discoverer - in principle, if not in name - of nitrogen. In common with previous Regius Keepers, he trained as a doctor, but his interests lay more in chemistry and the study of the atmosphere than in the medico-botanical world.

The Garden thrived during Rutherford's 33 years at Leith Walk thanks to a succession of talented Principal Gardeners (later called Curators). No less than six spanned his term of office. They included Malcolm McCoig, a respected systematic botanist, as well as a horticulturist, whose Flora of Edinburgh remained unfinished on his death in 1789; John McKay, a plant collector since childhood and able nurseryman whose interests embraced everything from tropical rarities to alpines; and George Don, a companion of John McKay's on many long and arduous explorations of Scotland's flora. Don was so obsessed with plant collecting that he was easily distracted from his responsibilities in the Botanic Garden and resigned after a few years to tend his extraordinary plant collection which included 60 different sedges and every known species of hardy grass.

Rutherford's sixth and last Principal Gardener - William McNab - was to hold the position for 28 years. He rose through the ranks of apprentice gardeners at Kew,

Among the exotic specimens cultivated by William McNab was the sacred lotus, *Nelumbo nucifera*.

moving to Edinburgh in 1810 to take up the Curatorship. McNab developed the Garden with enthusiasm and originality, introducing many new plants such as rare mimosas, Australian banksias and tropical water lilies.

A report published in 1812, just two years after McNab's appointment, states that the Botanic Garden contained over 4000 species in about 1000 genera. The Leith Walk garden was running short of space, so Rutherford set about acquiring a still larger site, but died in 1819, leaving the task to his successor, Robert Graham.

Robert Graham, William McNab and the move to Inverleith (1820-45)

A graduate of Edinburgh University, Robert Graham practised medicine in Glasgow and became the first Professor of Botany there in 1818. Two years later, he returned to Edinburgh as Regius Keeper, King's Botanist and Professor of Botany and Medicine. His first task, in addition to his medical and teaching duties, was to continue Rutherford's attempts to find an alternative site for the Botanic Garden. The final choice was at Inverleith, adjoining the garden of the Royal Caledonian Horticultural Society. The site consisted of 14½ acres (5.9ha) purchased from Mr James Rocheid, a wealthy agriculturist whose ostentatious lifestyle was the talk of the town. It was separated from the rest of the estate (which was at that time known as Broompark) and from the Rocheid residence - Inverleith House - by a wall.

Moving all the plants from Leith Walk to Inverleith took the best part of two years, the transplanting of mature trees being a major problem. This was solved admirably by William McNab's invention of a transplanting machine. The largest tree moved was a cut-leaved alder which measured 43ft in height. Through his skills and endeavour, the Botanic Garden was transformed - as well as transplanted - and grew in both size and prestige.

In 1833 the annual grant from the Government for the Garden's upkeep was a mere £1000, which had to cover wages, fuel, plants, equipment and the running of a museum which had recently been established. The situation was so bad that on occasions Graham contributed out of his own pocket. His repeated requests for an increase were eventually successful and the Government

Above. The West Indian fan palm, *Sabal bermudana.* Now more than 200 years of age, this specimen originates from the Leith Walk garden and now makes a historic centrepiece in the Tropical Palm House.

Left. Robert Graham.

Right. A monkey puzzle, *Araucaria araucana,* being moved in William McNab's renowned transplanting machine.

John Hutton Balfour.

The Temperate Palm House nearing completion c.1858.

advanced over £1500 for a new palm house, which was completed in 1834.

As well as practising medicine, teaching botany and materia medica, Graham published numerous papers, including descriptions of over 200 species in Curtis's *Botanical Magazine*. In 1836 he helped found and became the first President of the Botanical Society of Edinburgh, whose collection of books and dried plant specimens were subsequently to provide the nucleus of the Garden's library and herbarium.

John Hutton Balfour and expansion at Inverleith (1845-80)

On his death in 1845, Robert Graham was succeeded as Regius Keeper and Professor of Botany by John Hutton Balfour. Under his direction, clinical medicine was discarded from the curriculum in favour of laboratory work, a significant stage in the eventual separation of botany from medicine.

Balfour's seriousness as a scientist was offset by an imperturbable sense of humour and field trips were undertaken with typical Balfourian *joie de vivre*. The general cameraderie did not, however, detract from the customary tasks of collecting, identification and recording, in addition to which was added the ecological study of habitat, succession and distribution. Balfour's skills as a teacher extended to compiling textbooks for his students and contributing to encyclopaedias in order to impart the latest scientific knowledge to a wider audience. Essentially a religious man, Balfour was shocked, rather than excited by the theory of evolution in Darwin's *Origin of Species*, which was published in 1859. To many such a split between science and faith had previously been unthinkable, and Balfour, then aged 51, shared the confusion experienced by many scientists at the time.

During J H Balfour's 34 years of office, the Botanic Garden expanded in both scope and size. A new classroom was built in 1850, and the following year a museum of economic botany was established. By now the palm house erected in his predecessor's time was cramped, with the tallest trees pushing through the roof. Balfour campaigned for a new palm house and in 1855 obtained a grant of £6000 from the Government for the purpose. The Temperate Palm House as we know it today was opened in 1858 and is still the highest in Britain.

Towards the end of 1862, the Royal Botanic Garden became embroiled in a controversy which kept public opinion at fever pitch for well over a year. The Garden, financed by the Treasury, was open from 6am to 6pm on weekdays and until 8pm on Saturdays in summer, but was closed on Sundays. In effect, this meant that the average working man and his family - whose taxes went to the Treasury - had little opportunity to benefit from the garden. Eventually 14,000 working men signed a petition to the Lords of Her Majesty's Treasury that the Garden be opened on Sundays. This provoked outrage and a counter-petition with 34,000 signatures was sent by The Sabbath Alliance. The controversy raged so fiercely that the matter was put to the vote in the House of Commons in June 1863. By this time, the pro-Sunday lobby had 36,897 men's signatures, whereas 48,522 men, women and boys had signed in opposition. Lord Palmerston, then 80, spoke wittily and succinctly in the debate, saying that he personally had nothing against Sunday opening and had no doubt that public opinion in Scotland would change - as it already had in England - but that until such time, it should be respected. The vote was 107 for and 123 (including 22 of the 28 Scottish MPs) against. The issue was settled for the time being, and for another quarter of a century the Royal Botanic Garden continued to lock its gates on a Sunday. Despite more protestations from The Sabbath Alliance, the first Sunday opening took place on 7th April 1889, following the transferral of the Royal Botanic Garden into the care of the Commissioners of Her Majesty's Public Buildings and Works. Over 27, 000 people visited the Garden on the Sundays in that month alone.

In 1858 2½ acres (1.1ha) west of this new Palm House were added to the Garden, followed in 1864 by a further expansion when 10 acres (4.5ha) of the neighbouring Royal Caledonian Horticultural Society's experimental ground were acquired. The latter included an Exhibition Hall, originally erected in 1843, which for the next century served as the Botanic Garden's Herbarium, and a Curator's house, now the East Gate lodge. The land was developed as the Rock Garden and was completed in 1871. An even larger addition was made in 1876 when Inverleith House and its immediate grounds - some 30 acres (13.5ha) - were purchased. The grounds were to be planted as an arboretum, largely for the instruction of students with an interest in forestry, and Inverleith House was intended as the Regius Keeper's residence.

In 1873 the Royal Botanic Garden's collection of living plants numbered about 86,000 registered specimens. Balfour lectured to 354 students and on a single day as many as 7000 pieces of plant material were cut for demonstration purposes. All this was managed, with increasing difficulty, on an annual grant which in 1878 was only £1400. J H Balfour argued strongly for an substantially larger amount but nothing materialised before his retirement in 1879.

J H Balfour was ably supported by his curators. James McNab succeeded his father, William, as Curator in 1849, having previously spent 12 years as the Curator of the Royal Caledonian Horticultural Society's experimental ground. He was closely involved with the new Palm House, for which he designed the heating system, but is

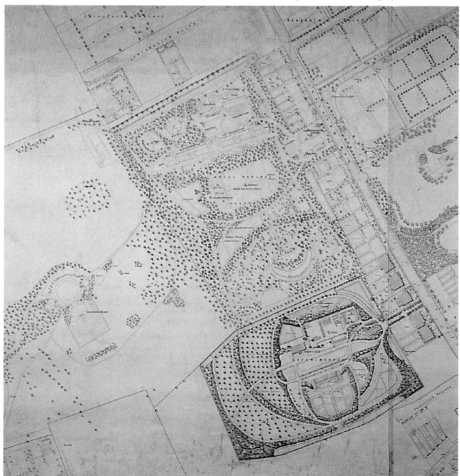

The policies at Inverleith c.1852, including the Experimental Grounds of the Royal Caledonian Horticultural Society and the grounds of Inverleith House.

Above. The former show hall of the Royal Caledonian Horticultural Society, which served as the Garden's Herbarium until 1964, is now known as the Caledonian Hall.

Below. James McNab's original Rock Garden was divided into over 4000 sections using stone from the demolished wall which had previously separated the Botanic Garden from the Royal Caledonian Horticultural Society's grounds.

Alexander Dickson.

best remembered for retubbing and moving the palms to their new quarters - a monumental and often dangerous task for which he devised methods so efficient that he became an authority on the subject. Some of the palms weighed about eight tons and had been grown for many years in bottomless boxes which measured over 4ft square. The giant *Livistona chinense* was 6ft round the base and 42ft high, while the *Sabal umbraculifera* had a crown 28ft across. Despite the hazards, both plants and men survived the move.

Great skill was also required for transplanting trees during major redevelopments in the Garden, such as took place when the Botanic Garden acquired the neighbouring garden of the Royal Caledonian Horticultural Society. For this purpose, James McNab used the transplanting machine which had been invented by his father 30 years before, making several modifications to enable a greater weight to be lifted by fewer men. The new version was such a success that it went into commercial production. Again, he pushed beyond the accepted limits, moving mature trees successfully even in summer.

1870 was the bicentenary of the Botanic Garden. It now ranked among the most important in Europe, with spectacular glasshouses, major collections of economic and medicinal plants, newly introduced trees (such as Douglas firs and Chusan palms), extensive formal beds, a well-stocked Museum and Herbarium, classrooms to accommodate 300 students, and an ambitious Rock Garden under construction. James McNab died in 1878. A year later, J H Balfour retired and the post of Regius Keeper went to Alexander Dickson.

Alexander Dickson: a brief and troubled reign (1880-87)

Dickson's appointment in 1880 marked another stage in the separation of botany from medicine, as medicine was no longer included in his academic title, which was solely Professor of Botany. He was primarily a research scientist and published many papers on the form and structure of plants.

On the administrative side, Dickson had inherited many unresolved problems concerning the newly acquired Inverleith House and the surrounding land, which was now designated as the Arboretum. The latter was still separated from the rest of the Botanic Garden by a high wall and was open as a public park on every day of the week, including Sunday when the rest of the Botanic Garden was mandatorily closed. Dickson refused to open the connecting gates until the proper provisions were made. Although ultimately the Treasury intervened and the Regius Keeper was instructed to open one of the three connecting gates, with a member of staff on duty to guard against plant thefts, many difficulties remained unresolved when he died suddenly at the age of 51.

In charge of the Garden at the start of Dickson's short term of office was John Sadler, a botanist by training who had served the Botanic Garden since the age of 17. For 25 years he had been J H Balfour's assistant, prior to being made Curator in 1879. Before officially taking on the new Arboretum, he had planted over 9000 trees and shrubs to shelter the boundaries. His death occurred in 1882 as a result of a chill caught while planting in severe weather. He was succeeded in 1883 by Robert Lindsay who had started his working life at the Botanic Garden as a boy when James McNab was Curator. Apart from the day-to-day maintenance of the Botanic Garden and the major task of planting the new Arboretum, Lindsay made some distinctive contributions in plant breeding. One group of plants that interested him was the genus *Hebe* (then included in *Veronica*). As a consequence of his enthusiasm for these shrubs, the Garden boasted a collection of some 40 species and varieties in 1891.

Isaac Bayley Balfour: a man with a mission (1888-1922)

The Royal Botanic Garden was in something of a trough when Alexander Dickson died in 1887. There were unresolved problems over integrating the Arboretum and Garden; the glasshouses urgently needed attention; the administrative and teaching facilities were inadequate; and the establishment as a whole needed modernising. Little short of a revolution was called for, and it came in the form of Isaac Bayley Balfour, son of J H Balfour. He gave a graphic description of the Botanic Garden at the time:

> '... the Establishment had as an educational institution and as a Scientific garden sunk from its previous high estate. So far as its staff were concerned it had come to be very much a place in which to pension off old men unable to get other work to do - I do not know what the average age of members of staff was, but I well recollect one old man, the chief painter of plant labels, who was only about eighty and whose fitness for work may be gauged by the fact that he was practically stone-blind ...'

Bayley Balfour was appointed Regius Keeper in 1888 and with consummate skill he steered the Botanic Garden into the 20th century.

Born at 27 Inverleith Row (then the Regius Keeper's residence), he spent his entire childhood in and around the Botanic Garden. His student days were spent in Edinburgh too, reading natural sciences at the University. He held the distinction of being the first candidate to receive a Doctor of Science degree at Edinburgh, which he obtained with First Class Honours in 1875 after carrying out research on the Royal Society's expedition to Rodriguez (an island near Mauritius in the Indian Ocean). He then went on to lecture in botany at the Edinburgh Royal Veterinary College until 1878.

The high standard of work he achieved on his first expedition led to a second - this time to Socotra at the mouth of the Gulf of Aden, under the auspices of the Royal

Left. Begonia socotrana *was first discovered by Isaac Bayley Balfour in 1879 and has recently been recollected by Garden staff working on the Flora of Arabia.*

Right. Isaac Bayley Balfour.

Society and the British Association. He studied the botany and geology of this unusually rich island. In just seven weeks during the winter of 1879 to 1880, he collected herbarium material of some 70 endemic lichens and over 200 endemic flowering plants.

On his return from Socotra, Balfour became Professor of Botany at Glasgow, and five years later - when still only 31 - he moved to Oxford as Sherardian Professor of Botany and Keeper of the Botanic Garden. He returned to Edinburgh in 1888, having proved himself to be an astute and dynamic administrator, as well as a first-rate scientist. Isaac Bayley Balfour's close association with the Royal Botanic Garden for most of his life gave him an immediate grasp of what needed doing and the commitment to carry it out. The first thing he did was to get the Royal Botanic Garden Edinburgh put on the same administrative footing as its counterpart at Kew. The proposal in the Universities (Scotland) Act of 1889 that the Botanic Garden be transferred to the University, was seen as a move that would turn it into a purely scientific institution and narrow its scope considerably. Balfour's arguments against this proposal were so persuasive that he won over the University authorities, the Town Council and public opinion. The outcome was as he intended: the Royal Botanic Garden Edinburgh, like Kew, was placed entirely under the Commissioners of Her Majesty's Works and Public Buildings.

This change of administration not only meant greater efficiency and better funding but also - at long last - that the Garden would be open from dawn to dusk every day, including Sundays. The popular response to this improved access inspired him to begin Saturday evening public lectures on a range of botanical and horticultural subjects. The two-way exchange had begun: more people than ever before were visiting the Garden which was in turn reaching a far wider public.

In 1890 a committee was set up to examine all aspects of the Garden and plan for future developments. Among the committee's recommendations were that the University Chair of Botany should remain linked to the Botanic Garden, but that teaching should extend to non-university students. Bayley Balfour attached great importance to Edinburgh's role in teaching and by the end of his reign it was regarded as Britain's leading institution for the teaching of botany.

Botany now led a separate existence from medicine and a University Botany Department had been created at 20A Inverleith Row in premises erected between 1910 and 1912 (though additions continued until 1920). The construction of the Botany Building also meant that the original east entrance to the Botanic Garden had to be moved from between numbers 20 and 21 Inverleith Row to its present position between numbers 7 and 8. Balfour also created a number of new scientific posts, including lecturers in various branches of botany; a full-time keeper of the Museum; a keeper of the Herbarium; a librarian; a photographer and artist; and a laboratory assistant. Communicating 'the condition and progress of the Garden, records of scientific investigations carried on in the Garden, and notices of points of interest relating to plant-life which come under the observation of the staff' was another of Bayley Balfour's aims. This was achieved through the publication of *Notes from the Royal Botanic Garden Edinburgh*, a scientific journal which he founded in 1900, both to sell to the public and to exchange for similar publications with other institutions.

In line for major changes were the now run-down glasshouses. The remaining old glasshouses of the Royal Caledonian Horticultural Society were demolished to extend the Rock Garden. The Palm House was reorganised, with a glass partition erected between the old (1834) and new (1858) houses in order to create temperate and tropical sections which could be kept at different temperatures. The main glasshouse range was entirely rebuilt and its 20 original boilers replaced by four

Above. The Botany Building provided premises for the University Botany Department and laboratories for the Botanic Garden.

Below. The title page of the first issue of the Garden's scientific journal.

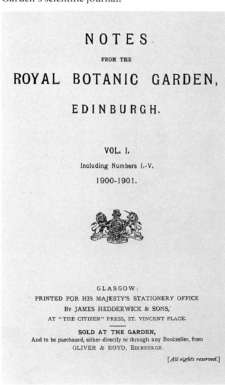

NOTES

FROM THE

ROYAL BOTANIC GARDEN,

EDINBURGH.

VOL. I.

Including Numbers I.-V.

1900-1901.

GLASGOW:

PRINTED FOR HIS MAJESTY'S STATIONERY OFFICE

BY JAMES HEDDERWICK & SONS,'

AT "THE CITIZEN" PRESS, ST. VINCENT PLACE.

SOLD AT THE GARDEN,

And to be purchased, either directly or through any Bookseller, from

OLIVER & BOYD, EDINBURGH.

[*All rights reserved.*]

modern units. By 1895 the first two houses - one for orchids and the other for stove plants - were complete. Three years later, the main house was finished. It was an impressive 340ft (103.6m) long, with a centre section for cool-growing shrubs such as camellias and acacias, and two side sections for economic plants and succulents. Smaller separate houses followed: ones for heaths and both tropical and temperate ferns in 1908; a rhododendron house and two alpine houses in 1915; and others for carnivorous plants, aroids and bromeliads.

Attention was also given to outdoor plantings. In about 1903, a herbaceous border 600ft (183m) long was laid out along what was then the north boundary. James McNab's Rock Garden was famous and attracted large numbers of visitors. Although it had been greatly admired in 1907, it was described as 'the Devil's Lapful' by the outspoken Reginald Farrer in his first book, *My Rock Garden*. Farrer's sensibilities had been well and truly offended by what he saw at Edinburgh: 'The plan is simplicity itself. You take a hundred or a thousand cart loads of bald, square-faced boulders. You next drop them all about absolutely anyhow; and you then plant things amongst them. The chaotic hideousness of the result is something to be remembered with shudders ever after.' Bayley Balfour decided to demolish the whole thing and start again. Work began in 1908 and continued each winter until 1914. The new Rock Garden was carefully constructed to resemble natural formations, using conglomerate from Perthshire and red sandstone from the Dumfries area. It covered 3 acres (1.4ha) and was thus one of the largest and finest in the world.

Bayley Balfour depended upon his Curators and the skilled labour of his gardeners for the success of his horticultural developments. Several of the gardeners were students on the horticulture and forestry courses that Balfour had started in 1892 to improve standards in these fields. The classes were free in return for labour, which enabled the Botanic Garden to increase staff without adding greatly to expenditure. Courses ran for two to three years, during which students worked from 6am to 5.30pm (7am to sunset in winter), with little in the way of holidays. Despite the gruelling routine, the courses were remarkably popular and successful,

Aerial view, from the south, of the glasshouses and botany buildings in 1929, when the surrounding area at Inverleith was far less developed than today.

Above left. The Rock Garden during its redevelopment 1908-1914.

Above right. Part of the Rock Garden today.

Below left. George Forrest, Scotland's foremost plant collector.

Below right. Forrest collected prolific quantities of seed each season. This image from the Botanic Garden's Forrest photographic archive shows material being dried prior to despatch - September 1913.

with a record of producing some of Britain's leading horticulturists and foresters. Something of importance happened in almost every one of Bayley Balfour's 34 years in office, but in 1902 he made an appointment which was to change the course of the Botanic Garden's history. The post was a minor one in the Herbarium and the successful candidate was George Forrest, a young man who had just returned from several years in the Australian bush. He was meticulous, well-organised and had a keen eye for plants. These qualities - together with his physical fitness and pioneering spirit - obviously impressed Bayley Balfour so that when, in 1904, a wealthy Liverpool cotton broker asked him to recommend a plant collector, George Forrest immediately sprang to mind. The patron was Arthur Bulley whose garden at Ness in Cheshire was both a plantsman's paradise and the base for his successful commercial venture under the company name of Bees Ltd. Bulley was interested in obtaining plants new to cultivation, and on the advice of Bayley Balfour, George Forrest was

Primula forrestii. This beautiful plant from western China was named by Isaac Bayley Balfour in honour of George Forrest.

dispatched to western China. His first trip took place between 1904 and 1907, to be followed by six further visits, on the last of which, in 1932, he died from heart failure. Balfour's judgment of Forrest had been right. He turned out to be a methodical and energetic collector who covered vast areas by recruiting and training local people to assist him. The result was that he introduced unprecedented numbers of plants into cultivation and brought back over 30,000 herbarium specimens. His introductions included some 300 new rhododendrons, as well as camellias, magnolias, Himalayan poppies, lilies, primulas and gentians which were of such horticultural potential that they aroused a fever of interest in gardening circles. Many of today's finest gardens were planted in this era as landowners both vied with each other and co-operated in acquiring and cultivating the latest introductions. There was particular interest in Forrest's collections of rhododendrons. John Williams, a leading member of the newly formed Rhododendron Society, had started hybridising these shrubs at Caerhays Castle in Cornwall as early as 1885, and both he and the Society gave Forrest financial support for the later expeditions.

Almost everything George Forrest collected went first to Edinburgh, where it was sorted and classified. Surplus seed was then distributed to those who had given financial support for the expeditions. Every area of expertise at the Botanic Garden was called upon to document, propagate and cultivate this massive influx of new material. The task took the best part of half a century, and was the driving force behind some of the developments that have already been described - notably the Rock Garden for alpine and dwarf species, and various glasshouses for those needing protection. Bayley Balfour himself took on the classification of the two largest genera, *Rhododendron* and *Primula*, which occupied him for the rest of his life. He also visited China and Japan in 1909 to learn about the cultivation of these and other Asiatic plants, having already established that he was an able horticulturist as well as a great botanist.

The impact of Forrest's collections was far-reaching. British gardens, for example, never looked the same again once the finest species and their hybrids became commercially available. More specifically, Edinburgh found itself with an unrivalled collection of Sino-Himalayan plants, both living and dried, and became the leading botanical authority on this area. Building on strengths is always a good strategy, and much of the collection, research and cultivation carried out by the Botanic Garden

since Forrest's time have been focused on this rich and important part of the world's flora. Bayley Balfour retired in 1922, expressing confidence both in his chosen successor, William Wright Smith, and the expectation that 'while the traditions of the past would not be forgotten, they would not be allowed to stand in the way of progress.'

William Wright Smith had been appointed by Balfour in 1902 as assistant lecturer. In 1907 he took on the challenge of running the herbarium at the Royal Botanic Garden, Calcutta, and in the following year assumed responsibility for the Botanical Survey of India. In 1911, with a substantial knowledge of the flora of India, Burma and the Himalayas under his belt, he returned to Edinburgh as Deputy Regius Keeper, and on Balfour's retirement in 1922 became Professor of Botany and Regius Keeper. In a letter to William Wright Smith, in which he explained his reasons for wanting him as his successor, Balfour wrote: 'The appointments which I am resigning are a unique combination and make Edinburgh a teaching centre different from others in the country - University interests in the ordinary sense and National interests have alike to be considered.'

William Wright Smith.

Opposite. Puck's Hut at the Younger Botanic Garden Benmore was erected as a memorial to Sir Isaac Bayley Balfour.

William Wright Smith and the founding of Younger Botanic Garden (1922-56)

Edinburgh was now one of the world's leading botanic gardens in terms of teaching and research, with up-to-date laboratories, new glasshouses, a renowned garden, extensive herbarium and living collections, and major areas of expertise. Throughout his last 10 years of office, Bayley Balfour had been seeking sites for growing plants that disliked Edinburgh's poor soil and relatively dry, cold climate - especially west coast locations suitable for rhododendrons and conifers. It was left to William Wright Smith to finalise an agreement with the Forestry Commission for a property in Argyll. In late 1929 part of the policies of the Benmore Estate in the Cowal Peninsula, initially 90 acres (36.5 ha), became the first specialist garden of the Royal Botanic Garden Edinburgh. Establishing the Younger Botanic Garden Benmore, as it became known, must rank as William Wright Smith's greatest contribution to the Botanic Garden's development. His success was based on previous collaboration with the newly-formed Commission to establish, in 1923, a forestry nursery at Inverleith in a field adjoining the north boundary (an area that was eventually to become the Demonstration Garden).

Wright Smith made considerable contributions to taxonomy. He had assisted Bayley Balfour with Forrest's Himalayan collections, publishing descriptions of some 550 new species between 1912 and 1921, together with an account of the lilies of China. He revised sections of *Primula* with George Forrest and carried on with *Rhododendron* and *Primula* where Bayley Balfour left off on his death in 1922, laying the foundations of much subsequent work on these demanding groups.

By 1930, Wright Smith's workload had increased to the point at which he needed the support of a Deputy. The man for the job proved to be John Cowan (1892-1960), an Edinburgh graduate who had also studied botany and forestry at Oxford before joining the Indian Forest Service. Cowan's first-hand knowledge of the vegetation and ecology of tropical forests was impressive, as was his experience of rhododendrons in the wild. Much work remained to be done on *Rhododendron*. George Forrest's last collection was still unnamed and material brought back by other collectors was piling up. Cowan threw himself into this work with his customary energy and enthusiasm, devoting the best part of 20 years to it. The research into rhododendrons carried out by Wright Smith, Cowan and their colleagues was of such quality and quantity that it confirmed Edinburgh as the

The Heath Garden, first established in Wright Smith's time provides colour all year round.

undisputed authority on the subject - a mecca for 'rhodoholics' and students of the genus worldwide.

Two major additions were made to the garden in Wright Smith's time. The first was the establishment in 1935 of a Heath Garden, situated to the east of the Rock Garden. Here there was a natural transition from steep contours and outcrops to an undulating coat of many colours - just as mountainous country gives way to moorland. The second new garden - the Peat Garden - came into existence in 1939 in order to solve some of the problems of cultivation posed by certain Sino-Himalayan plants. Many species found conditions on the Rock Garden too dry, warm and alkaline. Temporary success had been achieved by growing these in 'rooteries' - tree stumps bedded into peaty soil - but eventually these plantings succumbed to honey fungus. The solution was found by copying a technique devised by the McDouall brothers in their garden at Logan, Wigtownshire (which was later to become Edinburgh's second specialist garden). The Peat Garden was constructed on the northern side of the Woodland Garden: a site which provided the necessary shade and shelter, and an appropriate setting, for these woodland, alpine and lime-hating species, such as lilies, primulas, gentians, dwarf rhododendrons and Himalayan poppies.

In addition to these new areas, William Wright Smith made substantial changes to the Rock Garden at intervals during the 1930s and 1940s. Again, most of the modifications were made to accommodate the influx of Sino-Himalayan plants - both in terms of the sheer numbers and to cater for cultivation requirements that were not otherwise available at Inverleith. A scree was constructed on the northern side of the Rock Garden for plants that needed especially sharp drainage; a simulated dried-up river bed increased the range of ecological niches to the west; and the entire southern flank was redeveloped. This period also saw the diversification of the Arboretum, giving rise to the Woodland Garden and the Copse which gave shelter to rhododendrons, magnolias and other new acquisitions that showed sensitivity to late frosts.

In 1911 the Garden created a new post of Plant Propagator, to which Lawrence Stewart, who subsequently became Curator, was appointed. His success rate with subjects regarded as exceedingly difficult, if not impossible, was so high that the results merited description in scientific papers. Stewart's successor as Curator was

The Peat Garden at Edinburgh supports a rich variety of Sino-Himalayan plants.

Roland Cooper whose ties with the Botanic Garden were unusually strong. Having been orphaned as a child, his guardianship was transferred to William Wright Smith in 1907 when he was 16 years old. Wright Smith took the boy to Calcutta and on several Himalayan expeditions. When they returned to Edinburgh in 1910, Cooper began as a horticultural student in the Garden. While still a student, he made a return visit to the Himalayas as one of Arthur Bulley's collectors, discovering new rhododendrons, primulas and other plants of horticultural potential.

The period of Cooper's curatorship - 1936 to 1950 - was dominated by World War II and the ensuing shortages of staff and materials. A number of key staff were seconded, including the Deputy Keeper, John Cowan, who was put in charge of timber production for western Scotland by the Ministry of Supply. Though maintaining the Garden and teaching facilities under wartime conditions was a considerable strain, Wright Smith's worst fears were never realised; no actual bomb damage was sustained other than a few broken panes of glass.

The post-war years proved equally trying for Wright Smith (now Sir William Wright Smith, as he was knighted in 1932). Though in his seventies, he adapted remarkably well to the retirement and loss of those with whom he had spent most of his working life and the changes that came with an almost entirely new staff. Other than that, his only complaint was that 'My step was once so light on the heather, now I puff and blow if I climb the brae from the Laboratory to my house'. Despite this, he had no inclination to retire and died 'in harness' at the age of 81.

Expansion and rebuilding under Harold Fletcher (1956-70)

Harold Fletcher began his career at Edinburgh as assistant lecturer in 1934. After an interval of three years as Director of the Royal Horticultural Society's garden at Wisley, he returned in 1954 to become Deputy Regius Keeper, succeeding John Cowan. Following Sir William Wright Smith's death in 1956, Harold Fletcher became Regius Keeper. However, it had been decided by the University of Edinburgh and H M Minister of Works that the posts of Regius Keeper and Regius Professor should no longer be held by the same person, due to the ever-increasing workloads. The University Chair of Botany was filled in 1958 by Robert Brown, a plant physiologist. In 1965, the Royal Botanic Garden and the University of Edinburgh

Harold Fletcher.

were further separated when all but the taxonomy section of the University's Department of Botany vacated its premises at Inverleith and moved to a new complex, the King's Buildings, in south Edinburgh. However, though the two institutions had moved apart in physical and administrative terms, in other respects their links remained as close as ever. Thus in 1968 the Regius Keeper was appointed Honorary Professor in the University Department of Botany. The previous year Fletcher was appointed to the historic title first held by James Sutherland - that of Queen's Botanist in Scotland.

The first significant changes under Harold Fletcher concerned Inverleith House and the Herbarium. As the former was no longer required as an official residence for the Regius Keeper, the Ministry of Works refurbished it in 1960 to become the first home of the Scottish National Gallery of Modern Art. Since 1864 the old Exhibition Hall of the Royal Caledonian Horticultural Society, adjacent to the Rock Garden, had served as the Botanic Garden's Herbarium. The building had many shortcomings, including lack of space for expansion and its distance from the Library, which meant a cycle ride or tidy walk in all weathers for staff needing to consult materials and references. By the mid-1950s it was full to overflowing, its irreplaceable contents were in some jeopardy and the working conditions were near intolerable. Similarly, the Library was bursting at the seams, with storerooms crammed full of books and periodicals that could not be accommodated in the main room. In addition, scientists and administrative staff were desperately short of space. The solution to these pressing problems was an entirely new building, housing a purpose-built Herbarium and Library, together with laboratories, offices and

From 1960 until 1985 Inverleith House served as the home of the Scottish National Gallery of Modern Art, some of whose collections graced the surrounding lawns.

photographic studio. The site chosen was immediately south of the University Botany building on Inverleith Row, which since Bayley Balfour's time had been occupied by huts, two of which contained the museum collections. The new Herbarium and Library was opened by H M the Queen on the 29th of June 1964.

At the opening of the Herbarium and Library building, models and plans were displayed of the next major development: a new range of glasshouses for both propagation and display. Cooper's successor as Curator from 1950 was Edward Kemp, whose research and experience greatly influenced the designs of G A H Pearce, a Department of Public Buildings and Works' architect. The new range of exhibition plant houses was heralded as the most innovative since Decimus Burton's Palm House at Kew in the 1840s. The main house measures 420ft (128m) long and 60ft (18.25m) wide, with a distinctive external framework of latticed metal tetrahedrons to provide maximum light with minimum interference to the plantings. Built on two levels, it is divided internally into five climatic zones and remains a showpiece of the Garden at Inverleith.

The construction of these glasshouses involved the contractors and staff in a monumental amount of work and called for prodigious quantities of plants and planting materials. The mountain of top soil needed for the new plantings was obtained in 1966 from roadworks around the Forth Road Bridge. It was, however, too compacted to be used straight from the pile and had to be spread out 9in (23cm) thick and cultivated for several months to restore its structure. This was carried out at the Experimental Ground in Inverleith Place, an 11-acre (5ha) site to the north of the Botanic Garden which had been acquired in 1958 as the Temperate Nursery,

The new Herbarium and Library building, the headquarters of the Garden's scientific research work, is a striking feature in the northeast corner of the Garden.

The innovative design of the new glasshouse range, opened in 1967, is especially dramatic when viewed from the roof of the adjacent Temperate Palm House.

An armillary sphere in the Formal Garden at Benmore commemorates Harold Fletcher.

replacing the former forestry plots established by William Wright Smith.

Planting of the glasshouses took place throughout 1967 and well into the following year. A well-established look was given to the surrounding lawns and borders by moving mature trees. Large specimens, carefully saved from the old range of houses, were also used to good effect. The *pièce de résistance* in the new Tropical Aquatic House was a giant Victoria water lily (*Victoria amazonica*). Borne triumphantly from its temporary lodgings on the 24th of September by the Curator and six students, it opened its first flower with perfect timing on the 25th of October when H R H The Princess Margaret officially opened the new range.

A few months after the opening of these magnificent glasshouses, the Botanic Garden sustained one of the worst natural disasters in its history. On the 15th of January 1968, a hurricane swept across central Scotland. Compared with the garden at Benmore, which lost many hundreds of trees, Edinburgh came off lightly, with only about 30 destroyed. Of these, the saddest loss was James Sutherland's 300-year-old yew. To everyone's great relief, the new glasshouses were unscathed, losing but three panes of glass.

The following year saw another major development in the history of the Garden when it acquired part of the Logan estate in Galloway, in the extreme southwest of Scotland. The property, which consisted of a walled garden and its surrounding woodland, was given by the Hambro Trustees to the Department of Agriculture and Fisheries for Scotland as a new specialist garden for the Royal Botanic Garden Edinburgh. Blessed with an unusually mild climate, this subtropical garden was to provide a valuable opportunity to grow tender plants outdoors that seldom succeed in Edinburgh.

1969 was also an epoch-making year from an administrative point of view. The Botanic Garden had come under the Ministry of Public Buildings and Works since 1889 but on the 1st of April responsibility was transferred to the Department of Agriculture and Fisheries for Scotland (DAFS) within the Scottish Office.

Fletcher's retirement in 1970 coincided with another historic event - the tercentenary of the Royal Botanic Garden Edinburgh. He contributed to the celebrations with the publication of a history of the Garden from 1670 to 1970, which he wrote in

The 11 acre Nursery to the north of the Garden at Inverleith provides space for vital research collections as well as material for teaching and display.

collaboration with the librarian, William Brown. The task of writing the Garden's history had been started many years before by Isaac Bayley Balfour and continued (but only as far as 1738) by John Cowan. Now out of print, Fletcher and Brown's volume is a treasure house of archival material about Scotland's national botanic garden.

Douglas Henderson and the Garden's new status (1970-87)

Douglas Henderson became Regius Keeper in 1970 after 20 years in charge of the non-flowering plant collections. A mycologist by training, he was involved in the start of the British Fungus Flora project and co-authored a book on the British Rust Fungi. When Douglas Henderson took over, he brought with him the experience of having worked under two previous Regius Keepers. His first years at Edinburgh were spent under William Wright Smith and toward the end of Harold Fletcher's term of office he had assisted in management and administration. Taking charge was therefore more of a continuation than a new departure. Fletcher had already initiated a policy of acquiring plants of known wild origin, wherever possible, for the Garden and this was further developed under Douglas Henderson. The scientific policy of the Garden was the subject of a seminal Review by the Department of Agriculture and Fisheries for Scotland in 1970. This led to a significant recruitment of new staff between 1973 and 1975, and thereby laid the foundation for much of the Garden's current research.

During Henderson's 17 years of office, herbarium specimens increased by 250,000 to 1.8 million, including collections from the Garden's expanding programme of worldwide botanical explorations. Over this period the Library continued to grow, acknowledged as northern Britain's leading botanical library and achieving an international reputation. It acquired an additional 14,000 volumes between 1970 and 1987, and received over 1770 journals on a regular basis. The interests of the library were always very close to Douglas Henderson's heart, having been in the position of library supervisor from 1961 to 1970. With perfect timing, *The History of the Royal Botanic Garden Library Edinburgh* by Manjil Mathew (Garden

Douglas Henderson.

Librarian since 1967) - a detailed, finely illustrated account of an important aspect of the Royal Botanic Garden's development - was published in 1987, the year in which he left and Douglas Henderson retired.

The last phase of the major glasshouse rebuilding programme, which had started in 1962, was the provision of a new range of 'behind-the-scenes' houses for propagation, quarantine and research, together with buildings for materials and staff welfare. These developments were completed by 1976. In the following year, the new alpine area, designed to accommodate plants that were either too precious or too sensitive for display on the Rock Garden, was opened and soon became a popular garden feature. Display houses for Edinburgh's exceptional collections of gingers, gesneriads and tender rhododendrons were officially opened in 1978. Both the Alpine House and frames, and the Peat and Tropical Rock houses were valuable additions to the range of exhibition houses, revealing interesting aspects of the particular collections for which Edinburgh is world famous.

During this period there were several significant increases in the Royal Botanic Garden's lands: the Mediterranean or Silver Garden at Inverleith was created from a former tennis court; a vital shelter belt of 10 acres was acquired at Logan; some 65 acres were added to Benmore, comprising the Benmore Hill and Glen Massan arboreta; and the garden at Dawyck was acquired. In 1978 Lt Col. A N Balfour and family made a gift to the nation of part of the policies surrounding their house at Dawyck, near Peebles. The new Dawyck Botanic Garden covered 60 acres (24ha) and boasted a remarkable collection of trees, some dating back to the 17th century. More extreme in climate than Edinburgh, and considerably drier and colder than Benmore and Logan, it had the right conditions - and ample space - for growing a range of hardy trees and shrubs that were not well-represented elsewhere.

Edward Kemp's successor as Curator was Richard Shaw, who from 1956 to 1965 had gained particular expertise in the cultivation of rhododendrons while in charge of the Younger Botanic Garden at Benmore. In 1972, when he returned to

The Alpine area, comprising a timber-framed house with troughs, frames and south-facing wall, was opened in 1977.

Edinburgh as Curator, he began to overhaul Edinburgh's rhododendron collection. The timing was opportune, as James Cullen, the Assistant Regius Keeper, and other staff had started work on a major revision of *Rhododendron*. This resulted in a close co-ordination of the latest taxonomic thinking on the genus and the organisation and display of the Garden's plants. Assessing and replanting the Garden's long-established rhododendron collection was a mammoth undertaking and involved restructuring a number of areas. The project was finally completed in 1987, the year in which Richard Shaw retired.

Shortly before Douglas Henderson took office, the Royal Botanic Garden had come under the Department of Agriculture and Fisheries for Scotland (DAFS), with the Ministry of Public Buildings and Works managing all the buildings and the Scottish Office being responsible for staff. As part of a policy to permit greater independence to institutions, the Botanic Garden was established as a trustee body under the National Heritage (Scotland) Act 1985, becoming a grant-aided institution from April 1986. This Act defined the general functions of the Trustees as: research into plant science and related subjects; disseminating the results; maintaining national reference collections of both living and archival material for the purpose of study; providing advice, information, education and services related to plants or associated areas; and affording access to the gardens for the general public to derive knowledge or enjoyment from the collections. The Board of Trustees was appointed by the Secretary of State. Its chairman, Sir Peter Hutchison Bt., proved eminently well-suited for this position, having had many years of involvement with botany and horticulture.

So, as Douglas Henderson's term of office drew to a close, the Royal Botanic Garden had acquired partially independent status and had expanded dramatically in terms of both buildings and land. During the 1970s, in addition to being part of a scientific research institution, the Gardens increasingly reflected their role as public amenities. Educational activities in particular grew apace, stimulated by the donation of

The Azalea Lawn provides colour and scent for the enjoyment of visitors, as well as tracing the development of the main groups of hybrids.

The Garden's first Board of Trustees pictured in the Cactus House in 1986.

£50,000 to construct a Plant Exhibition Hall. Completed in 1970, this provided a venue for interpreting both botany and horticulture. In 1986 Inverleith House was returned to the Garden as a Gallery and Exhibition centre. The public face of the Garden was well-projected by the 1978 film 'Capital Garden'. With increased public and media attention, and the growth in leisure and tourism, visitor numbers surged. In 1970, when Douglas Henderson took charge, Edinburgh (which opened all year) had 401,480 visitors, and the specialist gardens (opening spring to autumn) had 21,230 and 18,200 at Younger and Logan respectively. By the time of his retirement in 1987, visitor numbers had risen: Edinburgh 761,145; Younger 43,003; and Logan 32,620. Meanwhile Dawyck was beginning to attract a modest audience, receiving over 6000 visitors during 1987.

Recent years: John McNeill (1987-89) and David Ingram (1990 onwards)

The late 1980s were very much a transition period for the Royal Botanic Garden. In addition to becoming a Non-Departmental Public Body, it also had to adapt to Douglas Henderson's retirement and the departure of several other long-serving senior staff, including the Librarian, Curator and Assistant Keeper.

The new Regius Keeper was John McNeill, an Edinburgh man and graduate of its University who was head of the Department of Botany at the University of Ottawa. The new Curator was John Main, formerly Curator of the Royal Horticultural

Society's garden at Wisley. Unfortunately, John McNeill's term of office lasted only two years, cut short by his return to Canada for personal reasons. During this period a computer network was installed and, in order to broaden the interface between the Botanic Garden and its public, a seasonal newsletter, *The Botanics*, was launched. In addition in 1989 the Garden's scientific publication, *Notes from the Royal Botanic Garden Edinburgh*, originally founded by Isaac Bayley Balfour in 1900, adopted a new format and title becoming the *Edinburgh Journal of Botany*. McNeill's successor was David Ingram previously Reader in Plant Pathology at the University of Cambridge and Fellow, Tutor and Director of Studies in Biology at Downing College. Being unable to take office immediately the Board of Trustees appointed mycologist Roy Watling as Acting Regius Keeper for the intervening period, confident that his energy and dedication would continue the pace of change.

In 1988 a landmark in the recent history of the Royal Botanic Garden took place; the tenth and final volume of the *Flora of Turkey* was published, ending a project which had spanned a quarter of a century. Following hard on the heels of this event came the retirement of its 'director', Peter Davis. Originally a student in the University Botany Department in the late 1940s, Davis was appointed lecturer in 1950 and eventually became Head of the Plant Taxonomy section - a position he held for 20 years. Many research students developed their expertise under Professor Davis, before becoming key staff in the Botanic Garden. His retirement marked the final severance of a formal Edinburgh University presence at the Botanic Garden. However, under David Ingram active collaboration not only continues through the joint supervision of postgraduate students who spend much time in the Library and Herbarium, and in the lectures given at the University by Botanic Garden staff, but also has been reinvigorated with the launch in 1992 of a new joint MSc course in Plant Taxonomy.

With an impact that echoes that of his illustrious predecessor Isaac Bayley Balfour a century before, David Ingram's arrival in 1990 has heralded a period of dynamic change for the Garden. To the new post of Deputy Director and Head of Science he appointed Dr David Mann, a phycologist from Edinburgh University. In line with the Strategic Plan for Scientific Research, programmes have been initiated to embrace the new disciplines of information technology and molecular biology. To integrate the Garden's core research on an international scale, a Scientific Advisory Group comprising eminent botanists from other institutes has been established.

Following the appointment in 1991 of the Garden's first Business Development Director, a post created to ensure that grant-in-aid will be supplemented through sponsorship and commercial activities, the Botanics Trading Company was launched in 1992 and is proceeding to develop visitor centres and shops with plant sales at each of the four gardens. In addition a Friends of the Royal Botanic Garden has been established to encourage the active support of the public.

Notwithstanding these changes, great care is being taken to ensure that they are never at the expense of the central work of the Garden, which always has been and will continue to be the curation of the collections and pursuit of plant science research, horticulture, conservation and education activities of the very highest quality.

It is a far cry from the days - not so long ago in the Botanic Garden's history - when botany and horticulture were fairly parochial occupations. The urgency of change to avert ecological disaster has given a new vision. Now local and global, but definitely not parochial, botany and horticulture come under the umbrella of plant science whose role is to safeguard and enhance the primary resource of both natural and man-made environments. And that, in its widest sense, is where the future of the Royal Botanic Garden Edinburgh lies as it goes forward into the 21st century.

A FASCINATION FOR FUNGI
August 15—October 18, 1987   Monday—Saturday 10-5   Sunday 11-5

Agaricus augustus by Beatrix Potter   © Armitt Trust Collection, Ambleside

Inverleith House · Royal Botanic Garden Edinburgh

The exhibition "A Fascination for Fungi" was presented in honour of Douglas Henderson on his retirement. Among the original works shown were several watercolours by Beatrix Potter.
© Armitt Trust Collection, Ambleside.

David Ingram with Professor Sun Handong, Director of the Kunming Institute of Botany in Yunnan celebrate the official twinning of the Chinese Institute with the Royal Botanic Garden Edinburgh in 1991.

So what exactly does the Royal Botanic Garden do? A visit to any of the four gardens might give the impression that their main purpose is the meticulous growing and labelling of plants, many of which have names that even keen gardeners have never previously encountered. In part this is true, for the Garden's Living Collection contains representatives of all the world's flora, not just those popular in cultivation, and maintains and displays them to the very highest standard. But the work of the Royal Botanic Garden can be likened to an iceberg of which only a small proportion is displayed above the surface. While its crowning glory, the living plants and gardens, are highly visible, a great deal of the Botanic Garden's work goes on behind the scenes.

Opposite. An Edinburgh botanist examines *Rhododendron adenogynum* in the Yulong Shan in Yunnan during the Sino-British Li Chang Expedition.

Meconopsis grandis was first collected by Ludlow and Sherriff on their expedition to Bhutan in 1933. This striking plant has been in cultivation at Edinburgh ever since.

BEHIND THE SCENES AT THE BOTANICS

The Royal Botanic Garden's collections do not consist solely of living plants. There is also the Library - the largest collection of botanical works in northern Britain - and a vast Herbarium of preserved plants. These collections contain much that is rare, priceless and irreplaceable. Maintaining them as part of our national heritage and as resources for staff and visitors is a major part of the Garden's work.

It is largely on the expert curation of each of these collections that the core of the Garden's work depends. This can be divided into three main areas: research, education and conservation. First and foremost, the Garden carries out research into plants (including fungi) as living organisms. It describes and names species, discovers how they evolved and where they are distributed, and learns how they grow and interact with other living things. Understanding plants at these levels provides the basis for effective conservation, plant breeding and genetic engineering. The educational side of the Botanic Garden's work has changed significantly in the course of its history: originally for medical students only, it now embraces everyone, from casual visitors to full-time students and from small children to senior citizens. Much of the education programme has a conservation slant and is designed for schools and the general public, but the Garden is also involved with formal education, running a world-famous horticultural training course and supervising postgraduate botanical research students. Whereas the work of the Garden has centred around curation, research and education since its very beginnings, conservation is a comparatively new undertaking. Plant species are becoming extinct at an alarming rate, and the plant diversity upon which we depend for food, vital raw materials and many medicines is ebbing away as habitats such as wetlands and rainforests are destroyed. Research, education and conservation are bound up with

Wholesale clearance of the Chilean conifer *Fitzroya cupressoides* leaves its indelible mark on a temperate rainforest. More than 230 of the world's 662 conifers are listed as threatened. The Garden's Conifer Conservation Programme seeks to secure a future for these important species.

each other. To quote Baba Dioum from Senegal: 'in the end we will conserve only what we love; we will love only what we understand; we will understand only what we are taught.'

From herbals to microfilms:
the Library's 300 years of botanical literature

In the early days of the Botanic Garden, the only books available for consultation were those owned by the Regius Keeper of the time. Books have always been synonymous with learning and, as might be expected, both the Garden's founders, Andrew Balfour and Robert Sibbald, were avid book collectors. Andrew Balfour was reputed to have the finest library in Scotland, consisting of over 3000 volumes and numerous manuscripts. The majority of works were on medicine and natural history, and though the library was his personal property, he was unfailingly generous in allowing access to it.

If anything, Robert Sibbald was even keener on books than his partner. 'From the tyme I entered to the Coledge, any mony I gott, I did imploy it for buying of books.' In 1723, six months after Sibbald's death, his personal library went the same way as that of Balfour's - its 5500 or so works, including a number he had written, being put up for auction. The entire library was bought by the Faculty of Advocates and two centuries later, in 1925, it was presented to the nation, forming the nucleus of the National Library of Scotland.

The Garden was endowed with its Royal Charter and first Regius Keeper (James Sutherland) in 1699. By this time Sutherland also held the Chair of Botany at the Town's College (later the University) and had written his *Hortus Medicus Edinburgensis: or, a catalogue of the plants in the Physical Garden at Edinburgh*, which was published in 1683. Before this, the Town Council gave instructions that the College should have a special room for keeping books and seeds. Sutherland therefore built up the embryo departmental library at his own expense and most probably took it with him when his teaching post was terminated in 1706. The following year it too passed into the hands of the Faculty of Advocates.

Charles Alston's library was similarly extensive and kept at the Garden for others to consult. Likewise, it was auctioned after his death. Fortunately, some of his own works and manuscripts escaped this fate and remain in the Library to this day. After 1763, when John Hope obtained an annual grant from the Treasury toward the upkeep of the Garden, books were purchased specifically for use by staff and students. Not all were destined for the Library; some being sent abroad in exchange for plants and seeds. The majority of books at the Garden were nevertheless those belonging to Hope himself, and when he died, these were removed by his family. In 1899, as a bequest from Hope's grandson, these 200 volumes, including James Sutherland's catalogue of 1683, were returned to the Garden.

The Library continued to increase through purchases made during Daniel Rutherford's term of office. The next two Regius Keepers, Robert Graham and John Hutton Balfour, exerted considerable influence on the Library's development. Both had been instrumental in founding the Botanical Society of Edinburgh in 1836 and took a keen interest in establishing its library and herbarium. The Botanical Society's library acquired several major collections from some of the many other specialist societies that came and went during the early 19th century. In 1872 the Society's library and herbarium were gifted to the Royal Botanic Garden via the Government 'on the understanding that the Government will provide for their accommodation and keeping, and that they will be open for consultation to the members of the Botanical Society, as well as to the public ...'. The decision was made not because the

The first page of Robert Eliot's *Hortus Siccus*, a bound volume of pressed and dried plants.

John Hope's personal bookplate, from one of the many volumes ultimately bequeathed to the Library.

Botanical Society was defunct - on the contrary, it was flourishing then as it still does today - but for the reason that its library was superior to that of the Botanic Garden and would be better and more conveniently used at the Garden where most of the Society's members based their research activities. The entire library comprised 1000 or so volumes, botanical manuscripts (including those of Robert Graham), correspondence from all over the world and a number of journals, notably a complete run of Curtis's *Botanical Magazine*.

Despite these developments, Hutton Balfour was far from content as the Library still lacked many standard works. His successor, Alexander Dickson, managed to obtain an allowance from the Government for purchasing books. Though a decided step forward, it proved inadequate and Dickson overspent; undeterred, he paid for certain journals out of his own pocket so that no gaps occurred.

The problem of a small and underfunded Library was taken up by Isaac Bayley Balfour and in 1889 a basic £30 per annum was agreed by the Government for the purchase of books. Five years later this was increased to £100. The Royal Botanic Gardens Kew further supported the improvement of the Library at Inverleith by sending large numbers of books that were surplus to requirements. So keen was Bayley Balfour on improving the Library that he scoured the second-hand market himself and bought anything of interest. One of his great finds was a 15th-century *Latin Herbarius* that once belonged to James Sutherland. His perception of the importance of botanical reference books, especially on systematic botany, was such that he bought certain works for the express use of the Garden's plant collectors. A set of Hooker's *Flora of British India* was purchased in 1905 and sent to George Forrest in Rangoon and 75 years later these valuable volumes were given back to the Royal Botanic Garden by Forrest's son.

Journals were also high on Bayley Balfour's list of priorities. In addition to founding *Annals of Botany* and *Notes from the Royal Botanic Garden Edinburgh*, he made agreements with the Botanical Society of Edinburgh for the exchange of journals, many of which are still in force. By 1900, the Library was receiving 140 different journals, mostly from abroad.

Under Isaac Bayley Balfour the Library grew so large that it called for full-time maintenance and organisation. In 1912 he persuaded the Treasury to employ a librarian. The first person appointed to the post was James Johnstone, an antiquarian bookseller from Dumfriesshire and a descendant of Robinson Crusoe. Johnstone had a passion for lavish bookbindings, as can be seen in books that date

R K Greville's *Flora Edinensis* contains drawings of local plants, including cryptogams accompanied by notes in Greville's own hand. This fungus (*Cucurbitaria elongata*) was found on twigs of gorse.

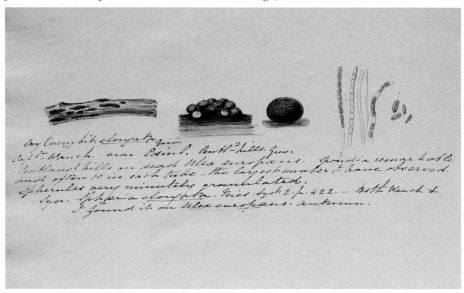

back to his time. The Library was then housed in various rooms and corridors which were crammed from floor to ceiling with all manner of items. The system devised for finding each item was to record the location on its cover and in a master catalogue. Clarity, if not brevity, was the system's greatest virtue, certain items being catalogued as 'on top of tea-chest in Room 4'!

Bayley Balfour never tired of asking the Treasury for more money to spend on books and he passed on a number of tips to his successor, William Wright Smith, on how best to continue the campaign. But the situation, and thus the priorities, changed: war-time economies intervened; and it also became obvious that adding to the collection was not necessarily the best policy while the present accommodation was so restricted. The problem of accommodation was brought sharply into focus in 1941 when the entire Cleghorn Memorial Library and botanical artefacts of the Royal Scottish Museum were transferred to the Royal Botanic Garden.

In 1928 Wright Smith wrote to the Board of Works:

> *'I need hardly emphasise the importance of a combination of botanic garden, a botanical library, a herbarium and a botanical museum. The full value of each can only be secured when they are associated. Our herbarium, the most valuable outside London, is housed in an old building used a century ago for flower shows by the local Horticultural Society. The library accommodation is far from adequate either for the visits of the public or for the proper arrangement of the books. It seems to me therefore, well worth consideration that the whole of the problem should be solved by the erection of one adequate building which would accommodate museum materials, library and herbarium. All three are shorn of the greater part of their usefulness when separated from each other as they are at present.'*

It took five years to record and find space for the 4000 volumes, which included classics and rare works that would have filled Bayley Balfour's heart with joy.

Under Johnstone's successor, J Marguerite Alford, the Library - now totalling some 35,000 volumes - was completely reorganised according to the Bliss Biographical Classification system, modified so that items in the Library could be readily cross-referenced to specimens in the Herbarium. With this reorganisation, the Library became a fully fledged professional institution, albeit in cramped and outdated surroundings. The elements of personal contribution - for so long a major part of its history - were still present however, and some of Wright Smith's own books remain there to this day.

In 1962 the University requested that all books and journals belonging to the Botany Department, which had been housed since the beginning in the Botanic Garden Library, be extracted so that the Department could assemble a separate library. This was a time-consuming task as the joint arrangement had been so long-standing and apparently permanent that few items were marked as University property. The separation was nevertheless accomplished, though University staff were to remain the largest category of borrower from the Library at Inverleith.

Meanwhile, the new Herbarium and Library building was under construction and in 1964 the Library's contents were transferred to it. During the same year the Botanic Garden received a major bequest of some 40,000 photographs, diaries and manuscripts belonging to the American plant collector Joseph Rock. Some were shared with the Deutsche Morgenländische Gesellschaft in Berlin but the majority stayed in Edinburgh. The Library now contained about 17,000 books and 25,500 volumes of journals, and received over 700 periodicals. The move to new premises

The Library's collection of rare works includes John Parkinson's '*Paradisi in sole . . .*' published in 1629. The book contains many fine wood engravings showing plants in cultivation.

occurred under the guidance of Librarian William Brown, who is also remembered for his co-authorship of the tercentenary history of the Royal Botanic Garden. His successor, Manjil Mathew, also contributed an important Garden publication, *The History of the Royal Botanic Garden Library, Edinburgh*, which was published in 1987.

During Douglas Henderson's Regius Keepership, Library stock doubled in size: gaps in the collection were filled; the second-hand market was more widely exploited; valuable archival material such as paintings by Margaret Stones and papers belonging to Beatrix Potter, George Forrest and other major figures was acquired; and microfilm copies of unobtainable works were ordered.

The Royal Botanic Garden's Library is now the largest and most comprehensive collection of literature on botanical and horticultural subjects in northern Britain, with over 75,000 books and some 2000 different journals. Among its treasures are some very old herbals, including the *New Herball* (1551) by William Turner and John Gerard's *Herbal* (1597) - standard works in the days when the Botanic Garden was founded.

Right. A porter stands beside *Rhododendron rufum in* Min Shan, China. The image is from the Joseph Rock archive, gifted to the Garden in 1964.

Below. *Rhododendron forrestii* seed capsule painted by Lillian Snelling in 1918.

Plant portraits: illustration and photography

The flowering of something new or rare is an event both publicised among staff and recorded for posterity in photographs, drawings or paintings. In many cases the final record of the event is preservation as a herbarium specimen.

There is a long tradition of commissioning botanical artists and of calling upon the artistic talents of staff members. Early records are few and far between but by the 18th century, botanical illustration played an important part in recording and teaching. Regius Keeper John Hope was an accomplished artist, as was his pupil James Robertson who drew native plants for his Professor. The volume of illustration burgeoned in the 19th century, when botanical illustration was considered a social accomplishment. Alexander Dickson illustrated his lecture notes with meticulous coloured drawings and Isaac Bayley Balfour commissioned Lillian Snelling (who subsequently became Kew's principal artist) to paint many of the finest rhododendrons and primulas that were then being introduced by collectors such as George Forrest.

Ironically, the heyday of botanical illustration marked the beginning of its decline as the passion for recording was increasingly satisfied by photography. Recognising his talents as an artist, Bayley Balfour appointed the former gardener Robert Adam to

This portrait of *Rhododendron lineare* by Mary Bates, painted in 1990 is one of a series of illustrations of selected species from the Garden's unique collection of Vireya rhododendrons.

the new post of Photographer and Artist in 1915. Over a period of 35 years, Adam gained a reputation not only for photographing plants, both in the Garden and in the Scottish countryside, but also as one of the country's foremost landscape photographers.

With advances in photography, the contribution made by photographs to research, education and conservation has increased considerably, and today the Garden's photographers record the plants at all four gardens, both *in situ* and in the studio, and supply photographs for publicity, publication and display purposes. They also process the photographic results of microscopic studies carried out by the scientific staff. The Royal Botanic Garden's collection of images includes archival material, photographs taken by staff members and donations from private individuals. *The Royal Botanic Garden Edinburgh Book of the Scottish Garden* published in 1989 featured photographs of over 50 of Scotland's finest gardens, with emphasis on their more unusual plants and was drawn from this collection.

The bulk of illustration required by the Royal Botanic Garden consists of line drawings for Floras, monographs and revisions. Some are drawn from living plants; many from herbarium specimens. In recent years botanical illustration has emerged from its mid-20th century doldrums and is once again appreciated for the aesthetic and scientific contribution it makes to recording plant life.

Dried and pickled:
plants for research in the Herbarium

A herbarium is a collection of preserved plants generally stored according to a scientific classification. The Royal Botanic Garden's Herbarium is of international importance, containing over two million specimens. Though comprehensive, it is particularly rich in the plant groups and geographical areas in which the Garden specialises. It holds, for example, major collections of the rhododendron family, conifers, gingers and all lower plant groups - ferns, fungi, lichens, mosses and algae. The Edinburgh Herbarium is the authoritative reference collection for Scotland's flora. Surprisingly, it is also regarded as the world's leading herbarium for Chinese material outside China itself. There is an emphasis too on cultivated plants, which are seldom well-represented in herbaria.

The bulk of material consists of dried and pressed plants which are mounted on sheets of thin card. Drying is an extremely effective way of preserving most plants, retaining many features unaltered. The sheets are protected by folders and stacked in fire- and pest-proof steel cabinets. The cabinets are arranged in family order, within which the sheets of specimens are filed according to genus and species and split into geographical areas. Specimens of mosses, liverworts and small algae are often put into paper packets before being mounted. Each specimen is labelled with the scientific name of the plant, the

Left. Labels on herbarium sheets give the scientific name of the plant, the locality where it was collected and other valuable information. This one is written in Forrest's own hand.

Right. A herbarium sheet; this beautiful specimen of *Gentiana sino-ornata* was collected by George Forrest in 1910.

exact locality and date it was collected, any significant information (such as habitat, local name and uses for food or medicine), the collector's name and a number. All specimens of the same kind collected at one time are given the same number, and duplicate specimens are distributed to various herbaria. Each species has what is known as a 'type specimen' - usually one of the original specimens from which a formal description of the species was first made. The importance of this specimen lies in the fact that in any dispute over the name of a species, the type specimen is the final 'arbiter'. Any specimens judged to be the same as the type can bear the same name; others cannot. Plant parts that are not amenable to mounting on sheets are stored in various other ways. Fleshy material or particularly complex flowers are pickled in jars of preserving liquid and kept in cupboards as the Spirit Collection. Seeds and dry fruits make up the Carpological Collection which is packed into labelled boxes. Samples of timber are also stored separately. Fungi, lichens and slime moulds are not pressed, but carefully dried in warm air cabinets. Microscopic algae are mounted on microscope slides or pickled. Botanical illustrations and photographs (mainly in the form of slides) also play an important part in herbarium records, showing details of habit and colour that are usually lost in processing. Where relevant, specimens are cross-referred to material in the Library and to the Living Collections, simplifying the task of locating various data on a particular plant.

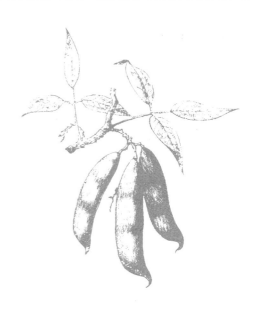

Fresh plant material is compared with reference specimens from the Herbarium to ensure accurate identification.

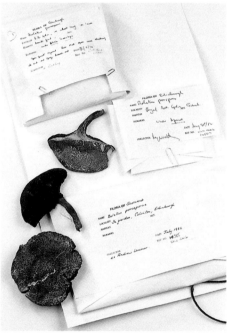

Top. Arisaema speciosum, although bleached, retains its features when preserved in pickle.

Bottom. Fruitbodies of fungi such as *Boletus porosporus* are air dried and lose some of their shape but their identifying features can still be observed under a microscope.

The main enemy of herbarium specimens, other than fire, flooding or damp, is insects, especially the larvae of skin beetles (Dermestidae). Aromatic plants, such as those of the carrot (Umbelliferae), sage (Labiatae) and daisy (Compositae) families offer the greatest attraction, whereas grasses and ferns are rarely attacked. In order to protect the dried specimens from pests, newly acquired material is deep frozen for two days and the entire herbarium is fumigated periodically.

Pressing plants in order to preserve them was probably done to some extent from the very start of the Royal Botanic Garden's history. Well-kept herbarium specimens last almost indefinitely. Edinburgh's oldest, of *Myrsine africana* is dated 1697. There is, however, no evidence of a herbarium as such until the 18th century when the Regius Keeper of the time, John Hope, encouraged the systematic collection and preservation of Scottish native plants. One of his students, Archibald Menzies, compiled an important herbarium of grasses, sedges, ferns, mosses, lichens and algae beginning while still a student and continuing during two epic voyages around the world. Its specimens may still be consulted today.

It was the 19th century, however, with its passion for collecting, that established the Herbarium as an important resource for research. Much of this was in fact carried out by the Botanical Society of Edinburgh, rather than the Royal Botanic Garden itself. The Botanical Society numbered among its objectives 'the formation in Edinburgh of an Herbarium of Foreign and British Plants'. To this end, the regulations specified that members had to contribute 50 species (plus duplicates) a year, with foreign members agreeing to an initial 500 specimens of at least 100 species, with a subsequent minimum annual donation of 300 specimens, representing at least 50 species. Far from daunting prospective members, this requirement appears to have been a positive incentive. The collection began in 1836 with 300 specimens from Switzerland and was soon followed by others from far and wide, including many from members in the colonies.

Dried the specimens might be, but dry as dust - never! Collectors were rarely trained botanists but rather were missionaries, doctors, military officers, geologists and so forth, many of whom took part in dramatic voyages of discovery. There are specimens from Charles Darwin's voyage in the *Beagle* and from Livingstone's exploration of the Zambezi. Not all collectors were men. Victorian women played a no less heroic role in plant collecting and often possessed considerable artistic talents which enabled them to draw or paint specimens as well as pressing them for future research. Among them was the Countess of Dalhousie who in 1839, two years before her death, received the unusual honour of being made an Honorary Member of the Botanical Society of Edinburgh. Apparently she turned to botanising 'as a solace in circumstances of severe domestic affliction', being stationed abroad with her husband who became Governor General of India. She spent all her time collecting and died with a list of wanted plants in her hand. The Countess of Dalhousie's East Indian collection of about 1200 specimens is one of the Herbarium's most treasured possessions.

Within a year of its founding, the Botanical Society's herbarium boasted 60,000 specimens, about half of which were foreign. The next year it almost doubled in size again and became a victim of its own success. Already too large for the Society to handle, it was merged in 1838 with the University herbarium. Further growth made even this arrangement unmanageable and in 1863 the collection was moved to the Royal Botanic Garden to combine with the Garden Herbarium. The amalgamated Herbarium was housed in the former Exhibition Hall of the Royal Caledonian Horticultural Society (today known as the Caledonian Hall), finally moving into its current purpose-built premises in 1964.

Rhododendron rarum (*Left*), in common with
certain other rhododendrons, has protective scales
on the underside of its leaves. These are clearly
portrayed in the scanning electron microscope
(*Right*). The scale shown is c.0.1mm in diameter.

Herbaria tend to grow in leaps and bounds, depending on sudden influxes of
specimens from donations, purchases, exchanges or expeditions. Two of the largest
accessions were the Glasgow University herbarium, consisting of well over 100,000
specimens, which was deposited on permanent loan in 1965, and the collections of
George Forrest, whose seven Chinese expeditions yielded some 30,000 specimens.
In recent years the emphasis has been on building up collections in which Edinburgh
specialises.

A great deal of research into herbarium and living plant materials is carried out in the
laboratory. Of particular importance is the detailed anatomy and morphology of
specimens revealed in the transmission and scanning electron microscopes. It is here,
for example, that the details of pollen grains - the 'finger prints' of the plant world
which are perfectly preserved by drying - are studied to throw new light upon the
relationship between different species. The core work on classifying lower plants
such as fungi and lichens is especially dependent on such laboratory facilities.

The herbarium is the cornerstone of botanical research, the entire scientific system of
naming plants being based upon it. It also serves as a vast filing system on the physical
characteristics of the plant world that is otherwise quite impossible to amass in one
place. The specimens are used by scientists in various ways, most commonly for
direct observation and comparison, but also for dissection and examination using
microscopes or chemical analysis. Having specimens of every known species from a
region is of great value in naming unidentified plants, compiling floras and
determining new records or new species. Though herbarium studies were originally
concerned mainly with identification and classification, the range of information
they can now supply has widened to cover every aspect of the plant world, including
ecology, evolution, economic and medicinal uses. With environmental concerns
now to the forefront, such information on the natural resources of an area is of
increasing importance for conserving species, saving damaged ecosystems and
formulating aid and development projects.

A meal break in Pari La during a plant collecting expedition for the Flora of Bhutan.

WILD FLOWERS OF THE WORLD: FLORISTIC RESEARCH

According to popular opinion 'a rose is a rose is a rose', but this is singularly unhelpful when communicating about specific roses in contexts such as hybridization, landscape design, medicinal uses or endangered species. The accurate naming and description of plants is vital, for each species - and even subspecies - differs from its close relatives not only in form and structure but also in cultural requirements, pollinators and pests, as well as in biochemical make-up, and thus in nutritional and medicinal value. To do this, botanists classify plants according to their differences and similarities and give each a scientific (Latin) name, following rules agreed in The International Code of Botanical Nomenclature. This facet of their work is known as taxonomy.

The work of taxonomists can be likened to doing a large and complex jigsaw puzzle that has many parts missing (the missing parts, in the case of plants, often being extinct or undiscovered species). It begins with observation and description, then comparison, and finally with classification - putting the piece in its place. With over a quarter of a million species of flowering plants alone and relatively few taxonomists - and only a handful in most tropical countries where the majority of the plants occur - it is not surprising that the jigsaw is far from complete. New species are still being discovered; extinctions are occurring all the time; and plants that were first described when botany was in its infancy have to be reclassified (and renamed) in the light of new information.

Taxonomic research has two main directions: Floras which are comprehensive accounts of all the plants within a certain country, region or area of interest; and monographs or revisions, that describe just one group of plants and their inter-relationships. A Flora is fundamental to many branches of research, from conservation and land-use, forestry, agriculture and horticulture, to crop protection and plant breeding. It can also promote greater interest in a region's native plants once this information is passed through books, films and tourist literature.

The classic Flora is a hefty work of impeccable scholarship which stands the test of time. However, it is not always 'user friendly', usually being physically far too large for field work, often unillustrated, and though comprehensive, containing descriptions that virtually only trained botanists can understand. For this reason there is now a move to produce a more accessible type of Flora, somewhere between the academic flora and a popular guide, which will be easy for all specialists to handle and use in the field. Increasingly, Flora projects now hold their information on computer databases. This allows selected information - for example, on economic plants or medicinal uses - to be extracted as required.

The Royal Botanic Garden is one of the comparatively few institutes worldwide that specialise in taxonomic botany. It both organises and contributes to a wide range of Floras. Recently completed is the *Flora of Turkey*, which describes some 8800 species of flowering plants and whose tenth and final volume was published in 1988. This collaborative project between the Botanic Garden and the University of Edinburgh on the Flora of Turkey project spanned some 25 years under the leadership of Professor Peter Davis. Expeditions during the 1950s and 1960s resulted in large additions of Turkish material to the Living Collections and Herbarium. This served to expand the interest and expertise in southwest Asia - more popularly known as the Middle East. Commencing in Isaac Bayley Balfour's time, it continues to this day in the Edinburgh-based *Flora of Arabia* and through contributions to *Flora Iranica* (based in Vienna) and *Flora of Pakistan* (compiled in Karachi and Rawalpindi). In addition, it had the effect, through contacts and co-operation, of increasing the numbers of botanists in Turkey itself, many of whom visited Edinburgh to carry out research and receive training.

Interest in the information contained in published Floras is by no means confined to botanists. The Floras of Turkey and Iran, for example, are widely used by horticulturists, as many popular plants, such as *Cyclamen* and *Iris*, have their centres of distribution in this region. And it has encouraged interest in the conservation of these plants, many being collected from the wild for the horticultural industry. More important still, the Middle Eastern Floras hold the key to wild ancestors of some of the world's major foods, such as wheat, grapes, figs, dates, peas and lentils, onions, almonds and olives. Wild ancestors of these foods are of critical importance in the breeding of new resistant strains when those currently in cultivation succumb to epidemics of pests or diseases. Determining the identity and distribution of these species is of singular importance in areas where the natural vegetation is under threat from development, erosion or overgrazing.

A Flora of the Arabian Peninsula and Socotra was initiated jointly with the Royal Botanic Gardens Kew in the late 1970s. The region covered by the *Flora of Arabia*, far from being a vast desert, includes grasslands, lush forests and mountains rising over 12,000ft (3650m). Up to 20% of the plant species are found nowhere else. Many are highly adapted to arid conditions and may prove of value in halting or reversing desertification in other parts of the world.

Of outstanding interest is the island of Socotra - a mere 75 miles (120km) long and 25 miles (40km) wide - which is home to 750 species of flowering plants and ferns, of which a third occur nowhere else. They include some very distinctive plants, such as the dragon's blood tree (*Dracaena cinnabari*), which yields a red resin used in varnishes and medicines, and the obese cucumber tree (*Dendrosicyos socotranus*), as well as the horticulturally important *Begonia socotrana*, from which winter-flowering begonias were bred. The uniqueness of Socotra as one of the few undeveloped dry tropical islands has attracted the involvement of the Worldwide Fund for Nature (WWF) and a project to advise the Yemeni Government on sustainable development that will leave the delicate ecosystem intact is based at the Royal Botanic Garden Edinburgh.

Concentrating for many years on the flora of a particular country almost inevitably develops an active interest in nearby regions. Peter Davis and others collected in Greece as well as Turkey, giving the Royal Botanic Garden a continuing involvement in Eurasian plants which is currently manifest in contributions to the Copenhagen-based *Flora Hellenica*. Meanwhile, the plant life of extensive areas of Asia remains to be documented. Contributions to the Floras of Thailand and Malesia, with the islands of New Guinea, Borneo, Sulawesi, Java and Sumatra, and the Malay Peninsula, are currently being made by botanists at the Royal Botanic Garden, and the involvement in Himalayan Floras is continuing.

Deep in central Asia lies Bhutan, a kingdom the size of Switzerland which is hemmed in from the north by inaccessible stretches of the eastern Himalayas. Disputed since the 18th century by Britain, Tibet, China and India, it has only recently been opened to westerners and entry is unpredictable. With a sparse population and traditional systems of land management, the natural vegetation remains relatively undisturbed, with over 5000 species ranging from alpine to subtropical. It is particularly rich in plants with economic potential: rhododendrons, orchids, wild cereals and species with medicinal uses. Exploration of Bhutan's flora began in 1838 when the first European botanist, William Griffith, collected 1200 plants that formed the basis of Bhutanese entries in J D Hooker's *Flora of British India* (1875-97). Roland Cooper, who was later to become Curator of the Royal Botanic Garden, made important

Woodland with frankincense (*Boswellia sacra*) and dragon's blood trees (*Dracaena cinnabari*) in the mountains of Socotra.

Pressing plants in Dhofar, with Jebbali tribespeople looking on.

collections during 1913/14, many of which ended up at Edinburgh. Further significant collections were made by the expeditions of Frank Ludlow and George Sherriff (between 1933 and 1950) who brought back plants, seeds and over 6000 herbarium specimens.

In 1974 the Royal Government of Bhutan asked the Overseas Development Agency in London to compile a Flora based on these early plant collections. The request was eminently reasonable, as the country of origin had so far failed to benefit in any way from the exploration - one might say, the exploitation - of its flora. With the largest existing herbarium collections by far being at the Royal Botanic Garden Edinburgh, botanists at the Garden were duly invited to undertake this project.

The Flora of Bhutan, in nine volumes, is now well under way, the first part being published in 1983. It is a 'new style' paperback flora, economically produced so that it is readily available and affordable, especially in Bhutan. The project has been funded by the Overseas Development Administration (ODA) and the Department of Agriculture and Fisheries for Scotland (DAFS), with support from the Royal Government and Forestry Department of Bhutan. Contemporary explorations for the Flora began in 1975 when 700 species were collected in just three weeks. A major expedition in 1979 yielded 2150 higher plant and 1100 moss and liverwort specimens from both montane and subtropical forests.

While some Edinburgh botanists trek to remote regions to document and collect plants, others spend their time studying those much closer to home. Since the 1970s the Royal Botanic Garden has collaborated with the Nature Conservancy Council (now Scottish Natural Heritage) to survey the occurrence and distribution of both higher plants and cryptogams in various Scottish habitats, especially uplands. This close working relationship led in 1991 to the Scottish Rare Plants Project which will provide a database for each rare plant species in Scotland.

Quite literally on the doorstep are the plants described in the Botany of the Lothians, the area of southeast central Scotland which includes Edinburgh. This project, launched in 1981, is led by the Botanical Society of Edinburgh (recently renamed the Botanical Society of Scotland). It involves active participation by staff and extensive use of the Herbarium at the Garden.

Cultivated plants are a particularly difficult area for taxonomists as they involve many complex hybrids, cultivars and unverified or illegitimate names. To complicate matters further, even correctly named true species may develop uncharacteristic habits in cultivation. For many years there has been consternation among botanists and horticulturists at the proliferation of inaccurate scientific names for cultivated plants. The problem is that some plants are misidentified when introduced; others are given different names by different growers; and many are cultivars or hybrids whose origin and consequent name may be dubious. The situation is made worse by the fact that standard reference works continue to be used by growers for naming plants even when they are considerably out of date. Also, gardeners become familiar with - and attached to - the scientific names of favourite plants and fail to appreciate the (often highly technical) reasons for taxonomic revisions.

In order to bring some semblance of order to this taxonomic chaos, a *European Garden Flora* was proposed which would combine botanical accuracy with a degree of accessibility to the layperson. The project began in 1979, co-ordinated and edited at Edinburgh, and published by Cambridge University Press. This six-volume Flora will describe some 17,000 species, providing both an indispensable reference work for horticulturists and a basis for more popular illustrated guides.

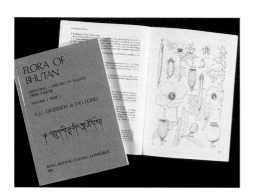

The first volume of the *Flora of Bhutan* was published in 1983.

Recording the locality of the close-headed alpine rush (*Carex norvegica*) in the Grampian mountains as part of the Scottish Rare Plants Project.

FOCUS ON FAMILIES:

Research into plant groups

In the course of preparing Floras, it may become apparent that the taxonomy of certain groups of plants is out of date and in need of revision. Detailed scientific descriptions of the physical appearance of the plants themselves form the traditional basis of revisions. However, there is an emphasis now on considering their chemistry, cytogenetics and detailed cell structure, as well as the wider contexts of evolution, geographical distribution, ecology and ethnobotany. Taxonomy at Edinburgh has focused on a range of major plant groups including rhododendrons and other members of the heath family, orchids, gingers and conifers.

Left. George Forrest's collections included this gentian found in Yunnan in 1906. Named in his honour, *Gentiana georgei* is photographed here in Nepal.

Right. Ceratostemma charianthum, a tropical member of the Ericaceae from the mountains of Ecuador.

Rhododendrons and their kin

The genus *Rhododendron* belongs to the heath family (Ericaceae), which has 100 genera and over 3000 species, many of which are important in cultivation. In addition to rhododendrons and azaleas, this family includes such popular garden plants as heathers (*Erica* and *Calluna*), *Pieris* and *Gaultheria*, as well as cranberries and blueberries (*Vaccinium*). The Royal Botanic Garden holds major collections of both living and herbarium specimens of Ericaceae and has a long history of research into the family.

The name of the Garden has been inextricably linked with rhododendrons since George Forrest brought back over 300 new species from Tibet and China in the early part of this century. The impact of these collections was enormous, more than doubling the number of known species and occasioning the first major monographic work undertaken by Edinburgh taxonomists. To begin with, the emphasis was largely on Himalayan species of rhododendrons and other Ericaceae, most of which are hardy. But as time went on, research turned increasingly to the poorly known tropical members of the family - a trend which has gained urgency with the destruction of forests in the tropics.

In order to deal as quickly as possible with George Forrest's collections, Isaac Bayley Balfour devised an *ad hoc* temporary classification based on groups of related species

The red-flowered form of the New Guinea orchid *Dendrobium cuthbertsonii*, a diminutive plant with disproportionately large blooms.

The shell ginger, *Alpinia zerumbet*, is a popular ornamental plant with arching racemes of waxy, fragrant flowers atop elegant canes.

- 'Series' - each of which was named after the most typical or common representative. Unfortunately, the preliminary system was then adopted by many taxonomists and rhododendron growers, including the Rhododendron Society. With further introductions by collectors such as Frank Kingdon Ward, Reginald Farrer, Joseph Rock, Frank Ludlow and George Sherriff, it was obvious that more taxonomic work on the genus was needed and a revision of Balfour's 'Series' was started at Edinburgh in the 1940s. This work was largely based on plants in cultivation, as field work in China and the Himalaya was almost impossible at that time. In the mid-1970s a major new revision of the genus was undertaken. The first parts to be published dealt with the scaly-leaved or lepidote rhododendrons (subgenus *Rhododendron*), comprising some 450 species, followed by the main grouping of non-scaly (elepidote) species (subgenus *Hymenanthes*), with over 250 species. Within each subgenus, related species are grouped in sections and subsections. This reclassification is now reflected in the Living Collections, particularly at Edinburgh and Benmore, where representatives are planted according to sections and subsections.

Gardeners in temperate parts of the world are familiar with the hardy rhododendrons which originate mainly in the Sino-Himalaya, but about a third of the genus (nearly 300 species) are tropical, occurring largely in southeast Asia. These belong to section *Vireya* in subgenus *Rhododendron* and include some of the loveliest of all rhododendrons, with a great variety of colours, shapes and scents. The Royal Botanic Garden has about 100 species of Vireya rhododendron in the Living Collection, many of which are new to cultivation, having been introduced by recent expeditions to Sarawak, Sabah and New Guinea. A selection can be seen in the Peat House where they flower mainly in winter and spring.

Orchids, Gingers and African Violets

The huge island of New Guinea is home not only to many Vireya rhododendrons and gesneriads, but also to vast numbers of orchids. Among these is a group of *Dendrobium* species which were virtually unknown until recently. Belonging to section *Oxyglossum*, these dendrobiums have large, often brightly coloured flowers borne on diminutive plants. Interest in the group began quite by chance in 1962 when an Australian plantation owner in Papua New Guinea, asked the Royal Botanic Garden for a botanist to collect orchids in the Owen Stanley Mountains behind his land. An expedition to Malaya and Sarawak to collect gesneriads was already underway and a diversion was made to New Guinea.

The orchids found on this and a subsequent expedition were of both botanical and horticultural interest. They included the translucent blue *Dendrobium hellwigianum* with a red lip, *D. cuthbertsonii* which may be red, pink, white or bicoloured, and the equally variable *D. vexillarius*, whose yellows, purples and scarlets seem to occur within certain geographical areas. Work on the New Guinea orchids at the Royal Botanic Garden not only involved taxonomic revision but parallel experimentation to determine their cultivation requirements.

Another offshoot of the 1962 expedition to Sarawak led to a programme of research into tropical members of the ginger family (Zingiberaceae) when a number of specimens were brought back to Edinburgh. The gingers are predominantly tropical, many being native to southeast Asian rainforests. There are about 40 genera and well over 1000 species, mostly with fleshy aromatic rhizomes, exotic orchid-like flowers, colourful fruits and attractive foliage. The family is of economic and horticultural importance, including the familiar ginger (*Zingiber officinale*), cardamom (*Elettaria cardamomum*) and turmeric (*Curcuma longa*), together with the ornamental ginger lilies (*Hedychium*), the hardy *Roscoea* and the handsome genus *Alpinia*, which alone has 250 species. Since then the Royal Botanic Garden has become an acknowledged centre of authority on the family.

Many popular ornamental plants belong to the family Gesneriaceae: African violets (*Saintpaulia*); hot water plants (*Achimenes*); Cape primroses (*Streptocarpus*) and gloxinias (*Sinningia*), to mention but a few. The gesneriads number about 125 genera and 2000 species, widely distributed throughout the tropics and into temperate parts of China, Japan, southern Europe and South America. Among their characteristics are attractive velvety leaves and often tubular or foxglove-like, brightly coloured flowers.

Several species of *Streptocarpus* and their numerous hybrids are popular in cultivation, making attractive and easily-grown pot plants for the house and conservatory. The genus is, however, of great botanical interest as certain species have a single enlarged cotyledon (seed-leaf) instead of true leaves. The single 'leaf' can reach extraordinary lengths: 32in in *S. dunnii* and up to 3ft long and 28in across in *S. grandis*. This peculiar form of growth is also found in the southeast Asian genus *Monophyllaea*. Many gesneriads throughout the tropics, from African violets in the Usambara Mountains of Tanzania to species of *Monophyllaea* in Sarawak, are threatened through loss of cover when forests are felled, as they thrive only in deep shade and high humidity.

Conifers

There are only about 660 species of coniferous trees - a relatively small number compared with many other groups - which belies their immense importance as the dominant

Specimens of *Pinus longaeva* are believed to be the world's oldest living organisms. This example in the Inyo National Forest, White Mountains, California, visited as part of the Conifer Conservation Programme, is around 4600 years old.

vegetation in many regions and as a major source of raw materials. They are also widely planted as ornamentals, hedging and shelter. Though several species are grown on a vast scale to provide 'softwood' for timber and paper, many are still cut from the wild - from virgin forests, including temperate rainforest. Conifers hold a unique place in palaeobotany (the study of fossil plants), being among the most ancient of land plants. The group includes the true conifers (Coniferales), such as the cypress, pine, podocarp and monkey puzzle families, together with the yews (Taxales) and the ginkgo - a 'living fossil' species. Most conifers are resilient and long-lived, found throughout the world in widely differing conditions. What they have in common is an ability to withstand stress, such as that caused by long dry periods, severe cold, high winds and a range of extreme soil conditions. The most typical weapon in their armoury is tough, needle-like foliage which is often coated in wax and filled with resin. Yet despite their longevity - in individual and evolutionary terms - 232 species are currently listed as vulnerable, threatened or endangered in the wild.

The Royal Botanic Garden is a major world centre for research into the taxonomy and conservation of conifers. This position has arisen partly from its location - Scotland being eminently well-suited for the cultivation of most temperate species - and partly from its comprehensive Living and Herbarium collections. Conifer research at Edinburgh aims to produce monographs on conifers worldwide, to study their evolution, distribution, biology and ecology, and to maintain living collections which support the Garden's conservation objectives.

Unlike tropical rainforest trees, which in many cases only thrive as part of a community, conifers do well in cultivation. The establishment of *ex situ* conservation breeding populations, with parents collected as seeds or cuttings from as many localities as possible, gives hope that species may survive even when the last of their kind has disappeared from the wild. The Royal Botanic Garden already has collections of young umbrella pines (*Sciadopitys verticillata*) and hiba Cedars (*Thujopsis dolobrata*) from various sources in Japan.

Seed collecting in North America to provide propagation material for the Conifer Conservation Programme.

A major challenge for conifer conservation concerns one of the most interesting collections at Edinburgh. This consists of young trees from New Caledonia, off the east coast of Australia. They are not hardy and must be kept under glass. Four-fifths of the island's plant species are endemic, including all of its 40 different conifers, many of which are threatened with extinction.

The ecological disaster now happening to many of the conifer-rich areas of New Caledonia can be accounted for by its underlying geology. Though partly covered by tropical forest, the southeast consists of mineral soils which are too toxic for most other trees. Many of these areas are subject to strip mining for nickel which entails the wholesale removal of the vegetation cover. Subsequent afforestation using alien trees only makes the situation worse as they include aggressive species that seed into surrounding fragments of conifer forest, outcompeting the last survivors. In order to build up a breeding population of these rare plants, cuttings of every species have already been collected.

A number of rare conifers are tender or nearly so. Some can be grown under glass in Edinburgh; others are tried in sheltered sites outdoors at Benmore and Logan. Arrangements are also being made to grow half-hardy conifers in several historic gardens throughout the British Isles. Among these rarities is the Taiwan catkin yew (*Amentotaxus formosana*) which was introduced to cultivation for the first time in 1976 when only one or two trees remained in the wild.

Certain conifer species which are quite common in cultivation are now threatened or extinct in the wild. There are, for example, more monkey puzzle trees (*Araucaria araucana*) in British gardens than in the wild in Chile; more Monterey pines (*Pinus radiata*) in Cornwall than California; and more cedars of Lebanon (*Cedrus libani*) in our parks and country estates than on Mount Lebanon, where only 50 remained as long ago as 1907. Seed and cuttings of cultivated plants are being sought in an attempt to harness and perpetuate genetic resources that are probably no longer available from the wild.

This plant of *Podocarpus forrestii* was collected as seed in Dali (Tali), Yunnan in 1990 and has been propagated at Inverleith under the Conifer Conservation Programme.

THE LAST FRONTIER:
RESEARCH ON FLOWERLESS PLANTS

Most floristic studies are concerned with the 'higher' plants (phanerogams), namely the flowering plants (angiosperms) and the conifers and their allies (gymnosperms). However, of equal importance, and far greater in number, are the 'lower' or flowerless plants (ferns, mosses and liverworts, algae, fungi and lichens), collectively known as cryptogams. The Royal Botanic Garden Edinburgh is Britain's only centre for co-ordinated research on all these groups.

Cryptogams tend to be far more widely distributed than flowering plants, and in many habitats it is the ferns, mosses and lichens that form the bulk of the ground cover. Yet all lower plant groups are poorly known - partly because they frequently prove difficult to observe and identify, and partly as a result of being considered uninteresting and unimportant compared with flowering plants. This situation has changed dramatically in recent years with the realisation that many cryptogams are important indicators of environmental change. Furthermore, advances in microscopical techniques have made accurate identification possible and opened up new fields of study. Research into cryptogams may be described as the 'last frontier' in botany, in which there are many discoveries to be made about their taxonomy, biology, ecology and evolution. The results of research currently in progress at the Royal Botanic Garden Edinburgh will be of particular value to ecologists and other specialists who are required to carry out biodiversity surveys for environmental monitoring.

Ferns

Ferns and related plants such as horsetails and club mosses - collectively known as pteridophytes - are an extremely ancient group which, with the conifers, dominated the Earth's vegetation for some 200 million years before facing increasing competition from the fast-evolving flowering plants. Those we see today are essentially woodland plants, found throughout the world from tropical rainforests to subarctic taiga (coniferous forests), predominantly in places which are too dark or damp for the majority of flowering plants. There are about 15,000 species

Adiantum asarifolium from Mauritius, probably the world's rarest fern, has been successfully propagated at Inverleith.

worldwide, many of which are threatened by loss of habitat, as more and more natural forests are cleared.

Since the 1970s, the Garden has played an important role in pteridophyte research and conservation with particular interest in the temperate ferns of Britain, Chile, Australasia and the Pacific Islands. Living collections of hardy species are distributed throughout the four gardens, with the more tender species being reserved for the Fern House in Edinburgh or outdoors at Logan. Rare species are also cultivated as an insurance against extinction in the wild. Indeed, the Garden possesses what is probably the world's rarest fern - a maidenhair (*Adiantum*) from the mountains of Mauritius. It may well be extinct in the wild but if the sole survivors produce spores they may at least be conserved *ex situ*, with the prospect of being returned to the wild if and when conditions are suitable.

Part of the research carried out in Edinburgh is concerned with establishing a spore bank and growing ferns from spores under laboratory conditions. By 'bulking up' the numbers of specimens and distributing them to other botanic gardens in order to reduce the risk, threatened species are given the best possible chance of survival.

However, not all research at Edinburgh is aimed at conserving rare species. The ubiquitous bracken (*Pteridium aquilinum*) has the distinction of being the most widespread vascular plant. Worldwide in distribution, it is an extremely invasive weed which is proving difficult to control in many countries, especially Britain where it covers an area equivalent to the size of Devon. Moreover, it is toxic to both man and beast, causing concern over its spread across grazing land and country used for recreational purposes. Work at the Garden suggests that there are several different kinds of bracken in Britain which may have interbred to form a 'super-bracken' that is now able to dominate vast areas of countryside. The aim is to devise a strategy for biological control based on a sound understanding of the plant and the conditions which have caused its spread. This is a good example of how taxonomic research can underpin the solution to a complex practical problem, supplying key information for applied research in other fields.

Mosses, liverworts and algae

Mosses (Musci) and liverworts (Hepaticae) belong to a division of the plant world known as bryophytes, which number about 25,000 species. The majority grow in damp shady places, though many mosses tolerate long periods of drought - in some cases surviving several years of desiccation and high temperatures. In common with other ancient groups, such as fungi and lichens, many bryophytes are far more widely distributed than flowering plants, having evolved long before the break-up of the Earth's land masses into continents. One tropical species, *Adelanthus lindenbergianus*, occurs in South America, Africa and Ireland, and in 1990 was also found in western Scotland. The British flora is in fact far richer in bryophytes than in flowering plants: the former numbering around 2000 species; the latter nearer 1500. The bryophyte flora of many parts of the world is incompletely known: recently a species thought to be endemic to Britain was discovered in China!

Though for the most part unobtrusive, lowly plants, bryophytes are ecologically important. Being sensitive to pollution, they are good indicators of both water and air quality. More specifically, mosses are among the first colonizers of bare ground, paving the way (where appropriate) for the succession to climax forest. In certain areas, such as tropical forests and temperate bogs, mosses may be the most abundant plant group. Their ability to hold large quantities of water is especially significant, on the one hand retaining sufficient moisture for epiphytes to thrive on the branches of

The moss *Tetraplodon mnioides*, which grows on animal remains, is a circumboreal species recorded here in East Nepal.

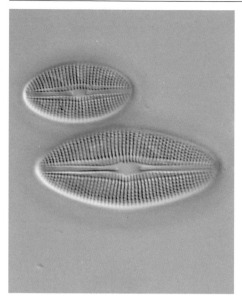

Diploneis sp., a freshwater diatom collected from a reservoir in the Pentland Hills near Edinburgh in the course of life-cycle studies of these beautiful microscopic organisms. The larger cell is c.0.05mm long.

tropical trees and, on the other hand, regulating the loss of water from uplands and wetlands. The sphagnum mosses are well-known in this respect, absorbing up to 16 times their weight in water. In addition, their dead remains are the main component of peat.

The Royal Botanic Garden has an excellent bryophyte herbarium, with outstanding collections from arctic and tropical regions. Research at Edinburgh in this area has expanded recently in response to the growing awareness of the importance of mosses and liverworts in environmental monitoring. Bryologists at the Royal Botanic Garden are involved in long-term taxonomic studies as well as carrying out biodiversity surveys at the request of various organizations. Taxonomic work concentrates on Scotland, the Himalaya and southeast Asia. The opportunity to collect bryophytes often arises on expeditions whose main purpose is to collect flowering plants during the preparation of major Floras. From collections such as these, provisional accounts of the liverworts of Arabia have been compiled and research on the mosses and liverworts of Bhutan, Nepal and Yunnan is underway.

Algae form a large and diverse group of mainly aquatic plants. They include microscopic diatoms and the spirogyra ('slime') of ponds and fish tanks, as well as seaweeds of all sizes and shapes, from tiny tufts of filaments to giant kelps over 50m in length. Though the Royal Botanic Garden holds important herbaria of the larger algae, it is upon some of the smallest algae - the diatoms - that research is concentrated.

An English country gentleman is credited with the first description of a diatom, which he saw in 1703 under a simple microscope while examining the roots of pondweed. Diatoms are single-celled algae, found in both marine and freshwater environments. The cell-walls of diatoms are impregnated with silica to give a glass-like shell that is virtually indestructible. The shell of each species has a unique and exquisite geometry, and it is upon the appearance of this skeleton that classification has, until recently, been based. New systems of classification being developed at Edinburgh are concerned particularly with the structure of the living cell and patterns of reproduction.

Diatoms play a major role in the carbon and silicon cycles, accounting for approximately one-fifth of all carbon fixed globally each year by photosynthesis. When they die, diatoms sink to the bottom of the sea or lake, forming vast deposits of silica. These sediments can be used to measure changes in climate. Diatoms are also known to be sensitive to water quality and are important indicators in lakes affected by acid rain or pollution by fertilizers. The Royal Botanic Garden is currently collaborating with other institutes and universities in Britain and Germany on diatom research, the aim of which is to establish a basic understanding of these organisms for the purposes of environmental monitoring. Its main contribution is taxonomic, with work in progress on a Marine Diatom Flora of the British Isles. Studies are also being made of archaeological remains and sediments. These should clarify the links between climate, glaciation, sea level and ocean currents, and show how environments have changed - information which may be of crucial importance in predicting the effects of global warming.

Fungi and lichens

Fungi hold a unique position in botanical science as they are, strictly speaking, neither plant nor animal. Resembling plants in structure and certain animals in the way they obtain nutrients, they are classified as a biological kingdom distinct from both. Fungi consist either of microscopic filaments called hyphae which grow through the living or dead material on which they feed, or exist as clusters of single cells called yeasts. Hyphae join together to form a network known as the mycelium, and in order to reproduce, they unite to form a fruiting body (the familiar mushroom or toadstool in some groups) - an elaborate device for producing spores from which new hyphal colonies may develop.

There are almost 6000 genera of fungi and some 70,000 known species worldwide, with an estimated 12,000 in Britain. Though some are useful, especially the yeasts, for making foods such as cheese, bread, yogurt and alcoholic drinks, others are exceedingly toxic, and a number cause diseases in plants and animals or structural damage in buildings. The Royal Botanic Garden has a long history of expertise in these interesting organisms, based principally on its unrivalled collection of herbarium specimens. Preparation of several fungal Floras is under way at present. As with flowering plants, fungal Floras describe the species found in a particular region. The British Fungus Flora gives an account of the mushrooms and toadstools that occur in the British Isles. These include the agarics (to which the familiar edible mushroom, *Agaricus bisporus* belongs) and the boletes (such as ceps) and their close allies. Started in the 1960s and with seven volumes already completed, this is the first comprehensive text of its kind.

With major advances in laboratory techniques, especially microscopy, during the last 30 years or so, research into fungi has progressed by leaps and bounds. But all investigations of fungal biology and any consequent exploitation of these organisms is only possible once there is a sound knowledge of the identity and relationships of the species concerned. The Garden's special expertise in this area has led to collaborative research programmes throughout the world, from controlling honey fungus in Australian eucalypt forests to the cultivation of edible fungi on oil palm waste in Cameroon.

It is now clear that fungi play a larger and more complex role in the global ecosystem than was first suspected, not just as decomposers but also as 'nutrient managers' through forming mutually beneficial relationships (mycorrhizae) with many kinds of higher plants. The complex interdependence between fungi and trees in temperate woodlands has been known for some time. One present line of research is into the effects of acid rain on these mycorrhizal fungi. A collaborative project between the Royal Botanic Garden and the University of Aberdeen has recently been set up on the arctic island of Svalbard. The aim is to establish whether the deterioration seen in trees exposed to pollution is caused by a breakdown in the mycorrhizal relationship. The existence of mycorrhizae in rainforests has only recently been discovered. Trees of the pea family (Leguminosae), for example, pair up with tropical relatives of the familiar milk-caps (*Lactarius*) and chanterelles (*Cantharellus*). It appears that fungi are even more vital to the rainforest ecosystem than to temperate woodlands, enabling mighty trees to thrive on poor thin soils by improving their nutritional status, and by cycling nutrients so efficiently that none are lost from the web of vegetation and root mats. This discovery explains why it has proved so difficult to replant rainforests, for the fungi - upon which the trees depend - are destroyed by burning, soil compaction and exposure to the elements. But it also gives hope that reafforestation with native species may be successful if young trees, complete with fungal partners, can be raised in nurseries.

Many fungi are parasites, causing disease in their living hosts. Rust fungi are a particular group of microscopic parasites which have been the subject of research at the Royal Botanic Garden for many years. About 250 species occur in Britain and these are described in the authoritative *British Rust Fungi* which was co-authored at Edinburgh by Douglas Henderson and published in 1966. Continuing work on rusts and similar microscopic studies of other parasitic groups, such as smuts and mildews, is carried out in the Laboratory. This research on fungal plant parasites is unusual in that it must respond rapidly to outbreaks of disease. With global warming

More than 3000 species of larger fungi, including the striking *Boletus calopus*, are being documented in the British Fungus Flora.

and the introduction of new crops, patterns of fungal plant diseases are likely to change, making the Royal Botanic Garden's unique expertise in this field of even greater importance.

Mycologists are also responsible for overseeing plant material in the quarantine houses, in which all plants collected abroad must spend at least three months (depending on type and origin) on arrival in Edinburgh. Identifying any pests and diseases that occur during this period is crucial in preventing the spread of dangerous pathogens into the rest of the Living Collection or, worse still, into the country as a whole. The identification of more general plant health problems, at the request of both Botanic Garden staff and outside agencies - from private gardeners to horticultural and agricultural concerns - is yet another task carried out at the Garden.

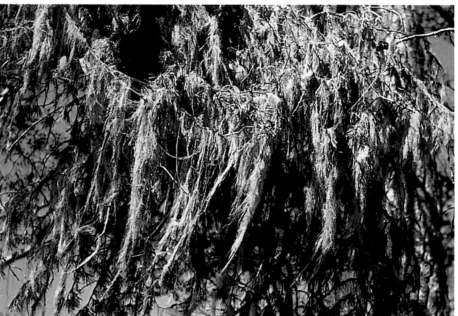

Left. Powdery mildew infection has become a serious problem on rhododendrons in cultivation worldwide and is the subject of detailed studies at the Garden.

Right. Alectoria sarmentosa growing epiphytically on Scots pine in Guisachan Forest. This lichen is an indicator of an ancient pine forest habitat.

Lichens are peculiar kinds of fungi that live in intimate association with algae. They form crusted, leafy or tufted growths in places few plants or other organisms can colonise, such as rocks, tree trunks and man-made structures of stone or wood. There are about 1600 species of lichen in Great Britain, many of which are found only in ancient woodlands, such as the native Scottish pinewoods. Though some lichens are used in dyeing, perfumery and medicine, their main importance today is in vegetation studies. Being precise in their requirements and exceedingly sensitive to pollution (especially to sulphur dioxide, acid rain and nitrogenous compounds), the presence of certain species is a good indication of air quality. They are also extremely long-lived, among the slowest growing of all organisms (a few millimetres a year is not uncommon) and often very limited colonizers, so the level of disturbance in a habitat can often be judged according to the distribution and abundance of lichens. For these reasons, interest in lichens and their conservation has increased greatly during the last 20 years alongside concern for the environment.

Unfortunately, lichens are not easy to identify and expert advice is often required; futhermore there is a constant demand for survey work in Britain, much of it for the Nature Conservancy Council (now Scottish Natural Heritage). Fundamental taxonomic research is also important, and significant contributions are being made to the new *Lichen Flora of Great Britain and Ireland*, as well as to lichen Floras of Chile, South Africa and Australia.

THE LIVING PLANT COLLECTIONS

The Royal Botanic Garden Edinburgh has the reputation of being among the best-maintained gardens in the world. Together with Inverleith, the gardens at Benmore, Logan and Dawyck form an important amenity for both local people and visitors. But first and foremost they are collections of living plants which are of scientific and educational importance. The Royal Botanic Garden in Edinburgh is the only botanical institute in Great Britain that can claim to cover the entire spectrum of plant life in its research programme. This diversity of interest is demonstrated, as far as is practicable, by the Living Collections which contain over 15,000 species - 6% of the world's flowering plants - from all corners of the globe.

The Living Collections, together with the Library and Herbarium, provide the basic

Propagation at Edinburgh involves the careful nurturing of seeds and cuttings of a vast range of plant species, many of which have never been in cultivation before.

materials for research. Unlike the Herbarium, however, most of them are accessible to the public, providing a link between the scientific institute and the community it serves. Admittedly, some of the plants currently being studied are kept behind the scenes in research glasshouses - especially if they need conditions that cannot easily be provided in the display areas - but the majority are grown for all to enjoy and learn from. Whether impressive, pretty or curious, it is the living plants that people come to see and which inspire the educational programmes of the Garden.

As a rule, the Living Collections are distributed through the four gardens according to the conditions that each provides. The garden at Inverleith is the only one with display glasshouses and facilities for quarantine, large-scale propagation and maintenance of research collections. The milder, humid climate and mountainous setting at the Younger Botanic Garden, Benmore, are ideal for many of the conifers and rhododendrons which fail to thrive at the other gardens. In contrast, Dawyck gives the opportunity for growing hardier trees and shrubs that prefer colder drier conditions. Both Benmore and Dawyck provide space not only for additional species but for the kind of plantings for which there is insufficient space at Inverleith. Logan has the mildest, sunniest climate of all and therefore accommodates mainly southern hemisphere species, including many half-hardy plants which are propagated annually for summer display. Some of the more tender conifers, which cannot easily be grown outdoors in any of the four gardens or under glass in Edinburgh, may find homes in gardens elsewhere in the United Kingdom.

The way that the Living Collections are displayed has changed over the centuries. In the 19th century there was an emphasis on 'order beds' in which plants were arranged according to their scientific classification. James McNab's famous rock garden consisted of uniform sections divided into angular compartments of various sizes, each of which housed a particular genus. Geographical areas provided another basis for groups. In Isaac Bayley Balfour's time, there was a thriving section of British plants, arranged in families, which he and his students had collected on their botanical excursions into the Scottish countryside. Grouping according to use was also popular: economic and medicinal plants being *de rigueur*.

Elements of all these arrangements are still important: traditional 'order bed' layouts and plantings to show specific uses serve this purpose in the Demonstration Garden; taxonomic relationships are important in the Arboretum, where many trees remain from Bayley Balfour's time; and a geographical arrangement predominates in the Rock Garden and Cactus House. Being of international importance, the main rhododendron and conifer collections at Edinburgh and Benmore are largely arranged according to their scientific classification, which is a great help to scientists and horticulturists.

However, alongside the more traditional layouts is a new approach, reflecting the widening of vision that has taken place over the past 30 years or so in the botanical world. The plants themselves are still studied in minute detail, but there is increasing interest in how they live in the wild and how they interact with the community of living things that make up ecosystems. Displaying plants to show this means re-creating habitats - a considerable challenge to the practical and aesthetic skills of the horticultural staff. The results are, of course, an illusion, as most habitats have characteristics that are quite impossible to reproduce on a small scale - not least of which are the insects and other animals. However, they do show the plants in a naturalistic setting and give a flavour of habitats that many visitors never experience

The naturalistic landscape of the Tropical Peat House provides ideal conditions to display valuable gesneriads and gingers from the research collections.

in real life. Landscaped glasshouse displays have now almost completely replaced rows of plants in pots, so that a walk through the different houses gives a vivid impression of different environments, from the dry air, bright reflected light and grey spiky foliage of arid lands, to the clammy heat and dripping dark greens of the tropics. Putting a stream through the Fern House has been particularly successful, bringing the plants alive - metaphorically speaking - by providing a feature that they are often associated with in the wild. Re-created habitats are also being attempted outdoors. A Cryptogamic Garden in Edinburgh and Bhutanese Glade at Benmore have recently been established, and a colony of Dawyck's Scots pines are being managed as a replica of the native Caledonian pine forest.

In addition to their importance as an amenity and research resource, the Living Collections are part of our national heritage. Combining outstanding beauty with historical, scientific and educational interest, the gardens are simultaneously a work of art, monument and nature reserve. Many of their plants and features recall the past: Edinburgh's Victorian Palm House and plants raised from George Forrest's collections; Logan's walled garden with its fragment of a medieval castle; Benmore's spectacular avenue of Sierra redwoods; and Dawyck's remarkable fastigiate (upright) beech *Fagus sylvatica* 'Dawyck'. But around this nucleus of cultural achievement revolves a host of mundane requirements: shelter belts, hedges, lawns and paths, cafes, car parks and visitor centres, guide books and signs, and the all-encompassing need for regular long-term maintenance. Whether august or workaday, all take their place in a kaleidoscope of priorities which constantly changes as one area of the Botanic Garden's fabric is strengthened and another wears thin.

Some things, however, do not change. Plants, like people and animals, need 'hands-on' care - plus the sixth sense known as 'green fingers' - if they are to thrive in competitive and often unnatural surroundings. Similarly, they are prone to ill-health

Transplantation of a semi-mature specimen of Brewer's spruce (*Picea breweriana*).

and do not live for ever, which entails remedial treatment and eventual replacement. Maintaining the Living Collections is therefore labour-intensive and time-consuming despite the advantages of modern technology, such as computer-operated watering devices.

The Living Collections are divided into six main areas of responsibility: Glass, Herbaceous and Alpine, Arboretum, and the Younger, Logan and Dawyck Botanic Gardens. Staff carry out maintenance tasks, which cover every horticultural skill from sowing the tiniest seeds to performing surgery on the tallest trees, under the watchful eye of Garden Supervisors. In turn, the Garden Supervisors come under an Assistant Curator who heads each department, and in overall charge of the Living Collections is the Curator.

Behind the scenes in the Living Collections

A plant may come into the Living Collection as a seed, a cutting, a dormant bulb, or well-established. Between two and three thousand accessions of living plant material are received each year, a large proportion of which is collected in the wild by expeditions. Regardless of whether it can be identified, each new collection is first labelled with an accession number.

The next stage after receiving an accession number in the case of seeds is cleaning, sorting and either sowing or storing. Seed from extreme climates may need special attention. In most tropical plants the seed has little or no dormancy and must be sown immediately, whereas alpine species usually require a period of subzero temperatures to mimic the long cold winters of high elevations. The progress of seed from expeditions in which Botanic Garden staff participated is always followed keenly and memories are rekindled as the bare pots show their first fuzz of foliage: rhododendrons as thick as mustard and cress, blades of seedling lilies, or the distinctive star-like seed-leaves of conifers. Other plant material from abroad is put into quarantine until the staff monitoring plant health declare it free from pests and diseases.

Plant records

Whatever its beginnings, records of each accession are kept from 'cradle to grave'. A card index system was started in 1938, which continued until the advent of computerisation in 1969. It took three years for the card index system to be transferred to disc, the first computer print-out being produced in 1972. Inevitably, there have been a number of advances made to the system since then and Garden Plant Records are now held on BG-BASE, a system developed for use in botanic gardens and widely used in the United States. The Royal Botanic Garden Edinburgh is only the third institution in Britain to operate this innovative database for its records. Though the Garden cultivates over 15,000 different species, Garden Plant Records now number 35,000 as in most cases there is more than one example of each. Exceptionally, annuals are not entered as the system requires each plant to have an accession number - a daunting and pointless exercise in the case of short-lived plants.

The records made for each plant contain many items of information which are vital for cultivation, research and conservation. They include the origin of the plant and name of collector or donor, its habitat and whether it is a species that comes under the Red Data Book categories of Endangered, Vulnerable or Rare. Last but not least, if unknown the plant must be correctly identified *or, if already bearing a name, must have its identity verified by a taxonomist. Key information can then be printed on to the plant label. Typically, a plant label shows the scientific name of the species (accompanied by its common name if important and widely used), its family (a Latin word ending in -aceae or -ae), origin and, in the bottom left-hand corner, the accession number together with the collector's (or expedition's) name and collection number. Some of this information is given as symbols: + or W = known wild distribution; * or T = threatened, rare or vulnerable; and V = identification verified. Until 1990 the accession number consisted of six figures, starting with the last two digits of the year in which the plant entered the collection and ending with its actual number within that year. An accession number 75.0538 thus indicates that it was the 538th plant to enter the collection in 1975. Anticipating the year 2000 and the fact that some venerable trees date*

Isoplexis sceptrum. The symbols on the label indicate that this plant originated as wild-collected material (+), that its identity has been verified by staff at the Garden (V), and that it is threatened, rare or vulnerable in its native habitat (*).

back to the 1890s, the accession number now has eight digits - the year being given in full. The first plant received in 1993, for example, will bear the number 1993.0001.

The Plant Records system provides the data used on labels throughout the Gardens. In addition, it allows staff to check information on particular plants. Entries are continually monitored, adding new accessions and updating existing ones in the light of information conveyed from all departments to the Plant Records office. Information from the records provides the basis for the *Catalogue of Plants* which lists every species (and subspecies, etc.) in the Living Collection, along with the collector's name and number where relevant. A list of 'conservation plants' is also issued periodically. This details species in the Living Collections which are under threat, giving their conservation status (extinct, endangered, vulnerable or rare in the wild), origin (wild, cultivated or unknown) and the numbers of each in the care of the Royal Botanic Garden.

Once documented, the new plant becomes part of the Living Collections. Before going on display, most newcomers are grown on in the complex of glasshouses reserved for research and propagation, or in the adjoining frames or else in the Nursery. This 10-acre (4.5ha) site to the north of Inverleith Place provides the necessary space for much of the Garden's temperate propagation, with extensive plantings of young trees, shrubs and herbaceous plants. For those destined to replace or add to plants already on display, this will be a brief sojourn; others that are either unsuited for display or are of particular scientific interest may spend their entire lives behind the scenes.

Research houses

The main block of research glasshouses consists of six large units, opened in 1978. In these are kept plants which are of prime importance to the Garden's research programmes. One of these buildings has been divided and landscaped as the Peat and Tropical Rock Houses, displaying some of the Royal Botanic Garden's collections of Vireya rhododendrons, tropical members of the heath family (Ericaceae), gingers and gesneriads. Vestiges of its life as a research house can be seen at the far end where there is staging and plants in pots - which is how all the other research houses are set out.

Plants coming into the Living Collections as new species cause a flurry of excitement as they develop. Flowering is eagerly awaited. Only when this happens can a new species be described and named by the herbarium taxonomists. Of considerable interest too are species already described and named but new to cultivation. There are always surprises - rather like meeting someone for the first time that one has heard a great deal about - as when *Rhododendron lowii* flowered for the first time in cultivation. This Bornean species is the giant of the genus, producing enormous clusters, some 14in in diameter, of up to 15 yellow to apricot, rose-scented flowers. Originally collected by Sir Hugh Low who made the first ascent of Mount Kinabalu on 11 March 1851, it was re-collected there by Garden staff in 1982. Six years later it produced its first flower buds. But as they developed it was realised that they were not going to open unless given a helping hand, for in the wild their thick coating of protective gum would be gradually washed away by the force of tropical downpours. In the nick of time, the imprisoning bud scales were removed and the magnificent flowers opened for the first time outside their native haunts. All newcomers present a challenge to horticultural staff, though trial and error are kept to the minimum by careful research into natural growing conditions.

BOTANICS FOR ALL

The Royal Botanic Garden Edinburgh has always been an educational establishment. In the beginning it provided instruction in the identification and use of plants for medicinal purposes. The role developed over the next three centuries so that today, alongside its primary function as a research institute, the Royal Botanic Garden offers two distinct types of educational programme. On the one hand it provides formal courses leading to qualifications, such as the Diploma in Amenity and Ornamental Horticulture (DHE) and the MSc/Diploma in Plant Taxonomy, and on the other hand it runs innovative educational programmes for colleges, schools and the general public.

Education and the visitor

The demand for educational services has increased greatly as awareness of the importance of plants has grown in society as a whole. The response has been to expand this aspect of the Garden's work and to widen the approach so that the educational net captures students, school children, plant enthusiasts and casual visitors alike. In rising to the challenge of catering for such widely differing interests, Edinburgh has pioneered the role of botanic gardens in areas such as environmental education and art inspired by nature. Where else, in the space of a few months, could one find: a botanical illustration summer school; action-packed family workshops on everything from batik to supermarket science; a shadow puppet show inspired by rainforest peoples; a radio science quiz; in-service training for teachers on life in the rainforest; a horticultural workshop on trees and shrubs for small gardens; a tour and tasting session of exotic forest fruits; and lectures on all things botanical, from 'a global plant conservation strategy', 'fungi in the diet' and 'plants for power' to 'woodcuts and herbals', 'plant collecting with a camera' and 'living off the land in the Scots tradition'?

Andy Goldsworthy constructing his Bracken Serpent in the Caledonian Hall for the 1990 Festival exhibition.

Inspired by Goldsworthy's creations, a young visitor produces his own art from nature during one of the Garden's summer Discovery Days.

As might be imagined, a programme of events as varied as this involves staff throughout the Botanic Garden as well as expertise, voluntary and commissioned, outwith the Garden. Information concerning forthcoming events, along with descriptions of various aspects of the Garden's work, is published in the Garden's seasonal newsletter - *The Botanics* - a title coined from the popular name by which the Royal Botanic Garden Edinburgh is locally known.

These activities are co-ordinated by the Public Services department. The very fact that such a department exists at the Garden is evidence of the profound changes that have occurred since the late 1960s. Before this time, it is fair to say that the work of the Garden was somewhat removed from the general public, interpretation being largely confined to plant labels, formal exhibitions of labelled artefacts, and equally formal lectures. The most significant change of approach has been to offer a wealth of more interactive events and displays for all ages and interests.

The change of approach was sparked off by the increased leisure, mobility and interest in natural history that occurred at this time, but a major impetus came with the opening in 1970 of a new Plant Exhibition Hall which, along with traditional lectures and guided tours, provided the foundation upon which today's visitor services were developed. An exhibition and education programme was initiated in Harold Fletcher's time and was further encouraged by Douglas Henderson. Progressively a team of specialist staff came together, including a nucleus of research scientists whose flair for communication enabled the Garden to develop this important aspect of its work.

Inspiring the next generation with a concern for, and interest in plants is a vital part of the work. Hence exhibitions and activities for school groups are a priority. To maximise this important educational opportunity, the Royal Botanic Garden has, since 1975, collaborated with a number of other institutions, such as Edinburgh Zoo and the Royal Museum of Scotland, in Interlink - programmes with themes ranging from 'Movement', 'Sea' and 'Prehistoric Life', to more recently 'Up the Amazon', 'Colour' and 'Deserts'. An Interlink Programme is far more than a school trip. Each runs for several weeks and is integrated with preparatory and follow-up classroom teaching. The participating organisations create imaginative settings and dramatic learning situations, using their own unique facilities. Those devised by Botanic Garden staff involve role-playing and all six senses so that the children discover for themselves what it is like, for example, to be in a rainforest finding food and shelter. The Living Collections are invaluable for this kind of approach. In a child's fantasy the landscaped environments of the glasshouses are lifelike jungles and deserts, complete with hosepipe snakes!

At secondary school level the Garden encourages exciting experimental teaching of plant science through a foundation named Science and Plants for Schools (SAPS). Their activities range from tissue culture of vegetables to work with 'fast plants' including a particular kind of cabbage (*Brassica campestris*) which has been bred to complete its entire lifecycle, from seed to seed, within five weeks. This 'rapid-cycling brassica' was originally intended to speed up the breeding of disease-resistant crops but has been found equally useful for teaching every aspect of plant science in schools.

Visitors come to the Garden at Inverleith for many reasons but the majority (nearly 50%) simply enjoy walking or relaxing in tranquil surroundings, often in the company of family and friends. Others (approximately 30%) are keen to see and take in everything; and a small number (up to 5%) have specific botanical or horticultural interests. The Living Plant Collections displayed in their landscaped settings are therefore of paramount importance. Maintaining, displaying and interpreting them to the very highest standards are crucial, from the smallest detail of a label to the grand plan of creating the educational ambience which serves to differentiate a botanic garden from a park. In support of this, the Garden provides leaflets and other publications, arranges guided tours (including glimpses behind the scenes) and offers specialist lectures and demonstrations, family workshops, evening classes and topical summer schools. Whenever possible, themes are developed to reflect aspects of the Garden's research. An example of this was 'A Garden in the Desert', an exhibition timed to coincide with the publication of *Plants of Dhofar*. This featured a reconstruction of an Arab suq (market) with products derived from local plants, accompanied by panels explaining their origin and uses. All this interpretative material was linked to a display of recently collected Arabian plants in the Cactus and Succulent House.

Such special exhibitions may take place in one of three distinct locations at Inverleith. The Exhibition Hall stages interpretive botanical and environmental displays, whereas the Caledonian Hall (the former Exhibition Hall of the Royal Caledonian Society) has resumed its original role in hosting a range of events, from flower shows to sculpture exhibitions. Inverleith House, which served as the Gallery of Modern Art from 1960 to 1985, was refurbished in 1990 as the main venue for gallery exhibitions. Occasionally the gardens themselves become a unique open air gallery, providing a superb setting for sculpture - a memorable example of which was the Barbara Hepworth exhibition in 1976. Sculpture in the Garden was also an element in the record-breaking 1990 Edinburgh Festival Exhibition 'Hand to Earth'. This retrospective of Andy Goldsworthy's work also occupied the Caledonian Hall and Inverleith House, attracting thousands of visitors and international media coverage. The success of a visit to the Garden depends not only on the peaceful setting or

Peace and tranquillity in the garden at Inverleith. Sculptures by Peter Randall-Page nestle beneath the grove of Sierra redwoods.

involvement in one of the host of educational activities, but also on certain essential facilities. With visitor numbers that can exceed 900,000 at Edinburgh, 40,000 at Benmore, 40,000 at Logan and 10,000 at Dawyck, cafes, shops, toilets and information centres are being developed and upgraded as a priority. Worth noting, for example are: the Terrace Cafe at Inverleith, with its panoramic views across the Garden to the city skyline; Logan's licensed Salad Bar which is regarded as one of the best tourist facilities in the area; not forgetting the 'superloos' in the recently restored Courtyard Buildings at Benmore!

At Inverleith an important part of the service is that provided by the Royal Botanic Garden Constabulary. These uniformed staff patrol and guard the Garden, preserving order, protecting life and property, and preventing the theft of plants,

Schoolchildren attending the innovative Living in a Rainforest education programme enjoy learning in the atmosphere of a specially constructed Bornean longhouse.

which they do with the same powers within the Garden boundaries as any police officer. The Garden had Park Keepers from the early 19th century until an Act of Parliament in 1872 raised their status to Royal Park Keepers with full police powers. They became the Constabulary in 1974, one of four forces protecting the Royal Parks and Botanic Gardens of Scotland and England. It is largely due to the Constabulary that the peace and decorum of the Garden at Inverleith is maintained even at the busiest times when visitor numbers may reach 17,000 in a single day.

Horticultural training

During the course of a visit, you will come across gardeners, a significant number of whom are students on a three-year course leading to the Diploma in Amenity and Ornamental Horticulture of the Royal Botanic Garden Edinburgh (DHE). In 1992 the horticultural training course celebrated its centenary, having been founded by Isaac Bayley Balfour in October 1892 to teach 'the Sciences underlying the Practice and the Principles of Forestry and Horticulture'. It was an important step in putting

the Royal Botanic Garden Edinburgh on a par with both the many forestry schools that were established at that time, and with the Course of Instruction for Young Gardeners at Kew. Training of this kind was in demand by owners of prestigious country estates which employed large numbers of gardeners, and who in many cases were avid plant collectors and knowledgeable plantsmen. It also contributed to colonial expansion, forestry having a high priority at home and throughout the Empire. The course was open to men under 25 who had worked as foresters or gardeners for at least three years. Then as now, the emphasis was on the practical. Lectures took place on two evenings per week and instruction was free, but students worked all day in the gardens. They were, however, paid a weekly wage of 21 shillings. Written certificates were given to successful students, stating the percentages gained in each subject which spanned chemistry, physics, botany,

Visitors to Inverleith may often see horticultural students working in the Garden and undergoing practical instruction.

geology, meteorology, surveying, entomology, forestry and horticulture. Like so many of Isaac Bayley Balfour's innovations, it went from strength to strength, producing many of Britain's leading horticulturists of the 20th century.

In William Wright Smith's time a new horticultural phenomenon arose. Successive town planning acts in the first half of the 20th century gave rise to local authorities whose responsibilities included open spaces, parks, roads and sites of historical or natural beauty. In practice, this meant maintaining large areas of trees, grass and flowerbeds. The result was that employment opportunities for well-qualified horticulturists increased in number and scope. Accordingly in the 1930s Edinburgh began to award diplomas to students successfully completing the training course. The Diploma in Horticulture Edinburgh (DHE) continues to be a much sought-after qualification in ornamental and amenity horticulture.

Harold Fletcher reformed the course in 1966, appointing a supervisor to oversee horticultural training and changing the curriculum. Lectures were concentrated into one day, the rest of the week being spent at work in the Garden. While Douglas Henderson was Regius Keeper, the course continued to widen in scope, encompassing new disciplines such as landscape design, nature conservation, public administration, turf culture, plant breeding and soil science. The course is open to men and women who have at least two years' practical experience and appropriate educational and horticultural qualifications, and continues to evolve to keep pace with advances in the horticultural industry.

Conservation

Conservation is integral to the work of the Royal Botanic Garden. For over 300 years the Botanic Garden has carried out investigations into plant life which have laid the foundations for conservation today, describing species and their uses, habitats and ecology. However, since the 1970s concern about destruction of habitats and loss of species has grown to such a pitch that conservation has become a stated objective of the Botanic Garden's work. This concern stemmed partly from interest in the tropics which included vegetation research in Brazil and southeast Asia. Though the tropics remain high on the list of priorities, the Garden also has an enormous challenge in its own backyard, for Scotland has lost many of its natural ecosystems in the last few hundred years.

Looking across the distinctive cerrado landscape in the Federal District in central Brazil.

Surveying the scene: vegetation studies

While Floras and monographs deal with plants in taxonomic groups, vegetation surveys provide details of the communities in which plants live. Along with an analysis of the geology, climate, animal life and human activity within an area, these surveys are a prerequisite for efficient resource management. They play a key role in resolving controversies over designating areas for conservation, notably Sites of Special Scientific Interest (SSSIs), and such development issues as road routes, agriculture and forestry schemes, and tourist facilities. Floras and monographs are essential tools for this kind of research. Conversely, vegetation surveys often turn up new records of plant distribution and, on occasions, new species.

As Scotland's national botanic garden, the Royal Botanic Garden plays a major role in surveys of Scottish vegetation. This is no mean responsibility as Scotland contains the greatest areas of upland, the highest mountains and the last remaining wilderness areas in Britain. It also has the most varied geology, scenery and wildlife. The main topics of investigation are montane vegetation, aquatic plant life and the rich cryptogam flora. Of particular interest are the types of vegetation unique to Scotland: the native pinewoods, western oak-hazel woodland, mountain top heath and grassland, the machair (shell sand) grasslands of the Hebrides and the flow country of Caithness and Sutherland (the world's largest area of blanket bog).

A quite different part of the world is also of great interest to scientists at the Royal

Botanic Garden: the cerrados (savannas) and tropical forests of Brazil. Surveys of these vast and complex areas began in 1967 with the Anglo-Brazilian Xavantina-Cachimbo Expedition organised by the Royal Society and the Royal Geographical Society. The plight of rainforests has received a great deal of publicity in recent years but little has been heard about the cerrados - regions of grassland and deciduous or semi-deciduous woodlands - which cover some 22% of Brazil (an area more or less the size of western Europe). Though generally occurring on poor soils, cerrado regions are more easily cleared than tall forest and have been much exploited for agriculture and charcoal burning. To give an idea of the scale of the problem, an estimated 50% of cerrado vegetation has already been destroyed, compared with about 12% of Brazilian Amazonian rainforest. Rich in endemic species and probably as ancient as the rainforest, the cerrados were the Cinderella of conservation in Brazil until surveys helped draw attention to their importance. Current research aims to identify key areas for conservation and to develop sustainable systems of land management on the fragile soils that have already been cleared.

Recent explorations in Brazil have included visits to the large island reserve of Maracá in northern Amazonia. Covered largely by forests of different kinds, it is almost free from human disturbance. Herbarium specimens of Brazilian plants found on the various expeditions number 15,000, constituting the first major South American collections in Edinburgh since Victorian times. Unfortunately, there are few examples of living plants from the cerrados in cultivation at Inverleith as they are adapted to high light levels and poor soils rich in aluminium - conditions difficult to reproduce in British botanic gardens.

Scotland and Brazil are just two of the countries in which staff from Edinburgh are well-equipped to conduct biodiversity surveys. Other areas include southeast and southwest Asia and the Sino-Himalaya. Several members recently took part in

Tree ferns on the upper fringe of montane rainforest, Gunung Binaiya, Seram, Indonesia.

surveying and establishing the Danum Valley Reserve in Sabah, Borneo, and vegetation studies have also been carried out on the Indonesian island of Seram in the Moluccas. In many of these areas the wholesale elimination of ecosystems and the extinction of species has become a daily event, emphasising the importance of this aspect of the Garden's work.

Protecting the Planet

The cornerstone of the Garden's conservation programme is taxonomic research. Such work on cataloguing the plant kingdom is a dedicated long-term task. Research at Edinburgh has followed lines predetermined by collections acquired in the 19th and early 20th centuries, spiced with a certain element of serendipity arising from the individual interests of Botanic Garden staff. Future programmes are being planned after wide consultation in order to maximize the Garden's contribution to botanical research, conservation and education on a national and international scale. Many plants are still undescribed or known in only the most superficial respects; countless species are in imminent danger of extinction; and taxonomists are thin on the ground. These facts point to the importance of gaining knowledge about plant life as rapidly and efficiently as possible.

To this end the Royal Botanic Garden Edinburgh is moving toward projects which entail an even greater degree of collaboration and integration with other institutes and disciplines. Though still primarily concerned with taxonomic research which is carried out by a core of Edinburgh-based botanists, it increasingly employs staff with other skills - in ecology or ethnobotany (the study of how people use plants in everyday life), for example. Other projects may involve contractual work taken on by the Garden. In 1991, for example, the Edinburgh Centre for Tropical Forests (ECTF) - which includes the Royal Botanic Garden Edinburgh as a member - was launched. This consortium of institutes and commercial operators undertakes consultancy in the tropics with the aim of managing forest and other woodland resources on a sustainable basis.

Although the conservation programme does not include campaigning or political activity, certain projects involve collaboration with organisations that are active in these areas. This is not to say that the Botanic Garden has no voice in decision making. Representation on advisory committees and bodies such as the Botanic Gardens Conservation International (BGCI) plays an important part in this process as various organisations, governments and regulatory bodies seek advice before formulating policies.

But it is not all talk: practical measures are being taken involving the cultivation, propagation and, in some cases, the re-introduction of endangered plants. More than 500 rare and threatened plants are grown in the four gardens, including the spectacular blue 'crocus' from Chile, *Tecophilaea cyanocrocus*, which is now extinct in the wild. Projects include establishing breeding colonies of endangered conifers from wild-collected seed, restoration to the wild of the Killarney fern (*Trichomanes speciosum*) and developing the first international spore bank for ferns. Another important development is the Ferguson Micropropagation Centre for the production of rare plants. Micropropagation using tissue culture is a technique developed in the 1960s for producing new plants using just a few cells from the original plant, which are grown in a nutrient under sterile conditions. Ultimately, thousands of new plants can be produced, each identical to the original. This may be the only way of reproducing certain endangered species which are extremely difficult to propagate by traditional methods. It can also be used for 'bulking up' rare plants,

One-flowered wintergreen (*Moneses uniflora*), now restricted to a few localities in native pine forests and old plantations in north east Scotland, is one of the subjects of the Scottish Rare Plants Project.

Manusela National Park, Seram, Indonesia. Scientists from the Garden have contributed valuable base-line data about the plant life to the management plan of this important rainforest conservation area.

either for re-introduction into the wild or, in the case of species coveted by collectors, to flood the market so that poaching from reserves and over-collection is discouraged.

Collaboration also takes the form of direct arrangements with other botanic gardens. The Royal Botanic Garden supports the Lipizagua Botanic Garden in Papua New Guinea, enabling staff there to keep in touch with developments worldwide via the Botanic Garden Conservation International. Twinning arrangements, which enable Garden staff to carry out research in other countries in exchange for training and technical aid, are being established. The first formal twinning agreement, with Kunming in China, was signed in 1991.

No less practical is the Garden's commitment to conservation through education, on the premise that raising awareness leads to caring, involvement and action. This is especially important for young people, whose habits and attitudes will determine the success of conservation in the future. Edinburgh is at the forefront of interactive education, particularly with primary school children, but also via training courses for teachers, gardeners and others with specialist interests. The Garden also helped to establish the International Botanic Garden Education Network to disseminate ideas and experiences in this new and exciting area. For the casual visitor, conservation messages are imparted through labels, guidebooks and special garden displays. The concerted aim is to reach as many people as possible at whatever age and stage of awareness so that conserving plant life becomes second nature.

Though physically far-removed from many of the countries where it is involved, in terms of commitment the Royal Botanic Garden is at the very heart of conserving their botanical riches, carrying out the research that inspires education and ultimately underpins all political and economic arguments. Unless we know exactly what plants exist and have an understanding of their distribution, ecology and uses, we cannot formulate strategies to protect them or their habitats.

The Garden at Inverleith is nothing short of a miracle and this is at no time more apparent than in spring when the lengthening days and warmer weather stir plants from all over the world into flower and new growth. It is proof that nature, given a helping hand from the gardener, can triumph over adversity and that the most luxuriant garden can be created on a thoroughly unpromising site. In Edinburgh adversity takes the form of poor sandy soil and low rainfall - only 24in (609.6mm) on average - which makes it the driest and least fertile of the four gardens. At the three specialist gardens - Younger, Logan and Dawyck - the horticultural staff have nature on their side for the most part, growing what does best, but in Edinburgh the majority of plants flourish in spite of the prevailing conditions, coaxed by liberal additions of humus and regular watering throughout the growing season. Over the centuries this beauty treatment has resulted in a woodland oasis where moisture-loving rhododendrons and even temperate rainforest trees thrive in the heart of a city.

SPRING

The seasons in Britain are notoriously unreliable but spring can be the most fickle of all. Undoubtedly the most floriferous time of the year, spring has nevertheless given rise to the expression 'nipped in the bud' as overnight frost so often spoils what was full of promise the day before. The vagaries of the weather are not, however, the only unpredictable thing about spring. In many plants the new season's flowering and growth depend on conditions in the previous year. This is especially true of woody subjects which often excel themselves after a good summer when growths are well-ripened. But whether braving blustery showers or basking in a precocious heatwave, there is always an enormous amount to enjoy in the Inverleith garden as its spring tide of flowers and new leaves gathers momentum.

Rhododendrons

The highlight of spring at Inverleith is undoubtedly the genus for which the Royal Botanic Garden is most famous: rhododendrons. Immensely variable, from diminutive shrublets to trees, they crop up throughout the garden - in alpine frames, the Rock Garden, the Woodland Garden, the Copse and the Azalea Lawn. In addition, Malesian rhododendrons, which require glasshouse protection, can be found in the Peat House, where they are at their best in winter and early spring. One of the earliest outdoors is *R.* x *praecox*, a cross between the free-flowering *R. ciliatum* and the hardier *R. dauricum*, which is a spectacular sight at this time of year. Very early too is the bright pink *R.* x *nobleanum*, one of the oldest rhododendron hybrids. One parent is the mighty *R. arboreum*, the first species introduced from the

Opposite. The Palm House seen from the Alpine terrace.

Rhododendron macabeanum from northeast India is more tolerant of windy, cold and dry conditions than most large-leaved rhododendrons, but is still a challenging plant to grow well at Inverleith. Its flowers are each three inches long, held above the leathery leaves in dense globular trusses.

Himalaya (around 1810) and a highly variable one, with flowers anything from pure white to blood red. This characteristic is its great virtue, providing a wonderful colour range for hybridisation, while its precocious flowering and need for shelter are compensated for by crossing with later, hardier species.

The great virtue of the rhododendron collection at the Royal Botanic Garden is that almost all its 400 or so species are from wild-collected seed. Many of them bear the names of great plant collectors on their labels, most notably of George Forrest who alone discovered some 300 new species and laid the foundations for the Botanic Garden's collection. Among his discoveries are three subspecies of *R. dichroanthum* which make dome-shaped bushes that flower in late spring.

Unusual in colour are some of the variants of *R. sanguineum*. As might be expected from the scientific name, which means 'blood-red', most have deep red flowers in clusters of three to six, but in *didymum* and *haemaleum* they are blackish-maroon. This is a striking example of the wide range of colours found in the genus, from near black to purest white, and every shade of red, pink, yellow and orange to the purple of *R. niveum* and the blue of *R. augustinii*. Although the main colour is what catches the eye, a closer look at rhododendron flowers often reveals a contrasting colour in the throat. In some species this forms decorative markings.

Left. Rhododendron sperabile var. *weihsiense* is a Burmese species which produces exceptionally lovely red flowers in April.

Right. The Japanese *Rhododendron reticulatum* is deciduous and flowers in April and May, before the new leaves appear.

Among the other 'famous name' rhododendrons at Inverleith is *R. strigillosum* which was introduced from Szechuan by E H Wilson in 1904. It is a stunning sight in full flower when spring is barely under way, its brilliant red flowers looking quite exotic on bleak days in early spring. The foliage is a feature too: incurved leaves and bristly new shoots. Another outstanding red-flowered rhododendron is *R. sperabile*, discovered in Upper Burma by Reginald Farrer in 1919. This neat shrub has a thick ginger-brown indumentum and exceptionally beautiful red bells at the height of spring.

The 'big-leaf' Himalayan rhododendrons - sections Falconera and Grandia - are the giants of the genus. Many reach 40ft or more and have leaves as long as a man's arm, leathery in texture and either suede- or silver-backed. More than most, they need moist woodland conditions with high humidity which is a constant challenge to provide in Edinburgh. In addition to being demanding plants, they also tend to be slow-growing and shy-flowering - indeed, many do not flower at all in their youth. Fortunately, the magnificent foliage, and striking bark of some species, is ample recompense for the patience and care they require. Big-leaf rhododendrons can be seen in the Woodland Garden. Look out for specimens of *R. rex* subsp. *arizelum*, *R. falconeri* subsp. *falconeri* and the magnificent *R. sinogrande* which was described by

Isaac Bayley Balfour and Sir William Wright Smith after its introduction by George Forrest in 1913. All flower in April or May.

Perhaps because yellow-flowered rhododendrons are in the minority, swamped by the more numerous and popular reds and pinks, they never fail to attract attention. *R. campylocarpum* is a small twiggy shrub with clear yellow, nodding, honey-scented flowers. It has been in cultivation since about 1850 when introduced by Sir Joseph Hooker from Sikkim. Even prettier is the subspecies *caloxanthum*. Far more conspicuous for its bristly, very blue leaves is *R. lepidostylum* which flowers in late spring and early summer. Several specimens of this compact, semi-evergreen shrub can be seen in the Peat Garden and Rock Garden. One of the finest displays of yellow-flowered rhododendrons can be seen beside the path that leads from Inverleith House to the Copse. Here are a number of specimens of *R. wardii*, a late-flowering Chinese species whose wide-open, primrose-yellow blooms are most effective above blue-grey hostas and the lilac flowers of *Geranium phaeum* var. *lividum*, a variety of the dusky cranesbill which is found in the southern Alps.

To see the real miniatures among rhododendrons calls for a visit to the Rock Garden. Here are hummocks of *R. forrestii*, a prostrate creeping shrub less than 12in high that bears comparatively large bright red flowers in ones and twos. Given time and

The formal Azalea Lawn seen through a natural planting of silver birches.

space, it can reach 5ft across. As might be expected from the name, it is yet another of George Forrest's discoveries, made in 1905 on the first of seven expeditions to western China. The circumpolar *R. lapponicum* can also be seen here, its tiny scaly leaves obscured by small clusters of purple flowers in May.

The difference between azaleas and rhododendrons confuses most people and has done since at least the 19th century when botanists disagreed over whether they were separate genera. Today, *Azalea* is a section of the genus *Rhododendron*, while the term 'azalea' is popularly used for a wide range of species and hybrids which are mostly deciduous, have five rather than ten or more stamens and whose leaves are clad in hairs instead of scales. However, this is no rule of thumb and there are numerous exceptions, such as the Kurume hybrids which are evergreen or semi-evergreen. Flowering on the Azalea Lawn, which faces the main range of glasshouses, begins in April with the bright magenta-pink *R. reticulatum*, a Japanese species which has been in cultivation since 1865, and continues throughout May and into June.

The main species used in hybridisation are located at the top of the hill and the hybrids are chosen to give a good range of colour over a long period. Interest is further prolonged by an interplanting of various kinds of rowan (*Sorbus*) which flower in spring and also produce brightly coloured fruits and autumn tints. There are three main groups of azalea hybrids. Hardiest are the fragrant Ghent azaleas which originated in the horticultural holdings around the Belgian city of that name in the early 19th century. They are derived from crossing the American *R. calendulaceum* (orange), *R. nudiflorum* (pink) and *R. viscosum* (highly fragrant white) with the common yellow azalea, *R. luteum*. The colour range is from white and yellow to pink and scarlet, but yellows predominate. Earlier and rather smaller are the Mollis azaleas which arose in the late 19th century from crossing selected forms of the hardy red *R. japonicum* with the tender yellow-flowered Chinese species, *R. molle*. Mollis hybrids have large but scentless flowers and good autumn colour.

These two main groups, along with the Kurume azaleas which flourish at Benmore, subsequently gave rise to three further groups. Rustica hybrids are double Ghents crossed with *R. japonicum*, forming sizeable late-flowering shrubs with large fragrant flowers in shades of cream, blush-white, salmon and orange. The Occidentale hybrids were produced by crossing Mollis hybrids with the North American *R. occidentale* to give fragrant pastel-coloured flowers late in the season. The popular Knap Hill and Exbury hybrids, bred from Ghent, Mollis and Occidentale hybrids from about 1945 onwards, include some of the largest-flowered azaleas in a wide range of colours, variable with regard to size and hardiness but generally late-flowering and in many cases having superb autumn colour.

The Arboretum in blossom

Originally the Arboretum referred to the grounds of Inverleith House which was acquired in 1876 to form the western two-thirds of the Botanic Garden. Today it embraces all the garden's main areas of trees and shrubs. Its importance in the Edinburgh garden cannot be over-emphasised. It is the backbone of the garden in structural terms, giving the illusion of woodland - that peaceful green leafiness which for many visitors is the garden's main attraction. However, its role as a background should not obscure the fact that virtually every specimen is of botanical or horticultural interest - a major difference between a botanic garden and a park. Most of the trees and shrubs in the Arboretum are planted in groups according to their botanical classification.

Whether coming into leaf or laden with blossom, trees are always a delight in spring. Everyone's favourites are the cherries (*Prunus*), most of which can be found on the Hill below Inverleith House. While the eye is drawn irresistibly to *P. sargentii* amid the daffodils, it is worth exploring the others nearby, including the wild apricot (*P. armeniaca*) and Manchurian apricot (*P. mandschurica*). Adjacent to the cherries are the crab-apples (*Malus* species). Cherries and crab-apples belong to the rose family (Rosaceae). So too do the hawthorns which mostly flower in late spring. There are a number of interesting Asian and North American species at Inverleith but the most characterful specimen is a dwarf thornless form of the native common hawthorn, *Crataegus monogyna* 'Inermis Compacta' - a gnarled old tree that dates back to 1904 and would provide a perfect setting for tales of wizards and goblins. Other rosaceous relatives include the rowans (*Sorbus*) which provide a succession of bloom throughout spring.

The Hill and adjacent areas of the Arboretum support a number of other trees which are of special interest as spring advances. Toward the West Gate is the main collection of horse chestnuts (*Aesculus*). Contrary to expectations, the common horse chestnut (*A. hippocastanum*) is not native to these shores but to Albania and

The sweet buckeye, *Aesculus flava*, grows wild in the southeastern United States. It is one of the few yellow-flowered members of the horse chestnut family.

northern Greece, whence it was introduced to Scotland in the 1650s. But the majority of the 20 or so species in the genus are North American, where they are known as buckeyes on account of the similarity between their glossy brown 'conkers' and the eyes of a deer. There is a fine specimen of a sweet or yellow buckeye (*A. flava*) - one of the few yellow-flowered species in the genus - near the Herbarium building.

Worth seeking out is the snowdrop tree (*Halesia carolina*) from the southeast United States which grows between the Pond and the Hill. In May the twigs are hung with white bells that look quite like snowdrops. The similar but larger *H. monticola*, seen near the East Gate, is native to the same area but grows at higher altitudes.

At the opposite end of the Hill from the horse chestnuts is a collection of ashes (*Fraxinus*). Perhaps because the common ash (*F. excelsior*) has inconspicuous brown flowers, we do not expect great things from this genus in the spring. The manna ash (*F. ornus*) is certain to change our expectations when in late May it is laden with creamy-white plumes of blossom which are heavily scented. This beautiful tree comes from southern Europe and western Asia. In Sicily it is grown in plantations and tapped for 'manna' - the sap which contains mannitol, an unusual alcohol used as a sugar substitute in diabetic foods.

Another surprise is in store from the poplars (*Populus*), a genus which is easily overlooked in spring when there is so much else of more obvious charm. However, a group of species known as the balsam poplars contribute to the season by filling the air with a delightful scent - not from their flowers, but from their aromatic new leaves. Balsam poplars of various kinds are found wild in both North America and eastern Asia. One of the commonest - and also tallest and fastest growing - is the black cottonwood (*P. trichocarpa*) whose new leaves have a powerful balsam scent when unfolding, which is very evident when climbing the hill from the West Gate.

If you stand to the south of the Hill in May and look up towards Inverleith House, you will see two patches of primary colour among the varied greens. On the brow of the Hill is a group of *Ceanothus thyrsiflorus* var. *repens* which when flowering

Left. The snowdrop tree, *Halesia carolina*, belongs to the styrax family (Styracaceae) and needs lime-free soil. Its delicate white bells open in May.

Right. The manna ash, *Fraxinus ornus*.

becomes mounds of deep blue covered with blooms from top to bottom. Higher still, to the right of Inverleith House, can be seen the top of a tree that in contrast is bright yellow. From a distance it looks like blossom but in fact is a red oak (*Quercus rubra*) in new leaf.

Also near the West Gate, adjoining the horse chestnuts, is the maple (*Acer*) collection. There are about 150 species of maple worldwide. The majority are found in China, with a scattering in Japan and under a dozen each for Asia Minor, Europe and North America. Though many are famed for their autumn colour, some also have delightful, if less flamboyant, spring foliage and decorative flowers - in lime green, yellow or wine red, according to the species. A close look at the flowers reveals the first signs of the typical winged seeds ('keys') which develop quickly as the flowers wither.

Right. The red oak (*Quercus rubra*) is native to Canada and the northeast United States. Its new leaves are bright yellow. They turn a dull green as they mature, flaring into colour again in the autumn - red in young specimens (hence the common name) but russet or brown in older trees.

Below. The primrose yellow *Corylopsis platypetala* var. *laevis.*

No description of trees in spring would be complete without mention of magnolias. The main collection is to the east of Inverleith House but there are others throughout the garden. In the Woodland Garden during early spring there is the white-flowered Japanese *Magnolia kobus*, together with the superb *M. sprengeri* var. *diva*. Also noteworthy for their fine show at Edinburgh are *M. denudata* and *M. stellata*. Much later comes the flowering of *M. acuminata*, known as the cucumber tree on account of its fruits which, though like small green gherkins to begin with, finally turn dark red. Specimens of this 'ugly duckling' magnolia can be found in the main collection and on the lawn in front of the Herbarium. The flowers are easily missed, being a glaucous green, but are worth examining closely - and there are plenty within easy reach - for their intriguing fruity scent.

The majority of shrubs that flower in spring are showy and well-known - forsythias, viburnums, flowering currants - and are unlikely to be missed. There are however some less familiar ones that are worth pointing out. The true witch hazels (*Hamamelis*) are autumn and winter flowering but the related genus *Corylopsis* hangs on until spring. Again, the flowers appear on naked twigs, making the display more spectacular. Most of the 20 or so species have primrose yellow, sweetly scented flowers in drooping racemes which are followed by hazel-like leaves that render the plants incognito for the rest of the year; all are from Asia. One of Edinburgh's finest is the specimen of *C. platypetala* var. *laevis* which grows at the entrance to the Copse. It forms a colourful partnership with an underplanting of five-leaved coral-wort (*Cardamine pentaphyllos*) which produces its pale magenta flowers at the same time. Most attractive too is the spring-flowering *Enkianthus*, a genus of the heather family (Ericaceae). A collection of these oriental shrubs can be found in the Copse and Rhododendron Walk areas. There are five species in cultivation at the Botanic Garden, the commonest being *E. campanulatus* which bears clusters of small rounded bells in a pale yellow striped with red, looking salmon in colour from a distance. Another interesting member of this family also to be found in the Copse is the madroña (*Arbutus menziesii*), a handsome tree all year round, with silky smooth red-bronze bark that peels attractively, large oval evergreen leaves and, in spring, conspicuous panicles of white flowers.

Left. The delicately veined bells of *Enkianthus campanulatus* open in May and last for three weeks.

Below. Helwingia japonica is an unusual member of the dogwood family, Cornaceae. Its flowers resemble small black pearls and are produced in the centre of the leaves.

Anyone with a taste for the unusual is sure to admire the odd little shrub *Helwingia japonica* which grows in the border facing the east side of Inverleith House. The purple-flushed ovate leaves have deeply impressed veins, neatly serrated margins and a glossy finish, and in the centre of each sits a flower which for all the world looks like a tiny black pearl - or perhaps more prosaically, a fly. The flower stalk has, in fact, fused with the midrib of the leaf. The same strange arrangement is found in a couple of other species in this genus which is usually included in the dogwood family, Cornaceae.

The main collection of lilacs (*Syringa*), which belong to the same family as olives (*Olea*), privets (*Ligustrum*) and ashes (*Fraxinus*), is on the Hill, and it is with the hardy members of these genera that several unusual lilac species can be enjoyed in May. The star of the show is *S. tomentella* from western China which was grown from seed collected by George Forrest. The delicate scented flowers are produced in great abundance and give a two-tone effect, their deep lilac paler on the inside and fading with age.

As spring turns into summer, it is the turn of the laburnums and brooms to flower. Two of these well-known members of the pea family (Leguminosae) can be seen simultaneously in the Demonstration Garden where they have fused together in the graft hybrid or chimera +*Laburnocytisus adamii*, in which the inner tissues are laburnum within an outer layer of broom. This freak of the horticultural world was produced by chance in Adam's nursery near Paris in 1825 during the routine grafting of a purple broom on to a laburnum in order to obtain a standard. The result is a mixture of the common laburnum (*Laburnum anagyroides*) and the purple broom (*Cytisus purpureus*), producing flowers of both species together with some that are half-way between the two. Judging by the amount of interest shown in the tree when flowering at Inverleith, it is a wonder that it is not more widely planted - as a conversation piece if not as a space-saving two-for-the-price-of-one tree for the small garden.

Springtime on the Rock Garden

Edinburgh's world-famous Rock Garden is guaranteed to have something of interest on any day of the year. Spring is, however, the period of peak activity when plants from all over the world start into growth after a winter which for many of them in the wild is spent in the bitter cold of mountainous regions.

There are eye-catching crocuses, scillas, muscari and chionodoxas, and alluring, if sombre, fritillaries - but for many visitors the most memorable early spring flowers are the daffodils (*Narcissus*) and the primroses (*Primula*). All members of these genera are attractive, if not entrancing. Outstanding among the daffodils is our own British wild daffodil or Lent lily, *N. pseudonarcissus*, which is smaller and has paler petals than the typical yellow trumpet hybrids. There are several subspecies, notably the Welsh Tenby daffodil (*N. pseudonarcissus* subsp. *obvallaris*) which has deep yellow petals and a six-lobed corona, and the creamy-white musk daffodil (*N. pseudonarcissus* subsp. *moschatus*). Daffodils with flat coronas are popularly known as narcissi. Smallest among these is *N. watieri*, a white unscented jonquil from the Atlas Mountains in Morocco.

Though the Botanic Garden grows many unusual and rare primulas, it is the familiar *P. juliae* from the Caucasus and its hybrids, notably *P.* x *pruhoniciana*, that steal the show in spring with their dazzling shades of magenta, wine red and purple. Brightest

Left. One of the strangest hybrids in existence, +*Laburnocytisus adamii*.

Right. The white flowers of the North American wake robin, *Trillium grandiflorum*, turn pink as they age.

of all is 'Romeo' which is almost fluorescent, drawing visitors to examine the label like moths to a flame. One of the best-loved of small primulas is the variable *P. marginata* with silvery grey-green leaves and mauve-blue, pink or white flowers. Though found wild only in the Maritime and Cottian Alps, few rock gardens and alpine houses are without it. Those at Edinburgh are no exception, where it can be spotted in nooks and crannies of the Rock Garden and is also displayed to perfection in its various forms in the Alpine House.

Two of the favourite plant groups after the daffodils and primulas are erythroniums and trilliums, both of which are members of the lily family (Liliaceae) and predominantly North American. In fact, many are woodlanders rather than alpines so to see the complete range grown by the Botanic Garden will entail visiting both the Rock Garden and the adjacent Woodland Garden. The only non-American species of *Erythronium* is the dog's tooth violet, *E. dens-canis* which has pinkish-mauve flowers and eye-catching foliage, heavily mottled with brown. A herald of spring in the high subalpine meadows of the Rocky Mountains is the yellow glacier lily (*E. grandiflorum*) which flowers *en masse* as the snows melt. Trilliums are so-named because their parts are in threes - typically with a whorl of three leaves, above which is borne a solitary three-petalled flower. The western wake-robin, *T. ovatum*, is found in montane forests from British Columbia to Colorado. Very similar but larger all round and with broader petals is *T. grandiflorum* which, because of its size is more at home in borders and woodland areas of the garden. In both species the long-lasting flowers age to pink.

Most people find pasque flowers (*Pulsatilla*) irresistible with their exquisite anemone-like flowers, ferny leaves and overall covering of silky hairs which acts as a fur coat to protect them against the elements. The common name has undergone a change of meaning over the centuries. Originally from the French *passefleur*, which can be translated as 'unsurpassable flower', it became pasque or paschal (Easter) flower through association with its early spring flowering and perhaps also from its use of the flowers to dye Easter eggs green. The genus *Pulsatilla* is widely distributed

Spring-flowering phlox, iris and penstemons in the North American section of the Rock Garden.

Celmisia is a large genus, almost entirely confined to New Zealand. *C. hookeri* stands out on the Rock Garden in May with its silver leaves and outsize daisies.

in mountainous regions of Europe, Asia and North America. About a dozen different species are grown on the Rock Garden and any you come across will repay a closer look - especially on sunny days when the flowers open wide to expose their golden stamens or are backlit by early morning or evening sun.

Many plants from montane regions have grey or silver foliage - an effect given either by a covering of hairs or by an encrustation of lime - which serves to protect the plant from low temperatures and high light levels. The large genus *Saxifraga*, with some 400 species, has numerous examples of lime-encrusted species. A great variety can be seen flowering on the Rock Garden in spring and early summer, nestling into crevices, forming mounds over rocks or on the scree, when both flowers and foliage can be appreciated to the full.

Silver foliage is also widespread among plants from the southern hemisphere, especially from New Zealand. Logan Botanic Garden has by far the best selection of southern hemisphere plants but a feature of Edinburgh's Rock Garden in late spring and early summer are various kinds of *Celmisia*. All have classic white daisies with yellow centres and many have grey foliage. One of the loveliest is *C. hookeri* with long, silky smooth, silvered leaves and 2in flowers. It is quite a large plant - 12in or more - and positively gleams when in full flower.

The structure of the Rock Garden and all its various microhabitats for alpine plants is dependent on boulders of immense size. Over and above these, a great variety of trees and shrubs - many of prostrate or dwarf form - have been planted to soften the outlines and provide further niches. Most of them go unnoticed, like settings for jewels, but in the spring several stand out when flowering.

The star of them all is a venerable Japanese bitter orange, *Poncirus trifoliata*. Actually from northern China, this hardy species is closely related to the true citruses and in favourable situations produces tiny oranges. It is however chiefly grown for its scented white flowers - translucent and much larger than those of citruses - which appear among the fearsome dark spines in late spring, just before the leaves unfold.

The Alpine House

Some distance from the Rock Garden is a complementary area - the Alpine House with its adjacent frames and raised bed. Though not a large area, it is one of the most attractive in the entire garden, with its accompanying borders and terrace of trough gardens. It also contains a surprising number and variety of plants, from the sensitive souls and rarities which are displayed in rotation under glass, to sun-loving herbaceous and bulbous plants in the borders, climbers on the rear wall and crevice plants in retaining walls. An area that can be walked round in a couple of minutes may easily absorb an hour or more, especially in spring.

The heart of the area is the Alpine House itself. In spring this is one of the highlights of a visit to the Botanic Garden, with colours rivalling those of summer bedding but coming instead from some of the world's most delicate wild flowers: high alpine drabas, dionysias and androsaces in yellow, pink and white; magenta pleiones; mauve and white cyclamen; pastel primulas; bronze fritillaries; red tulips; and gentian-blue Chilean crocuses. Every plant here is a gem, often challenging in the extreme but grown to perfection and displayed with obvious pride.

Some of the most difficult species shown in the Alpine House are those that form 'cushions' - the tight hummocks of foliage characteristic of high altitude plants which have to contend with howling winds. Trickiest of all are the dionysias - cousins of the more widespread androsaces - some of which grow naturally under rock overhangs and cannot tolerate water on their foliage. These slow-growing plants belong to the primrose family (Primulaceae) and come from the mountains of southwest Asia.

Other treasures of the Alpine House include pleiones, small deciduous orchids with disproportionately large flowers in purple, pink or white. They grow in mossy places on mountainsides in various parts of Asia, often up to the snow line, and are therefore mostly hardy - though they dislike winter wet. The most prized species is *P. forrestii* - the only yellow-flowered pleione - which was discovered by George Forrest in 1906 at 10,000ft (3000m) in western Yunnan.

Outside the Alpine House are more lovely sights: the creamy-white flowers of *Clematis alpina* subsp. *sibirica* and a large Siberian fritillary (*Fritillaria pallidiflora*) with pale yellow bells; the unusual white-flowered mezereon (*Daphne mezereum* 'Album') which later has yellow, rather than red berries; and masses of purple-blue *Synthyris stellata* in the retaining wall of the raised bed.

Top. Scarlet tulips, blue Chilean crocuses, and magenta pleione orchids - the colours in the Alpine House during spring rival those of summer bedding.

Bottom. Trough gardens are a feature of the paved terrace outside the Alpine House.

Woodland borders

The areas of the garden known as the Copse, Rhododendron Walk, Woodland Garden, Glade and Peat Garden are dominated by trees and shrubs. In and among these are borders and underplantings devoted to herbaceous and bulbous plants which enjoy the shelter of woodland conditions. Most of these are at their best in spring.

Some species of *Trillium* are equally at home in woodland or on the Rock Garden. One that is too large for the Rock Garden is *T. sessile* var. *chloropetalum* which reaches 18in. It is a handsome plant with marbled leaves and erect maroon flowers. Known as toadshade, it makes effective ground cover in several areas of the Woodland Garden and Rhododendron Walk. In contrast, one of the smallest

Trillium sessile var. *chloropetalum.*

trilliums, *T. rivale*, can be seen in the Peat Garden, where it forms a neat posy of flowers about 6in across. *T. rivale* and several other white-flowered trilliums have pink forms. The Royal Botanic Garden is famous for a pink form of *T. grandiflorum* which has been in cultivation at Edinburgh since 1914.

The Peat Garden solves the problem of growing plants that need a more acid soil, shadier conditions and higher levels of moisture and humidity than are provided on the Rock Garden. With the current concern about the removal of peat from wetlands, it is of interest to note that relatively little peat is used and that the tiers of peat blocks last about 15 years. Nevertheless, substitutes made from coconut waste are currently being tried. Late spring and early summer in the Peat Garden sees the flowering of *Paris*, with its characteristic solitary flower above a ruff of leaves. One of the most attractive is the Japanese herb Paris (*P. japonica*), which has a many-petalled white flower atop a disc of oval leaves.

The woodland areas are ideal for primulas that enjoy damp, shady conditions. These include *P. whitei*, whose lilac flowers coincidentally have a white eye, and candelabras such as the cerise pink *P. pulverulenta*. They are also home to most of the garden's Himalayan poppies (*Meconopsis*) which bloom from late spring to early summer. The Royal Botanic Garden is renowned for its collection of these plants - 18 species and several hybrids - which do exceptionally well in Scotland's cool climate. They are not, however, without their problems, several being short-lived and in some cases monocarpic (dying after flowering). These must be renewed every year or so from seed and the hybrids - which do not come true from seed - have to be divided regularly.

As the common name suggests, these poppies are found wild in various parts of the Sino-Himalaya. The favourites are those with sky blue flowers, notably *M. grandis* and *M. betonicifolia* - though in fact they are variable and may be anything from a dingy purplish-blue to deep purple or white. These two have crossed to give *M.* x *sheldonii*, a vigorous free-flowering hybrid with fine large blue flowers on plants 3-5ft tall. In addition to their lovely flowers, some Himalayan poppies also have attractive foliage, deeply lobed and densely covered in silver or gold hairs which are especially noticeable at the rosette stage. *M. napaulensis* has striking ginger hairs and red, pink or purple flowers; white and pale blue forms are also known, and several

can be seen in the woodland areas where they reach an impressive 6ft.

Peonies are another highlight of the garden's woodland areas in late spring. The borders of herbaceous plants along the Rhododendron Walk are protected by bamboos, European mountain pines (*Pinus mugo*) and North American beach pines (*P. contorta*), all of which tolerate Edinburgh's poor soil. Here can be seen *Paeonia tenuifolia* which was introduced to our gardens from Transylvania and the Crimea as long ago as 1735. It has finely cut leaves, which are ornamental in themselves, and single peony-red flowers. Nearby is a mass of single pink flowers belonging to *P. veitchii* var. *woodwardii*. Single peonies such as these are rarely seen in gardens today, having been supplanted by double-flowered forms which last longer - most of which are hybrids. The Botanic Garden is therefore one of the few places where one can see wild peonies.

Peonies are tenacious, frequently the last survivors in abandoned gardens and outliving the gardener who plants them. They do however, dislike disturbance and are carefully worked round when the borders are stripped and replanted - a task which takes place every five to six years to prevent overcrowding and the build-up of disease. Most peonies are herbaceous plants but the aristocrats of the genus are the so-called tree peonies which are shrubby. Of these, the most magnificent is *P. suffruticosa*. Known in China as the king of flowers, it has been in cultivation there since the seventh century. All early introductions to the West were of garden variants and it was not until the early part of this century that wild stock was collected by

Left. This small Himalayan poppy was a great favourite of Reginald Farrer, who found it by the million on the cold mountainsides of Kansu. He took exception to its scientific name, *Meconopsis quintuplinervia*, which he found singularly unappealing, and bestowed upon it the charmingly apt common name of harebell poppy.

Right. The single-flowered *P. mlokosewitschii* from the Caucasus - nicknamed Molly-the-witch by tongue-tied gardeners - is enduringly popular among peony aficionados. Its lovely flowers are complemented by blue-green foliage and followed by ornamental seed pods.

William Purdom and Joseph Rock. The true species has pure white flowers and the magnificent *P. suffruticosa* subsp. *rockii* produces huge scented 10-petalled flowers with a deep maroon basal blotch. There are specimens of the species in several locations, notably in front of the Herbarium, and of the subspecies in the Woodland Garden. All flower in May.

The Pond

The Pond was developed in the 1820s in an area of naturally boggy ground. Water is pumped from the Pond to the Rock Garden, whence it flows in a series of falls and pools back to the Pond again, creating a succession of damp habitats for moisture-loving plants. The Pond comes to life in the spring with the spectacular flowering of the skunk cabbages which produce massive arum-like inflorescences and a pervasive cabbagey, skunk-like odour. There are two species: the primary yellow *Lysichiton americanus* from western North America; and the less common, pure white *L. camtschatcencis* from northeast Asia. In cultivation they occasionally cross, producing an intermediate cream-flowered hybrid that is a pale reflection of its dazzling parents. In the wild this never happens, as the two species are decisively separated by the Bering Sea, having evolved after continental America and Asia drifted apart. As flowering ends, the enormous oval leaves develop which give the margins of the Pond a lush, exotic appearance throughout the summer. In contrast, the sword-shaped new leaves of *Iris pseudacorus* 'Variegatus' form smartly striped clumps, topped with yellow flowers as spring turns into summer.

Enjoying damp conditions beside the Pond is the dawn redwood (*Metasequoia glyptostroboides*). One of the few deciduous conifers, it produces light green new needles in late March. It is a conical tree with ascending branches and a deeply furrowed trunk clad in shaggy, reddish bark. In many respects it resembles the American swamp cypress (*Taxodium distichum*), but has softer leaves that are opposite rather than alternate on the twigs. Both species are planted near the Pond, but the most conspicuous specimen is the dawn redwood in the centre border.

No pond is complete without a weeping willow (*Salix alba* 'Tristis'). The curtain of foliage makes a perfect backdrop for the deep purple-blue flowers of *Iris sibirica*, a species which revels in rich damp soil.

The Glasshouses in spring

The glasshouses are of interest at all times of the year, most of the plants being perennial evergreens that are chosen for landscape effect as well as their intrinsic interest. Being largely tropical, seasonal changes are less pronounced but there are certain highlights which should not be missed. There are ten different houses altogether which may be explored by starting at the lowest level in the Temperate House.

A wide range of tender plants from the drier temperate parts of the world can be found in the Temperate House. Here is the largest of all the so-called 'hardy geraniums' (to distinguish them from the half-hardy bedding geraniums which are really pelargoniums), *G. maderense* from Madeira. Closely related and also in the Temperate House, but flowering in summer rather than spring, is another Madeiran geranium, *G. palmatum*, which is distinguished by its plain green or pink-flushed leaf stalks and much less divided leaves.

The first signs of spring in the Temperate House are the mimosas or wattles (*Acacia*), many of which come from Australia and turn bright yellow in spring under a mass of pompom or bottlebrush flowers. These members of the pea family (Leguminosae) include the kangaroo thorn (*A. armata*), the knife-leaf wattle (*A. cultriformis*) and prickly Moses (*A. verticillata*). *Acacia* foliage commonly consists of phyllodes (flattened stems) instead of true leaves. It varies greatly, being anything from fern-like or blade-shaped to needle-sharp, and either dark green or grey, according to the species.

The Australian honeysuckles (*Banksia*) are evergreen shrubs of the protea family (Proteaceae) which are handsome with or without their dense bottlebrush spikes of tubular flowers. *B. collina* does well in the Temperate House and attracts attention in spring when spiky rounded heads of cream flowers appear among the long narrow grey leaves.

As our eyes scan the glasshouses for the dramatic and showy - of which there is much - it is all too easy to miss the unobtrusive which may be equally interesting and, in its

Banksia collina is one of about 70 species of evergreen shrubs, known as Australian honeysuckles.

own way, just as lovely. Two examples are the purple anise or aniseed tree (*Illicium floridanum*) and the champak (*Michelia figo*), both of which flower in late spring and early summer. The former is native to the southern United States and is closely related to the Chinese star anise (*I. anisatum*) which is widely used both medicinally and as a flavouring. It has aromatic leathery leaves beneath which hang clusters of narrow-petalled, rather crinkled, purplish-brown flowers, followed by woody, star-shaped seed pods. *Michelia* bushes are detected by the sense of smell rather than by sight, for the small waxy flowers are powerfully scented of pear drops. Not unlike a miniature magnolia flower in appearance, they are cream, edged with maroon, and are few and far between among the glossy oval leaves.

Spring in the Tropical Aquatic House is also eventful. The peace lilies

Left. Brownea grandiceps produces spectacular pendent balls of red flowers.

Right. The new fronds of some tropical ferns bring a touch of colour to the lush greenery of the Fern House.

(*Spathiphyllum wallisii*) begin their lengthy display of pure white spathe-and-spadix inflorescences, and the last flowering stems of the Nigerian Cape lily (*Crinum podophyllum*) bow down to the water under the weight of their huge exotic white blooms. In the surrounding 'jungle', there are dense clusters of cream flowers produced by *Rudgea macrophylla* from Brazil, the pendent balls of red flowers of the leguminous tree *Brownea grandiceps* (literally 'big head') from Venezuela, and in complete contrast, the tiny sausage-shaped spikes of yellow flowers which belong to the bull's horn acacia (*Acacia spadicigera*).

The new leaves of many tropical plants can be almost as colourful and interesting as the flowers. From spring onwards, this is something to look for in the glasshouses. In the Fern House there are new fronds in shades of pink and bronze and in the Tropical Rock House the red new shoots of a tropical blueberry, *Vaccinium acrobracteatum*, show up from afar. Tropical trees tend to produce flushes of new leaves which are flaccid at first, drooping at the ends of the branches. They are commonly pink, red or white so that at a distance it looks as if the tree is flowering. Those of the cocoa tree (*Cacao theobroma*) in the Tropical Aquatic House are a pinkish-bronze. The colours are caused by compounds which protect the new foliage from the intense solar radiation of tropical regions.

The orchid family (Orchidaceae) is the largest family of flowering plants, with around 25,000 species in some 750 genera. This means that one in ten species of flowering plant is an orchid! - which would appear to contradict the notion that orchids are synonymous with the rare and exotic. In fact, though numerous in terms of genera and species, the majority are rare, being naturally confined to very small areas, mostly in the tropics. What the numerousness implies instead is that orchids are incredibly diverse, with every conceivable variation on the basic design - an arrangement of three sepals and three petals, in which one of the petals is differently shaped from the other two and is known as the lip.

Many of the orchids in the Orchid and Cycad House are grown on artificial trees, made from galvanised steel pipes clad with the bark of the cork oak (*Quercus suber*). This imitates the natural habitat, for the majority of tropical orchids are epiphytes which perch high up on the branches of rainforest trees. Before the 'trees' are planted with orchids, the spaces between the framework and the cork are filled with expanding foam to prevent pests from taking up residence. The orchids have to be tied on initially but soon produce roots that clasp the bark so tightly that it is impossible to remove them without damage. Terrestrial tropical orchids are, on the other hand, planted at ground level. These include the slipper orchids (*Paphiopedilum* and *Phragmipedium*), and reed-like orchids such as the orange-flowered *Epidendrum radicans*.

With such diversity, highlights among the orchids are many. The Royal Botanic Garden has a particularly fine collection of *Dendrobium* species - over 160 in all - of which a significant proportion are from New Guinea, collected from the wild by scientists carrying out research into this group, and are now on display in the Peat House. They range from the dwarf, pretty *D. vexillarius* to the bizarre *D. finisterrae*. Not all orchids have gaudy or strange flowers. It is worth finding the chain orchid (*Dendrochilum glumaceum*) in spring, as its spikes of tightly packed small white flowers, though individually unremarkable, arch gracefully downward and smell delightful. Scent is another feature of orchids which varies greatly, from entrancing to interesting or downright unpleasant. As foliage plants, orchids are undistinguished (and often undistinguishable), but when flowering there is never a dull moment!

The Temperate Palm House and the adjoining Tropical Palm House are the oldest glasshouses at Edinburgh, dating back to 1858 and 1834 respectively. Because of their age, the overhead walkways are no longer safe for visitors and so the high-level flowering and fruiting takes place unobserved. However, it is usually possible to catch sight of palm flowers or fruits which in many species are borne in large panicles in the crown. The flowers are mostly cream in colour and last only a day, followed by one-seeded fruits which may be brightly coloured to attract birds and mammals. Each year in May, the West Indian fan or thatch palm (*Sabal bermudana*) produces numerous round black berries, about the size of peas, which can often be found on the ground. Growing in the centre of the Tropical Palm House, this specimen was moved from the earlier Leith Walk garden and is now over 200 years old.

Palms epitomise the tropics where most of the 2800 species are found. Not all conform to the popular image, based on the coconut palm (*Cocos nucifera*), of a single trunk, unbranched but scarred where leaves have fallen and topped by a tuft of graceful, feather-shaped leaves. There are also palms with leaves like fishtails, bamboos or fans and ones which differ markedly in habit, being thorny-stemmed climbers known as rattans that form hazardous barriers in tropical rainforests. Discovering a new leaf unfurling is often as exciting as seeing flowers or fruits. Those of the fan palms are especially attractive as the segments draw apart, leaving threads between them. This can be seen in the Mediterranean dwarf fan palm (*Chamaerops humilis*), a cool-growing species which reaches only 5ft in the wild and usually less in a pot, making it popular for conservatories.

The palm houses are not exclusively given over to palms. In spring the bright orange flowers of the kaffir lilies (*Clivia miniata*) add colour to the Temperate Palm House, as do the small pink flowers of the not-quite-hardy, evergreen *Geranium canariense*. The Temperate Aquatic House is little different in terms of habitat from the Tropical

The Orchid and Cycad House displays an exciting range of tropical plants, from sophisticated orchids to the most primitive giant ferns and cycads.

Top. The grassy clumps of *Maxillaria tenuifolia* produce a succession of solitary, red-spotted yellow flowers in early spring which smell strongly of coconut.

Bottom. The Temperate Palm House dates back to 1858. Its overhead walkways provide excellent views of the tall vegetation but are no longer safe for public use.

Aquatic House - its name lingering on from when it was kept at significantly cooler temperatures. It too has a central pool but is bordered by bromeliads, small understory herbs, epiphytic cacti, climbers and a few feature shrubs, many of which are South American in origin. One of the first climbers to flower is a tropical American morning glory, *Pharbitis learii*, which blooms from spring to autumn. Known as the blue dawn flower, it opens a deep blue, turns purple by lunch-time and finally becomes pink as the flowers curl inwards and fade. Quite different are the delicate white flowers of the shrub *Psychotria jasminiflora* which appear in April. It comes from Brazil and belongs to the same family as coffee and gardenia, the Rubiaceae. The genus *Psychotria* is so-named because of its chemistry. Several species are used in the preparation of ayahuasca, a hallucinogenic drink which is central to the religious ceremonies of the Amazon Indians.

The Peat House is not only a focus for certain orchids, but also houses the Garden's remarkable collection of tender Vireya rhododendrons. The peak flowering time for these southeast Asian plants begins in winter and extends into spring. These are especially enjoyable during the early months of the year when inclement weather tempts even the hardiest visitor to seek a brief respite in the glasshouses. But as spring advances, the Peat and Tropical Rock Houses have other treasures too: the ericaceous vine *Dimorphanthera kempteriana* with large waxy pink bells; a shrubby Mexican member of the African violet family (Gesneriaceae), *Drymonia strigosa*, whose salmon-pink calyces remain long after the tubular yellow flowers have fallen; and, best of all, the jade vine (*Strongylodon macrobotrys*) from the Philippines which is now extremely rare or possibly extinct in the wild. Each May this massive tropical liana produces dangling racemes, up to 3ft long, of claw-shaped flowers in a colour unusual if not unique among flowering plants, which might best be described as peppermint green.

The Philippine jade vine, *Strongylodon macrobotrys*.

SUMMER

Edinburgh is at its busiest during the summer, especially in August when visitors from all over the world crowd into the city for the annual Edinburgh International Festival. The garden at Inverleith reflects this, and is itself a venue for Festival exhibitions and events.

Thankfully, it also retains its atmosphere of verdant calm, enabling visitors to escape from the urban bustle and restore their energies in the peaceful world of plants. The danger is that once inside the garden, there is so much to see that a relaxing interlude can turn into something of a marathon, especially for the real enthusiasts who, determined to see everything, are guaranteed complete though pleasurable exhaustion. A happy medium can, however, be achieved, either by taking advantage of guided tours, or by concentrating only on the highlights, some of which are described below.

Opposite and Right. The Herbaceous Border provides a spectacle of colour throughout the summer, backed by one of Britain's most impressive beech hedges.

The Herbaceous Border

If there is one feature that attracts visitors like bees to honey, it is the magnificent Herbaceous Border which is in full bloom throughout the summer. Edinburgh's Herbaceous Border is a triumph of skill over adversity where, with ample feeding and the protection of one of Britain's most splendid beech hedges, the full spectrum of colourful herbaceous perennials thrives in all its grandeur. For maintenance purposes the Herbaceous Border is divided into two sections, each of which is stripped and replanted every six years. In addition to feeding, weeding and removal of dead stems in winter, the most important task in maintaining the Border is staking, without which herbaceous plants are quite literally a flop. A combination of birch stakes and metal rings are used to prevent unsightly sprawl.

In winter and early spring the Herbaceous Border is bleak, the majority of plants having died down completely. As spring advances, there are signs of things to come. First in the run-up to flowering are the hardy geraniums and the hostas, both of which are blessed with attractive foliage as well as lovely flowers. Some of the hardy geraniums which begin flowering very early in the season include *Geranium* 'Johnson's Blue', a cross between *G. himalayense* and the meadow cranesbill, *G. pratense*; the double form of *Geranium himalayense*; and the long-flowering pink *G. endressii* 'Wargrave'. Early too are the oriental poppies, including *Papaver orientale* 'Olympia', with double orange flowers, and the doronicums, attractive yellow daisies which are often the first plants to bloom in the border.

As spring advances, the hosta foliage is at its immaculate best - blue in the case of *H. glauca*, irregularly waved and variegated in *H. undulata* and white-margined in *H. sieboldii*. When summer gets under way, sculptural details such as hosta leaves are lost amid the riot of colour - lupins, campanulas, catmint, delphiniums, phlox and, as autumn draws near, Michaelmas daisies, Japanese anemones and ice plants.

The Demonstration Garden

The Herbaceous Border is primarily of horticultural interest. On the other side of the beech hedge is the Demonstration Garden which has both horticultural and botanical features. The Rose Garden is more than ornamental in early summer, being planted to show the development of roses as garden plants. Modern varieties are grown in the central arbour which is surrounded by some of the original species used in their breeding: the heavily scented musk rose (*Rosa moschata*) which flowers from August to October; wild dog roses (*R. canina*); the deep pink French rose (*R. gallica*); the white-flowered polyantha rose (*R. multiflora*); and the Austrian briar (*R. foetida*) which introduced yellow into the colour range. Bordering the Rose Garden are more wild roses and varieties of interest to the gardener. These include

The Rose Garden is both ornamental and informative.

the sweet briar (*R. rubiginosa*) whose leaves smell of apples after rain and the Scotch or burnet rose (*R. pimpinellifolia*), a low-growing, thicket-forming shrub which grows wild on sand dunes and has unusual black hips.

The centrepiece of the Demonstration Garden in summer is a bed of hardy annuals which can be seen from half-way along the Herbaceous Border, framed by the arch in the beech hedge. The bed is sown in early May and is at its best in July and August. Being opportunistic plants that germinate, grow, flower and seed in the fastest possible time when conditions are suitable, hardy annuals need no encouragement to provide a colourful display. Of special interest is a wigwam of canary creeper (*Tropaeolum peregrinum*), a Peruvian relative of the nasturtium which reaches 12ft in a single season, making it a useful plant for temporarily covering eyesores while a more permanent climber is established.

Close by are beds of hardy culinary and medicinal herbs which have a particular fascination. Here one can see the actual plants whose names are familiar in recipes (such as coriander and caraway) or as ingredients in skin care preparations (marigold, for example) or, less obviously, may be the source of drugs. Important medicinal herbs include foxglove (*Digitalis purpurea*), used to treat heart failure, and valerian (*Valeriana officinalis*), a potent sedative. Many herbs in everyday use are not hardy however, and must be imported from warmer parts of the world. Some of these can be seen elsewhere in the garden: ginger (*Zingiber officinale*) and turmeric (*Curcuma longa*) in the Tropical Rock House; Saigon cinnamon (*Cinnamomum loureirii*) and lemon verbena (*Aloysia triphylla*) in the Temperate House.

The Demonstration Garden may be likened to a living text book in which are shown some of the basic principles of botany, together with some interesting aspects of cultivated plants. At one time, most of the Botanic Garden was arranged along these lines as it was primarily a teaching institution in which practical instruction played a major role. Two areas in particular are concerned purely and simply with botany: the traditional Scottish Order Beds in which native plants are arranged by family; and the area of beds devoted to botanical classification and plant structure. The information, for example, on types of plant, patterns of growth, seed dispersal, and pollination mechanisms, is given on large labels at a convenient height for reading,

Top Left. The bed of hardy annuals in the Demonstration Garden.

Top Right. Cranesbills (*Geranium*) and Himalayan balsam (*Impatiens glandulifera*) are among the examples of Exploding Seedheads in the Demonstration Garden.

Bottom. Soft colours and aromatic foliage predominate in the Silver or Mediterranean Garden, here seen in *Tanacetum densum* subsp. *amani, Artemisia* 'Silver Queen' and *Lavandula vera* 'Compacta'.

each feature described being illustrated by appropriate plants. There is, for example, no better way to appreciate the phenomenon of dehiscent fruits than by observing the bed of Explosive Seedheads on a warm sunny day as the cranesbills (*Geranium*) and Himalayan balsam (*Impatiens glandulifera*) fire seeds in all directions.

The north-east corner of the Demonstration Garden consists of a lawn with island beds of feature plants such as pampas grass (*Cortaderia selloana*), bordered on two sides by raised beds of predominantly grey-leaved plants. Because of its open sunny aspect, silver foliage and vibrant flower colours, this area is known as the Silver or Mediterranean Garden, although it contains plants from various regions with a similar climate. Truly Mediterranean in origin are the lavenders, in shades of mauve, purple and pink, which rub shoulders with American penstemons and tree poppies (*Romneya trichocalyx*) and that aristocrat of silver plants, *Tanacetum densum* subsp. *amani* from Turkey. Many of the plants are aromatic, especially in hot sunshine, though the pungent aroma of the curry plant (*Helichrysum angustifolium*) is often most apparent after rain. All these plants enjoy warm, well-drained soil. This is provided by the raised beds which are supported by setts purchased from the council after they had been removed from streets in the city. The walls themselves make an ideal habitat for plants such as mulleins (*Verbascum*) which grow wild on stony banks and rock faces.

Summertime in the Arboretum

With the fading of the lilacs and laburnums, spring is over and the Arboretum takes on its role as backdrop for the colourful displays of summer. For the majority of trees and shrubs, summer is a productive time; the new leaves expand and darken, casting pools of shade round each trunk, while green fruits swell in readiness for ripening. There are, however, some 'late starters' which flower in the height of summer, and some species which are of interest for other reasons. The highlights may be fewer than in spring and autumn but are memorable nevertheless.

The most scented summer-flowering shrub is the mock orange (*Philadelphus*), with a perfume which at close quarters is even more enjoyable than that of genuine orange blossom. The *Philadelphus* collection is concentrated on the Salix Lawn and the adjoining border which runs along the south boundary of the Garden. Sadly, few visitors make the minor detour necessary to explore this somewhat remote corner of the garden. Almost all the mock oranges planted in gardens today are hybrids or cultivars, many of which originated at the turn of the century at Lemoine's nursery in France. The original cross, named *P.* x *lemoinei*, was between the European *P. coronarius* and the North American *P. microphyllus*. This and a selection of its clones, together with the parent species can be seen in the collection. Mock oranges are found wild in Asia, as well as in Europe and North America. The most widely planted Asian species is *P. delavayi* which was discovered and introduced by the Abbé Delavay in 1887 and re-collected by George Forrest in 1919. It has large leaves with greyish undersides and a profusion of small, heavily scented flowers.

Viburnums are a very varied group as regards foliage, flowers, flowering time, scent and fruits. They also tend to be scattered throughout the garden, though the main collection is located along the east boundary and on the Pyrus and Hazel Lawn. Some are similar to hydrangeas in that the flower heads are composed of small fertile flowers surrounded by sterile florets. An example is *V. plicatum* forma *tomentosum* 'Mariesii' in which the lace-cap flowers are borne in tiers - one of the loveliest of all shrubs when well grown. A specimen of this can be admired in late spring and early summer at the Palm House end of the Copse. Several species are valued primarily as foliage plants, the most impressive being *V. rhytidophyllum*, which is situated near the Linnaeus Monument (behind the main glasshouse range). In May and June it bears stout cymes of beige flowers, but its large rhododendron-like leaves, with their deeply wrinkled texture, remain the principal attraction.

Magnolias are always thought of as spring-flowering, so much so that most of the summer-flowering species go unnoticed - partly also because the flowers are hidden among the leaves, rather than exposed on bare branches. In the Copse and Rhododendron Walk areas there are specimens of *Magnolia sinensis* and *M. sieboldii*, both of which have fragrant pure white flowers, and the quite different *M. hypoleuca* which has very large obovate leaves and waxy scented cream flowers facing upward at the ends of the branches. June is the peak flowering time for all of them, though *M. sieboldii* tends to flower intermittently from May to August.

The most spectacular summer-flowering tree must be *Davidia involucrata*, commonly known as the handkerchief tree on account of its huge white bracts that flutter in the breeze. There are davidias on the Hill, near the Herbarium and the Caledonian Hall. Though not as eye-catching from a distance, the tulip tree's flowers, which appear in July, are unusually lovely at close quarters - like pale green tulips, flamed with orange in the centre. The tulip tree (*Liriodendron tulipifera*) also has the most elegant leaves which are almost square with four lobes. A fine specimen stands beside the Herbarium. Easily grown but rarely seen in gardens are *Euodia daniellii* and *E. hupehensis*, Asian trees which are related to the citruses and, perhaps

The tulip tree, *Liriodendron tulipifera.*

more obviously, to *Skimmia*. Both have ash-like leaves and produce conspicuous clusters of off-white, strongly scented flowers in late summer, followed by black and red fruits respectively. Euodias are grown on the Pyrus and Hazel Lawn and on the Hill.

Catkins up to 20in long are produced in summer by the Caucasian wingnut, *Pterocarya fraxinifolia*. The leaves are even longer than the floral chains, and ash-like, adding to the ornamental effect. This large fast-growing tree belongs to the walnut family (Juglandaceae) and tends to sucker vigorously. It enjoys moist soil and tolerates flooding, making it suitable for wet situations. Edinburgh's specimen is on the Pond Lawn and was grown from seed sent from Rome Botanic Garden in 1922. Nearby is another tree worth finding in the summer: *Populus wilsonii* which, as the name suggests, was another of E H Wilson's 'firsts' from China (in 1907). It has purplish-green twigs and broad handsome leaves 8in long. The most enjoyable feature, however, is the sound that the leaves make - more of a rattling than a rustling - which must be the result of their thin but leathery texture.

Oddly enough, two plants which give visitors pleasure in the Arboretum during summer are 'weeds' - plants that by definition grow in profusion where they are not wanted. One of them is really rather a joke. Named *Pratia treadwellii*, this tiny creeping plant from New Zealand has insinuated itself into most of the Arboretum's lawns, having escaped from the confines of cultivation as an alpine. Here it celebrates its freedom each summer by studding the grass with starry white flowers that on close examination resemble those of a lobelia. Over the past 20 years it has indeed been well trodden upon, and mown repeatedly, to no avail and now outnumbers the daisies. The other is *Tropaeolum speciosum* from Chile, known as the flame creeper for its scarlet mini-nasturtium flowers which are followed by jewel-like berries of brilliant blue, set in a red capsule. Though devilishly difficult to grow in most parts of Britain, it verges on rampancy in some Scottish gardens which provide the requisite cool moist conditions. In summer it threads its way through the evergreens, turning their jaded greens into a tapestry.

Summer flowering comes to a climax in the Arboretum with the eucryphias -

Left. One of the Arboretum's rarest and most interesting trees is *Tetracentron sinense*. This 'odd man out' has no close relatives. Among its unusual features are the red spurs from which each leaf is produced and the symmetrical way that the heart-shaped leaves are arranged - in two rows down each branch and alternately so that the leaves overlap. The bark is also worth noting - pock-marked and marbled in shades of grey. Edinburgh's specimen dates from 1905 and can be seen on the Pyrus and Hazel Lawn.

Right. The flame creeper, *Tropaeolum speciosum*.

supremely beautiful shrubs that grow wild in Chile and Australasia. The garden at Inverleith has a number of fine specimens in the Copse, Woodland Garden and the border in front of the Herbarium. Perhaps the best specimen of all is the one beside Inverleith House. This is *E.* x *nymansensis* 'Nymansay', a choice clone of the cross between two South American species, the evergreen *E. cordifolia* and the hardier deciduous *E. glutinosa* which was raised at Nymans in Sussex in about 1915. In August and September it is completely covered in the most exquisite white flowers, each 2¹/₂in across with a centre of delicate gold stamens, which reverberate with the hum of bees.

The Peat Garden and Woodland borders

There is not as much to see in the Peat Garden during summer as in spring but what there is should not be missed. One of the last primulas to flower, and one of the most striking is *Primula vialii* which bears some resemblance to a dwarf red hot poker, with tapering heads of purple flowers that are bright red at the apex due to the contrasting colour of the flower buds.

The European *Lilium pyrenaicum*, a yellow Turk's cap lily, has been grown in the Garden since the 17th century.

Of a rather quieter beauty are the various species of *Nomocharis* which open their spotted blooms on slender stems of whorled leaves in July and August. In many respects they resemble lilies but the flowers are rather more delicate in structure and colouring. *Nomocharis* thrive only in consistently cool moist conditions and are at their best in Scottish gardens. There are about 15 species all told, the most commonly grown being *N. pardanthina* from China. When well-grown it bears up to ten pink flowers which are dotted with deeper pink and delicately fringed.

As summer draws on, the last flowers of the Himalayan poppies (*Meconopsis*) open at the top of the stems and their dominance of the woodland borders gives way to that of the lilies. The peak flowering time for lilies is July and August, but begins as early as May with the lovely but pungent *L. pyrenaicum* - a yellow Turk's cap kind that has been grown in the garden since James Sutherland's time - and ends in September with the magnificent golden-rayed lily of Japan, *L. auratum*, which in a poor summer barely opens before autumnal weather sets in.

Lilies are commanding plants, often architectural in form, beautifully coloured and deliciously scented. Visitors are invariably drawn to the garden's 80 or so species and numerous hybrids. The giant Himalayan lily, *Cardiocrinum giganteum*, is undoubtedly one of the wonders of the plant world. This extraordinary species was introduced in 1852 when it flowered for the first time in cultivation in Cunningham's Comely Bank Nursery in Edinburgh. It reaches 10ft tall with 20 or more fragrant white trumpets, each about 8in long. The leaves are quite unlike those of the true lilies, being broadly heart-shaped. Another very tall species is the leopard or panther lily (*L. pardalinum*) from California, which reaches 7ft. Its orange-red Turk's cap flowers open in July and are brown-spotted, numbering up to 20 per stem. Much less obvious, is *L. nepalense*, a Himalayan species which was introduced only in 1927. It spreads by runners but is by no means easy to cultivate outdoors, thriving more reliably in a cool greenhouse. The large waxy flowers are green with maroon centres and tend to hang downward.

The majority of hardy orchids flower in summer, making a fine show *en masse* which rivals bedding plants in impact. *Dactylorhiza* orchids are some of the best for this purpose, being about the quickest to reach flowering size from seed - usually in less than five years. Most *Dactylorhiza* species are variable in colour, ranging from pale mauve-pink or even white to vibrant magenta. This applies to the robust marsh orchid (*D. elata*) which can be seen in its most colourful guise in the woodland border near Inverleith House. Of great ecological interest is the colony of common spotted orchids (*Dactylorhiza fuchsii*) in the Woodland Garden which was rescued from a coal spoil tip at Gorebridge near Edinburgh in 1984, showing that orchids are in many cases resilient plants whose rarity is frequently caused by loss of habitat.

Summertime on the Rock Garden

Colour and interest on the Rock Garden flow uninterrupted from spring into summer, with sheets of pastel dwarf phloxes contrasting with mounds of yellow potentillas and the brilliant pinks of *Penstemon newberryi* and *P. fruticosus* var. *scouleri*. Singling out a few highlights from so many is partly personal choice and partly from observation of what appeals most to visitors. Campanulas, with their predominantly soft blues and bell-shaped flowers, are always popular. The easy and rampant thrive on the Rock Garden while the rare and fragile are confined to pots in the Alpine House. Closely related to *Campanula* is the much smaller genus *Symphyandra*. *S. armena* is a particularly graceful species, with arching stems of translucent bluish-mauve bells in July and August. Pinks (*Dianthus*) are just as attractive as bellflowers but in habit are more varied and in many cases are deliciously scented. An interesting example is *D. erinaceus* from southwest Asia, whose large cushions invitingly mould themselves to the shape of the underlying rock but are excruciatingly prickly to the slightest touch. In summer their sculptural curves are decorated in a random fashion with apparently stemless pink flowers.

A plant to rival *D. erinaceus* in its compact prickly habit is *Erinacea anthyllis*. This slow-growing leguminous shrublet comes from Spain and North Africa, where it grows in dry rocky places, exposed to full sun. In spring it produces a short-lived crop of soft leaves, followed in early summer by lavender-blue pea flowers. Thereafter, it brazens out the heat and drought - and no doubt hungry goats too in the wild - as a hunched mass of blue-green spines. These vegetable hedgehogs adorn the wall of the raised bed beside the Alpine House and several summits of the Rock Garden.

Royal blue is a scarce colour among flowering plants, guaranteeing admiration. The Chilean crocus (*Tecophilaea cyanocrocus*) holds centre stage in spring, as do the gentians in autumn, but in summer it is *Delphinium grandiflorum* and *D. tsatsienense* that steal the show. The latter is a short-lived Chinese species, 9-15in tall, which flowers in June and July; the former is a perennial, reaching about twice the height and flowering from July to August.

The cobra lilies (*Arisaema*) offer a glimpse of some of the more bizarre

Top. A colony of the marsh orchid (*Dactylorhiza elata*).

Bottom. *Verbascum dumulosum* forms waterfalls of yellow flowers on the Rock Garden and over the raised beds beside the Alpine House in early summer. This dwarf mullein was raised from seed collected by Peter Davis while working on the Flora of Turkey.

Left. Summertime colour around the pond and stream is provided mainly by astilbes. These moisture-loving perennials are mostly Chinese or Japanese in origin, and belong to the saxifrage family (Saxifragaceae).

Right. The intense blue of *Delphinium grandiflorum* and *D. tsatsienense* spellbinds visitors to the Rock Garden in summer.

manifestations of plant life in the Botanic Garden's living collection. Most flower in late spring and early summer. Being slightly tender and rather difficult to cultivate, the majority are given extra care in the Alpine House. Of the more robust species on the Rock Garden, the most spectacular is *A. griffithii* whose inflorescence is undeniably reptilian in appearance. From under the hooded spathe protrudes a spadix with a thread-like extension that reaches 12in or more, dangling along the ground to lure pollinators up into the vase of the spathe. The foliage of *A. griffithii*, in common with other arisaemas, is remarkably handsome, with dark mottled stalks and wavy-edged trifoliate leaves. *Arisaema* is a genus of predominantly woodland plants with about 150 species, 25 of which are grown by the Royal Botanic Garden. The frames beside the Alpine House show a number of oreganos (*Origanum* species) in the summer which need drier conditions than can be guaranteed on the Rock Garden. Outstanding is the Cretan dittany (*O. dictamnus*), which is found wild only on rocks in the mountains of this Mediterranean island. This sun-loving shrublet has rounded woolly leaves and flower heads of large purplish bracts surrounding pink sage-like flowers. All parts of the plant are highly aromatic and it has been prized since Classical times as a medicinal herb. Less rare and more accommodating is *O. rotundifolium* from Turkey, which has pale green bracts and mid-green leaves but is otherwise similar. It too needs a well-drained sunny position but generally thrives in the open if planted in an alpine trough or raised bed.

The Pond

In the course of the summer, more and more of the pond's surface becomes covered with vegetation, leaving only patches to reflect the sky. Much of the encroachment is done by the fringed water lily (*Nymphoides peltata*) which is not a water lily at all but a member of the bog bean family, Menyanthaceae - a group closely related to the gentians (Gentianaceae). This look-alike water lily has small fringed yellow flowers and the typical floating orbicular leaves.

Meanwhile, the margins of the pond and stream brim with interesting plants, such as the royal or flowering fern (*Osmunda regalis*), our most stately native fern species. Colour around the pond and stream is provided mainly by astilbes, with plume-like panicles of flowers in various shades of pink, double meadowsweet (*Filipendula ulmaria* 'Flore Pleno'), with its froth of hawthorn-scented cream flowers, and the similar but larger and pink-flowered *F. purpurea*. Here and there are monkey flowers (*Mimulus*) too, mostly yellow but scarlet in the case of *M. cardinalis*. Waterside iris stand aloof from the mêlée. They include the dainty purple-blue *I. sibirica*, the native yellow flag (*I. pseudacorus*) and the Japanese flag (*I. ensata*), an integral part of every Japanese water garden, whose flat, broad-petalled flowers range from deep purple to pure white.

The Glasshouses

The borders surrounding the main glasshouse range serve as a preamble to the tender plants within. Here in the shelter and extended warmth of the glasshouses grow a wide range of plants that would not normally survive outdoors in Edinburgh, notably African bulbous species such as the swamp lily (*Crinum* species); the pineapple lily (*Eucomis regia*); the pretty but garlicky *Tulbaghia violacea*; an elegant speckled orange wild gladiolus (*Gladiolus dalenii*) and the African lilies (*Agapanthus*). Once inside, the temperature rises and the scene becomes more exotic still. In the Temperate House, the purple satin flowers of the glory bush (*Tibouchina urvilleana*) open to 4in across. Climbing along the upper level walkway is the bat-pollinated cup-and-saucer vine (*Cobaea scandens*) from Mexico. It bears numerous large horizontal bell-shaped flowers all summer, into which (in the wild!) small bats delve for nectar and pollen, attracted by the musty floral odour which is said to resemble that of the bats themselves. Another interesting climber is the giant Burmese honeysuckle (*Lonicera hildebrandiana*) whose creamy-yellow flowers reach an impressive 6in and turn gold as they age. In spite of their striking appearance, they cannot compare in scent to our native woodbine (*L. periclymenum*).

Climbers contribute to the mystery and magic of the tropical houses too. The Peat House has its coral pink passion flower (*Passiflora racemosa*) and the Orchid and Cycad House its flamboyant *Bougainvillea* and golden trumpet vine (*Allamanda cathartica*). But it is the Temperate Aquatic House that has the greatest variety. These include *Thunbergia laurifolia*, a clock vine with pale lavender flowers, and the nightmarish pelican flower (*Aristolochia grandiflora*) whose massive convoluted flowers smell of rotting fish and are the colour of dried blood - a grotesquery designed to attract flies which are trapped inside the rear tubular section until pollination has taken place.

The luxurious growth of climbers serves the useful purpose of providing shade for the other denizens. In the Temperate Aquatic House, many of these are bromeliads (members of the pineapple family, Bromeliaceae) which are largely epiphytic in the wild - a habit demonstrated by the 'tree' upon which a number are perched. One of the most spectacular specimens in the collection is *Vriesia imperialis* which produces an inflorescence over 6ft tall with red bracts and two-ranked spikes of yellow flowers.

Top. Climbers such as the golden trumpet vine, *Allemanda cathartica*, add to the mystery and magic of the glasshouses.

Middle. Aristolochia trilobata is typical of its genus with foetid flowers, designed to attract flies.

Bottom. Vriesia imperialis, a giant relative of the pineapple.

Plants in the Orchid and Cycad House also benefit from the shade of climbers. Though summer is a relatively quiet time for orchids, when most are concentrating on growth, something can always be found in flower. Several members of the tropical American genus *Sobralia* are summer-flowering, their large but short-lived flowers produced in succession atop reed-like stems. In habit terrestrial rather than epiphytic, they are generally tall plants. *S. macrantha* grows to 8ft and bears magenta flowers up to 10in across. The palm-like cycads are interesting plants at any time of the year, being among the most primitive plants on earth. Male and female flowers are on separate plants, as indicated on each label. Summer is the best time to see the spectacular cones which in some species are a bright orange-red and 20in or more in length.

The centrepieces of the Tropical and Temperate Aquatic Houses are their pools, filled with fish and a great variety of floating and emergent aquatic plants which are at their best in summer. The temperate house has its water hyacinth (*Eichhornia crassipes*), a lovely but pernicious weed that chokes subtropical waterways with its exponential growth, and the sacred lotus (*Nelumbo nucifera*), an elegant plant with long-stalked circular leaves and tall stems of pink flowers which has since earliest times been a symbol of spiritual perfection in eastern religions. But it is the Tropical Aquatic House's Amazonian water lily (*Victoria amazonica*) which most captures the imagination. This immense plant is larger by far than any other water lily. It is also one of the fastest-growing of all plants, with each leaf expanding at a rate of a square foot in 24 hours, enabling a plant to develop a leaf area of over 200 sq.ft in five or six weeks. Though perennial, *V. amazonica* is treated as a greenhouse annual in temperate regions as there is insufficient light for it to thrive in the winter. Considering how far north Edinburgh is, the giant water lily does extremely well, though in poor summers the leaf size is reduced.

Other favourites in the Tropical Aquatic House include the American lobster claws (*Heliconia*), with their flattened, mostly red and yellow flower spikes that look more plastic than vegetable, and the Malaysian *Zingiber spectabile*, a ginger which produces leafy canes over 6ft in height and stout pale golden flower spikes, rather like waxy cones in appearance, from which protrudes a succession of black and cream flowers.

After the lushness and humidity of the tropical houses, the Cactus House in summer is a place of cool repose. In contrast to the hothouse scramble for space in which each plant seems intent on overpowering its neighbour, the cacti rise serenely from the dry stones, inching their way imperceptibly through each growing season. Summer is

Left. Cone-like inflorescences of a Malaysian ginger, *Zingiber spectabile*.

Right. The male cones of the cycad *Encephalartos hildebrandii* reach 20in in length.

nevertheless their most active time as regards growth and flowering. And for plants that tend to look rather lifeless and in some cases actually resemble stones, the flowers are remarkably fresh and colourful, causing much wonderment in visitors: primary reds and yellows in the prickly pears (*Opuntia*); magenta, cream, yellow or red in *Mammillaria*; and anything from pale peach to brick red in *Aloe*. In the giant *Cereus* they are creamy-white and open at night to be pollinated by bats or moths. Though difficult to see for this reason - and because they are produced at the tops of the 10ft columns - fallen flowers can often be found on the ground.

Both the Peat and Tropical Rock Houses are colourful in summer with various members of the African violet family (Gesneriaceae) in which the Royal Botanic Garden has research interests. Here are the wild ancestors of the many *Saintpaulia*, *Streptocarpus*, *Columnea*, *Achimenes* and *Aeschynanthus* hybrids that are so popular as houseplants. The royal red bugler, *Aeschynanthus pulcher*, was first introduced from Java in 1845 and was re-collected in 1968. The flowers are typical of the genus and characteristic of many bird-pollinated plants: tubular and bright red with a yellow throat.

Like the orchids, most Vireya rhododendrons flower earlier in the year, but one of the finest, *Rhododendron konori*, is summer-flowering. Named by the 19th-century Italian explorer Odoardo Beccari after a semi-mythical tribal leader, *R. konori* has been described as 'one of the most majestic of vireya rhododendrons with its huge white to pink, powerfully carnation-scented flowers: only a truss or two of flowers can fill a large display greenhouse with delicious perfume. This is as nothing to the thrill of smelling the same perfume drifting on the cool fresh air on an open New Guinea mountain and finding the fallen corollas often at the bottom of unclimbable trees.' The plant in the Peat House has several dozen trusses of huge pure white flowers in August - and at a level where they can be enjoyed to the full.

Left. The Amazonian water lily, *Victoria amazonica*, is the centrepiece of the Tropical Aquatic House.

Right. The Cactus House appears orderly and serene, in contrast with the lush riot of vegetation in the other glasshouses.

Autumn

As far as most plants are concerned, autumn begins in September: the evenings draw in; the mornings become silvered with dew; and even during a belated heatwave - an 'Indian summer' - the drop in night temperature ensures that growth slows down. The end of the growing season is not, however, a dull time. In most deciduous trees, the change in foliage is a daily drama, as if each successive frost induces a spasm that flushes or pales the leaves until the shocks become too great and the trees withdraw, stark and rigid, into dormancy. The glory of autumn leaves is somehow tinged with sadness as they fall and blow away or become sodden and disintegrate, but the sight of ripe fruits is sheer joy. Whether poisonous berries, hard nuts, dried seed pods or fruits which are recognisably edible, their variety of colours, shapes and textures is one of the most enjoyable features of autumn, and one which is of especial interest to children - though the child in all of us finds the appeal of conkers and acorns, newly fallen from their cases, quite irresistible.

For some plants, autumn is not an end but a beginning. Many from regions with a hot dry season take their vacation from active growth then, bursting into bloom and sprouting new leaves at the onset of cooler, wetter weather - which in cultivation here means the autumn. This pattern is common to a number of bulbous plants, such as *Nerine*, *Crinum*, *Amaryllis*, *Schizostylis* and *Colchicum*, which have become so popular that their flamboyant pinks are now as much a part of autumn colour in gardens as golden leaves and red fruits.

Opposite. The Persian ironwood, *Parrotia persica*, a wide-spreading small tree, native to northern Iran and the Caucasus overhangs the Stream. Its beech-like leaves take on a medley of colours, which vary according to climatic and environmental factors.

The southern African *Nerine bowdenii* flowers in autumn after several months of dormancy.

Autumn colour in the Arboretum

A walk through the Arboretum in autumn is a feast for the eyes, the bright colours of fruits and dying leaves standing out against the varied greens, drawing one's attention in new directions as the season progresses. The first show of autumn colour - any time from late August - is usually among the horse chestnuts or buckeyes (*Aesculus*), of which there are about 10 different kinds at Inverleith. Earliest is the sweet buckeye (*A. flava*) from the southeast United States, which turns yellow as the days shorten. There are several specimens, one of the best being to the front of the Herbarium. The horse chestnuts form their own small family, Hippocastanaceae. The sweet chestnuts (*Castanea*), on the other hand, belong to the beech family, Fagaceae. Three species can be found in various parts of the Arboretum, the best known and commonest being the sweet or Spanish chestnut (*C. sativa*). This magnificent tree has elegant serrated leaves which turn gold in the autumn, deeply ridged bark and clusters of extremely prickly green fruits that contain the familiar glossy brown chestnuts, prized for roasting, boiling or crystallising as marrons glacés. The species was apparently introduced to the British Isles by the Romans, as chestnut meal was one of the staple foods for their soldiers. Unfortunately, its southern origins make it late-flowering in this country and the chestnuts reach a decent size only in exceptionally good summers.

The walnuts (*Juglans*) and hickories (*Carya*) form another small family (Juglandaceae) whose members are both ornamental and useful, having ash-like leaves and producing fine-grained timber, edible nuts and oils. The aristocrat of the group is the common walnut (*J. regia*) which is native to southeast Europe, the Himalayas and China, but has been cultivated in Britain for many centuries. In common with other walnuts, the convoluted seeds are borne inside smooth rounded cases. There are specimens near Inverleith House and among the main collection of beeches and oaks. The North American hickories are very similar to walnuts in appearance but are generally less hardy and more graceful in habit, with better autumn colour. The hardiest is the bitternut (*Carya cordiformis*) which grows as far north as Quebec, and it is this species which thrives in Edinburgh. The large leaves have seven to nine leaflets and turn yellow in autumn. Specimens can be found in the wild garden and to the south of the West Gate.

All oaks (*Quercus*) bear acorns, but this seed-in-a-cup arrangement can vary greatly in appearance from one species to another, particularly with regard to the scales on the cups, which may be anything from closely set and mosaic-like to warted or long and curly. Exploring these variations on a theme is an interesting pursuit in autumn, and one that can be done conveniently in the main oak collection, between the Herbaceous Border and the West Gate, where about 35 species are grown side by side. In contrast to the horse chestnuts, oaks are among the last trees to change colour. Most turn golden brown - the large, deeply lobed leaves of the Hungarian oak (*Q. frainetto*) being especially fine - but the North American pin oak (*Q. palustris*), red oak (*Q. rubra*) and scarlet oak (*Q. coccinea*) are famed for their reds which in some trees - especially young ones - can be very striking. As the autumn tints develop, the evergreen oaks stand out clearly. These include the holm oak (*Q. ilex*), with its willowy leaves and pale cups, and the cork oak (*Q. suber*) which has sharp teeth, rather than lobes, round the leaf margins and thick spongy bark that in Mediterranean regions is harvested for cork products.

Some of the best trees for autumn colour are the rowans or mountain ashes and the whitebeams (*Sorbus*), which combine brightly coloured fruits with attractive leaves that turn various shades of red, yellow and gold. In a number of species, the fruits ripen in late summer before the leaves start to change colour. Others are better co-ordinated and in a few the fruits remain long after the leaves have fallen. Rapid disappearance seems to be the fate of red-berried species, such as the native *S. aucuparia*, while those with pink, white or yellow fruits are apparently less appetising to the birds - at least in this country. The fruits of the Chinese *S. hupehensis* are long-lasting, starting off deep pink and fading as they ripen. They contrast well with the large blue-green leaves that turn purplish-brown and finally red before they fall. Specimens of this handsome tree can be spotted in various parts of the Arboretum when in fruit. *Sorbus* is a member of the rose family, Rosaceae. So too are the hawthorns (*Crataegus*), crab apples (*Malus*), *Cotoneaster* and *Photinia*, all of which are renowned for their colourful fruits. These groups are concentrated in the south borders and on the large lawn to the south of the West Gate. Here also are several species of *Viburnum* which have brightly coloured berries.

Autumn colour in conifers is not something which immediately springs to mind, as the majority are evergreen. However, there is a handful of deciduous species and these rival many broad-leaved trees for interest as their needles go through the autumnal changes. Best known are the larches (*Larix*) which become a mellow gold before the needles fall. The most interesting specimen at Inverleith from a historical, if not aesthetic, point of view is the Dunkeld hybrid larch (*L.* x *eurolepis*) opposite the

The North American red oak, *Quercus rubra*, is famed for its brilliant autumn colour, which tends to be better in young specimens.

Herbaceous Border. As can be seen from its asymmetric shape, it originated as a cutting from a branch and has never developed a normal leader and radiating branches. The oddly swollen base is callus tissue that began forming as part of the healing process when the cutting was first taken. The cutting was obtained from the original hybrid Dunkeld larch at Blair Castle, the Duke of Atholl's estate at Dunkeld, in 1906 - two years after the existence of the hybrid was first discovered. The cross arose by chance, probably in about 1895, between the European larch (*L. decidua*) and the Japanese larch (*L. kaempferi*).

Other deciduous conifers are the bald or swamp cypress (*Taxodium distichum*) and the dawn redwood (*Metasequoia glyptostroboides*). As the needles change colour in the autumn, the two are easily distinguished; the dawn redwood turning a tawny salmon pink and the swamp cypress becoming a rich russett. Both can be found conveniently close together near the pond, and elsewhere in the Arboretum.

While looking at conifers, it is worth exploring the barberry (*Berberis*) collection which adjoins the main conifer area to the north of the West Gate. The Edinburgh collection is exceptionally good, with numerous species and hybrids, both evergreen and deciduous, grown for their (mostly) scented yellow flowers, vivid autumn colour (in the case of deciduous kinds) and attractive fruits, which are predominantly egg-shaped and red or black, often with a bluish bloom.

The late summer flowering of the *Eucryphia* collection continues well into the autumn. No other group of woody plants offers better continuity through this part of the horticultural calendar. In the case of *E. glutinosa*, the fading of its flowers is followed by rich colouration of its deciduous foliage.

The witch hazel family, Hamamelidaceae, has several members which colour well in the autumn. The popular winter-flowering witch hazels (*Hamamelis mollis* and the hybrid *H.* x *intermedia*) turn a pleasant if unspectacular yellow. More colourful is the Japanese *H. japonica* var. *flavopurpurascens* whose leaves become irregularly

The European barberry, *B. vulgaris*.

marbled in red, yellow and green. Several species of *Fothergilla* are also noted for their vibrant autumn colours. *F. major* from the Allegheny Mountains in the eastern United States is usually the best, turning bright yellow and red, though it should be remembered that autumn colour in this and many other deciduous trees and shrubs is variable, depending on factors such as the clone, age of the specimen, climate, soil and planting position. Fothergillas, for instance, tend to colour better in sun than shade, and like the witch hazels need acid soil. A representative group of this family can be found between the Alpine House and the Herbaceous Border.

No account of autumn colour is complete without mentioning the large and varied genus of maples (*Acer*). Many of the spectacular colours in the North American 'fall' belong to maples - largely to the sugar, silver and red maples (*A. saccharum, A. saccharinum* and *A. rubrum*, respectively). Specimens of all three can be found in the main maple collection, to the south of the West Gate. Equally colourful are the various forms of the Japanese maples, *A. japonicum* and *A. palmatum*, whose gnarled shapes and delicate foliage provide focal points in the woodland borders, especially as their colours change. The buttercup-leaved maple (*A. japonicum* 'Aconitifolium') and the vine-leaved maple (*A. japonicum* 'Vitifolium') are splendid both in leaf shape and autumn colours, and the *A. palmatum* cultivar 'Osakazuki' is one of the best reds. *A. japonicum* and *A. palmatum* had been subjected to hundreds of years of selection and hybridisation in Japan before their introduction here in the 19th century. In consequence, the wild species are rarely seen. This is not the case with other maples from China and Japan, which though popular have never been idolised to such an extent. Many of these are every bit as lovely as their highly bred relatives and are worth seeking out in autumn. Especially fine are: the Japanese red snakebark maple (*A. capillipes*) on the lawn between the azaleas and the Pond, whose foliage turns orange and yellow; the paperbark maple *A. griseum* in front of the Palm House, which turns red; and the unusual variegated snakebark maple (*A. rufinerve* 'Albolimbatum') near the East Gate whose pale leaves flush red and yellow.

The Royal Botanic Garden is famous for its display of autumn-flowering gentians.

Late colour in the Peat, Heath and Rock Gardens

Autumn is a surprisingly colourful time of the year in the southeastern corner of the Inverleith garden, where plants that enjoy special conditions - sharp drainage or moist acid conditions - are catered for in the Peat and Rock Gardens. A visit to these areas should ideally be followed by one to the Alpine House and its surrounds, where similar but rarer or more demanding species are grown under glass or in frames. The highlights of the season in all these areas are undoubtedly the gentians and colchicums. Close by, the Heath Garden goes from strength to strength, the tail end of the summer-flowering heathers hanging on into early autumn and the main autumn varieties being joined as the season progresses by the first touches of colour from those that span the winter and spring.

As befits an institution with a strong interest in plants from the Sino-Himalaya, the Royal Botanic Garden has an outstanding collection of gentians (*Gentiana*), with about 75 of the 400 species as well as various hybrids in cultivation - mostly at Inverleith. By no means are all gentians blue or autumn-flowering, but it is those that fit this description which make such an arresting display at this time of the year. Needless to say, it is the easiest - G. *sino-ornata* and G. x *macaulayi* that form great pools of blue in the Peat Garden. To the uninitiated, they appear from a distance like a mirage among the autumn leaves, drawing puzzled visitors like a magnet to find the explanation for such an improbable expanse of sapphire blue.

The deep blue G. *veitchiorum* from Sichuan remains a challenge to keep for any length of time, and propagation by seed invariably results in hybrids. This species is displayed in the Alpine House. Almost as tricky, but succeeding on the Rock Garden is G. *farreri* which was introduced by Reginald Farrer and William Purdom from northern Kansu in 1914. Edinburgh's gentians may be visible at some distance, but nowhere near the quarter of a mile from which Farrer could spot this resplendent species in the wild. His description of the flowers as of 'an indescribably fierce luminous Cambridge blue within, with a clear white throat, while, without, long vandykes of periwinkle-purple alternate with swelling panels of nankeen, outlined in violet and with a violet median line' is now almost an epitaph, for the true species is rarely seen, having joined forces with its relatives in the intimacy of cultivation to produce equally stunning - and more vigorous and floriferous - hybrids. Deserving of special mention, constituting several of the mass plantings, are: G. x *macaulayi*, a cross between G. *farreri* and G. *sino-ornata*, which grows as easily as the latter, flowers freely in September and October and tolerates partial shade; and G. 'Inverleith' (G. *farreri* x G. *veitchiorum*), which was raised in Edinburgh.

Colchicums have as many admirers as gentians but for the most part are easier to grow. Commonly known as autumn crocus or meadow saffron, *Colchicum* is neither a crocus nor does it have anything to do with saffron (which is the dried styles and stigmas of *Crocus sativus*). In fact it belongs to the lily family (Liliaceae). As in the case of the gentians, the Royal Botanic Garden has an excellent collection of this genus, its centre of distribution being Turkey and southwest Asia which have long been part of the Garden's floristic research programme. About 45 species and numerous varieties and hybrids are currently held. Not all are autumn flowering but the few that bloom at other times are nowhere near as popular or spectacular in cultivation.

Colchicums vary little in flower shape or colour. Most species have goblets of pink, mauve or light magenta, though some show a tessellated pattern and several have double and/or white forms. The great appeal of colchicums is that these sumptuous flowers open unobscured by foliage at a time when almost everything else seems to be dying back, and in generous numbers too - up to 20 per corm in *C. byzantinum*.

Gentiana x *macaulayi*, 'Kingfisher'.

The full range of autumn-flowering colchicums at Inverleith can be enjoyed by visiting the Rock Garden and Alpine House, followed by a wander around the woodland borders, where these colourful plants are a feature from late August to November.

Just as eye-catching are the African kaffir lilies (*Schizostylis*) and red-hot pokers or torch lilies (*Kniphofia*) which add their brilliant flame-coloured flowers to the more subtle shades of autumn foliage. Red-hot pokers are unmistakeable, with their dense spikes of downward-pointing tubular flowers which in many are two-toned orange and yellow, like flaming torches. Flowering time depends on the species or hybrid; some opening in June and July; others in full bloom from July to September; and a number a-blaze throughout the autumn. The three groups also vary in habit, the latest being slow-growing and the smallest, with grassy foliage and quite dainty flower spikes which seldom exceed 2½ft. One of the neatest is *K. galpinii* at little more than 1½ft, which lights up the Rock Garden with its orange torches in early autumn. *K. triangularis* is slightly larger and even later - often still flowering in December.

The structure of the Rock Garden is as dependent on shrubs and trees as on rocks. Some of these are at their most interesting in autumn - cotoneasters with red berries,

Top. Colchicums are one of the highlights of autumn. This is *Colchicum laetum*, growing at the foot of *Tsuga canadensis* 'Pendula' on the Rock Garden.

Bottom. Kniphofia galpinii is a small, slow-growing red hot poker or torch lily. It blooms to great effect on the Rock Garden in September and October.

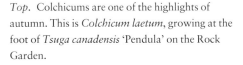

gaultherias and pernettyas with fruits in various shades of red, pink, black, white and, in the case of several gaultherias, blue. In terms of foliage, the brightest shrub on the Rock Garden is *Lyonia nezikii* from Japan, which is a fine sight in autumn with its deep red leaves and blue-black berries. The genus *Lyonia* is closely related to *Pieris*, occurring in eastern Asia and from North America into Mexico, Cuba and Jamaica. Like *Pieris*, it has white to blush-pink urn-shaped flowers and needs moist acid soil.

The area of the Rock Garden devoted to Japanese plants adjoins the Heath Garden - a rolling expanse of heathers, punctuated by tree heaths, birches and pines. It is hard to say when the heather season begins and ends, as the flowering times of the various species and varieties overlap to form a year-round mosaic of colour. Foliage also contributes to the effect, with various kinds grown not so much for their flowers as for their carpets of gold, silver-grey, deep green or bronze which in many cases burnish or redden as autumn advances. From late summer to October and November most of the cultivars in flower are derived from Scottish heather or ling (*Calluna vulgaris*), as for example is the attractive double pink 'H E Beale'. Bell heathers (*Erica cinerea*) are mainly summer-flowering but there are always some - such as the bicoloured mauve and white 'Eden Valley', and the bright purple Irish

Left. *Lyonia nezikii*, in the Japanese area of the Rock Garden.

Right. Few trees can rival the common beech, *Fagus sylvatica*, in its uniform rich russet.

cultivar 'Joseph Murphy' - that linger into October. The Cornish heath (*E. vagans*) is generally later, with about a dozen varieties flowering from August to October in cream, white and shades of pink. Quite distinctive on account of its size, both in terms of height, up to 18in, and large purple-pink or white bell-shaped flowers, is St Dabeoc's heath (*Daboecia cantabrica*) which is native to western Ireland and southwestern parts of Europe.

The Cryptogamic Garden

The Royal Botanic Garden's research interests in cryptogams or non-flowering plants, such as ferns, horsetails, mosses, liverworts, lichens and fungi, is reflected in the experimental Cryptogamic Garden which was established at the west end of the Demonstration Garden in 1990. The area was planted with Scottish native plants, interspersed with tree stumps and fallen branches. A number of cryptogams, notably woodland ferns and horsetails, have been progressively added. Theoretically, other kinds will appear in due course as appropriate conditions develop. The spores of mosses, liverworts, lichens and fungi, as well as ferns and horsetails, are readily dispersed. One fungus already present is the razor strop fungus (*Piptoporus betulinus*) which grows only on birch. Unmistakeable as a bracket fungus, it is white when young, becoming grey-brown and corky with age.

A *fruitful time in the Glasshouses*

Garden and glasshouses are worlds apart at this time of year. Outdoors, many plants are losing their leaves or dying down after undergoing profound physiological changes at the approach of freezing conditions - changes which we enjoy as inspiring autumn colours. In contrast, the overwhelming majority of glasshouse plants are evergreens from warm temperate and tropical regions where seasonal temperature changes are less extreme. True, growth slows down as daylight decreases and temperatures are lowered, but with a few exceptions - such as the Amazonian water lily (*Victoria amazonica*), which becomes completely dormant as autumn draws to a close - most look remarkably similar all year round. Yet these warm-growing plants also have their rhythms of flowering and fruiting which in many cases coincide with our growing season. Autumn is therefore as good a time as any to appreciate the exotic fruits, both strange and familiar, that can be seen in the glasshouses - a fruitful experience that can be enjoyed whatever the weather!

The yellow flowers, blood-red bracts and pale green fruits of *Musa sanguinea* are much admired in the Tropical Rock House.

The sight of a hand of bananas developing among the huge arching leaves of a
banana plant never ceases to delight visitors of all ages. There are some 30 kinds of
wild banana (*Musa*) in tropical Asia and East Africa. Virtually all cultivated bananas
are sterile hybrids that can only be propagated vegetatively by suckers, whereas wild
bananas contain hard pea-sized seeds. About 15 species of *Musa* are grown under
glass in Edinburgh. These include *M. acuminata*, a parent of the hybrid *M.* x
paradisiaca of commerce, which can be seen in the Tropical Aquatic House. This
southeast Asian species will reach 20ft, producing the typical pendent inflorescences
that last for months on end, simultaneously bearing flowers beneath large purplish
bracts, below which can be seen every stage of fruiting - from green and finger-sized
to the familiar long yellow ripe bananas.

Also in the Tropical Aquatic House is a clump of rice (*Oryza sativa*), a true aquatic
which can be seen weighed down with grains at the edge of the pond, and a towering
stand of sugar cane (*Saccharum officinarum*). Both are tropical members of the grass
family (Gramineae). Anyone with a sweet tooth will also be fascinated by the cocoa
tree (*Theobroma cacao*) in the Tropical Aquatic House. Strictly speaking, the plant
should be known as cacao, as cocoa refers only to the product obtained from the

Familiar tropical food plants such as rice, *Oryza
sativa*, are grown in the glasshouses.

seeds after fermentation, roasting, grinding and removal of fat. Chocolate is produced by the same process but retains the cocoa butter. The word 'chocolate' is derived from the Amerindian xocoatl, a foaming drink not unlike Guinness in appearance which was made from cacao seeds and various flavourings, such as honey and chilli - a recipe that gives new meaning to hot chocolate. So highly prized was the cacao that its seeds were used as currency and social status was measured by increasing consumption of xocoatl.

T. cacao is an understorey tree of tropical rainforests, reaching 18ft or more. The simple leathery leaves measure 1-2ft long and are produced in flushes which are a conspicuous pinkish-bronze at first. Clusters of up to 50 tiny scented flowers appear directly from the trunk. Most cauliflorous trees are pollinated by bats but the cacao

Left and Right. The cocoa tree, *Theobroma cacao*, produces its flowers and fruits directly from the trunk and branches - a phenomenon known as cauliflory, which is especially common in tropical species.

flowers are visited by midges. From such small beginnings develop very large furrowed fruits, each containing about 40 purple seeds in five rows. The fruits may be green, yellow or reddish when ripe, depending on the variety. Whether or not Edinburgh's cacao has adapted to pollination by Scottish rather than Amazonian midges, fruits are set regularly and can be seen at most times of the year.

Most of the passionflowers (*Passiflora*) have edible fruits, though all are full of hard seeds and some are more palatable than others. One of the best is the granadilla (*P. quadrangularis*) which bears extraordinarily beautiful flowers, with a halo of long wavy filaments in blue, purple and cream, followed (if pollinated) by golden yellow fruits up to 8in long. There are examples in the Tropical Rock House and in the Orchid and Cycad House. A number of cacti also have edible fruits. Indeed, for such deadly-looking plants they are remarkably benign and in many the green flesh is edible too. Best known are the prickly pears or Indian figs (*Opuntia*). *O. vulgaris*, which grows wild from Georgia through

Central America to Peru, and several other species can be seen in the Cactus House. In the adjoining Temperate Aquatic House is the Barbados gooseberry or lemon vine (*Pereskia aculeata*), a climbing cactus which can reach 30ft. It has deciduous leaves and fearsome spines, and in autumn produces fragrant pink to cream flowers which may give rise to smooth yellow fruits. Perhaps more tempting is the pineapple (*Ananas comosus*) growing in the border beside the pool. Most bromeliads are epiphytes, perching high up in trees, but this species is terrestrial and is grown in fields commercially. We take the fruit for granted but it is quite peculiar in structure, consisting largely of a swollen fleshy stem which is crowned by a tuft of leaves. When flowering, the inflorescence atop its stout 2ft stalk is scarcely bigger than a fir cone and at a glance looks rather similar. Each inflorescence produces some 150 blue

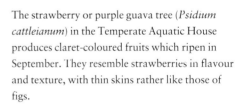

The strawberry or purple guava tree (*Psidium cattleianum*) in the Temperate Aquatic House produces claret-coloured fruits which ripen in September. They resemble strawberries in flavour and texture, with thin skins rather like those of figs.

flowers, after which the cone-like 'apple' starts to swell, ripening after about six months. Also in the Temperate Aquatic House is a large pawpaw or papaya tree (*Carica papaya*) whose mango-like fruits contain the enzyme papain which is used both to tenderise meat and in medications to improve protein digestion.

As its name suggests, the tree tomato (*Cyphomandra betacea*) is a small tree or large shrub which bears tomato-like fruits. Indeed, *Cyphomandra* is related to the tomato (*Lycopersicum esculentum*), belonging to the same family - the nightshades (Solanaceae). It is evergreen and reaches about 15ft with widely spaced branches of bright green heart-shaped foliage and attractive orange-red fruits which ripen from late summer onwards. The specimen in the Temperate House is the subject of much curiosity, often of a practical nature, that leaves the plant with fewer fruits as the season progresses - evidence, perhaps, of the plant's success in attracting mammals to disperse its seeds and of our hunter-gatherer instincts which are stirred by autumn's bounty.

WINTER

When the flaming colours of autumn have died away, the garden is left at its quietest and most sombre to face the cold and grey of a northern winter. Though stripped to its bare essentials, the garden is never without interest. Indeed, it takes on a new and different character in winter as views open beyond the leafless trees. The dormant season's delights - such as interesting bark, late berries, frail winter blossom or the new shoots of bulbs - may be few and far between but are nonetheless rewarding, challenging our powers of observation and sharpening the senses in an apparently monotonous world of browns and greens. And in the worst weather, when even the most stoical give up on the great outdoors, there are always the glasshouses where our love of colour - and warmth - can always be indulged.

The inconspicuous flowers of the Christmas box, *Sarcococca confusa.*

Opposite. Flowers of the witch hazel, *Hamamelis mollis,* decorate the bare branches in the New Year.

Winter in the Arboretum

Winter in temperate regions is a time for trees, their contribution to the landscape being most appreciated when herbaceous plants lie low. Evergreens have even more impact when the possession of foliage is a solo act, and deciduous trees, devoid of foliage, reveal the underlying structure of trunk and branches that gives each species and individual specimen its character. Taking time to look at the trees in the garden should therefore be on every visitor's agenda during winter. Whether the trees are storm-tossed or dripping wet, rimed with frost or laden with snow, it can be as visually stimulating as any other time of year.

Winter-flowering trees and shrubs are always a cheering sight and for this reason have been planted near the West Gate to welcome visitors at this inhospitable time of the year. They range from the fragrant primrose-yellow *Mahonia* x *media* 'Lionel Fortescue' which blooms from late autumn onwards, to the compact evergreen Christmas box (*Sarcococca confusa*) whose pale spiky flowers fill the air with a sweet perfume. The other main area for such delights adjoins the Alpine House, where there is a bank of winter-flowering viburnums and a lawn surrounded by witch hazels (*Hamamelis*). Coming across *Viburnum farreri* in full bloom is a fine sight throughout the winter, especially next to the later-flowering *V. grandiflorum* and their hybrid, *V.* x *bodnantense*. These viburnums produce their pink to white scented flowers on bare branches, making even more of an impact than the evergreen European *V. tinus*, which also flowers over a long period in winter. Quite different in appearance but naked-flowering too are the Chinese and Japanese witch hazels (*H. mollis* and *H. japonica*), and their offspring *H.* x *intermedia*. They all flower from about December to March, the species generally having spidery scented yellow flowers, while the hybrids are in shades of yellow, pale copper and bronze-red. These are joined in January and February by the North American Ozark witch hazel (*H. vernalis*) which has dense

Top. A fine example of the paperbark maple, *Acer griseum.*

Middle. The chalk-white bark of the Himalayan birch, *Betula jacquemontii,* stands out in winter.

Bottom. Interesting bark is a feature of many rhododendrons, such as *Rhododendron hodgsonii.* There is an outstanding specimen of this species in the border to the east of Inverleith House.

masses of yellow to orange or red flowers with a pungent fragrance.

One feature of trees that generally goes unnoticed in the growing season is the bark. For many species it is as much a fingerprint in identification as leaf shape and floral structure; a sweet chestnut (*Castanea sativa*) can be spotted from some distance in winter by the spiral pattern of deep ridges on its trunk, and the smooth grey boles of the beeches (*Fagus sylvatica*) are unmistakeable. Trees with interesting bark can be found throughout the Arboretum, but some of the most outstanding have been planted close to the East Gate. Here can be seen a snakebark maple, *Acer rufinerve,* a species from Japan whose green bark is marked with white striations; the Chinese *Betula albo-sinensis* which has pinkish bark overlaid with a grey bloom; and, also from China, *Prunus serrula,* a small cherry with rich mahogany-coloured bark. With the texture and gleam of satin, it is a cheering sight on a dull day and quite magnificent in the sun.

A walk through the Arboretum in winter will pass other splendid examples of snakebark maples, such as *A. capillipes* from Japan and the Chinese *A. grosseri,* as well as specimens of the paperbark maple (*A. griseum*) - the finest example of the latter being to the front of the Palm House. The main birch collection is on the lawn between the Hill and the south border, where an exceptionally fine specimen of *B. jacquemontii,* recently assigned the cultivar name 'Inverleith', makes one of the finest sights in the entire garden during winter. The native silver birch (*B. pendula*) has rather rugged grey bark by comparison with the smooth white bark of its Himalayan relative, but is nonetheless an attractive and characterful tree.

In winter evergreens come into their own, not just as foliage plants but as shelter for other specimens and for the wildlife - squirrels, birds and hibernating insects - that also inhabits the garden. Hollies (*Ilex*) are a particularly good example, being planted *en masse* as a windbreak for the rhododendrons and other shrubs in the Copse, while at the same time providing a great deal of interest throughout the winter. *Ilex* is a large widespread genus of around 400 species, not all of which are hardy. Neither are they all evergreen, prickly or red-berried, although the common holly, *I. aquifolium* is best-known on account of these features which are an indispensable part of Christmas decorations. All holly plants are either male or female, which explains why some never bear berries.

The holly collection contains about a dozen species, together with various hybrids and cultivars of the common holly. Most of the hybrids are forms of *I.* x *altaclarensis,* a vigorous, large-leaved holly with *I. aquifolium* in its parentage. These include 'Camelliifolia' with purplish twigs and new shoots, almost spineless slender leaves and large berries, and 'Camelliifolia Variegata' whose leaves are variously margined, piebald or entirely yellow. On a short walk round the collection, a wealth of variation in foliage can be seen, from the hideously spiny 'Monstrosa' to the virtually spineless 'Wateriana' (both males). Especially curious is the silver hedgehog holly ('Ferox Argentea' - also male) which has white-margined leaves with spines on their upper surfaces as well as round the edges. But perhaps best of all is the moonlight holly ('Flavescens' - female), whose gold-washed foliage brightens up the dreariest day.

Just as important as holly for Christmas decorations is mistletoe (*Viscum album*), an evergreen parasitic shrub which grows incognito beneath the host tree's foliage for most of the year, but is very obvious when the tree is bare. *Viscum album* belongs to a mainly tropical family of parasites, the Loranthaceae. Rare in Scotland, it can occur on almost any deciduous tree and, very occasionally, on conifers but is commonest on apple, ash and hawthorn. In the garden at Inverleith, a naturally disseminated plant can be seen on the sweet buckeye (*Aesculus flava*) to the south of the Herbarium. Mistletoe is famed for its association with the druids, who

ceremoniously cut it from oak trees with a golden knife for use in divination.
Another evergreen which was sacred to the druids is the yew (*Taxus baccata*). They
built their places of worship near yew trees - a tradition carried on in Christian times,
so that few churchyards today lack this conifer. Yews are immensely long-lived, the
oldest specimens in Europe being well over 1000 years old. James Sutherland's yew
was 300 years old when it succumbed to the hurricane of January 1968, having
survived the move from the original Physic Garden to Leith Walk and from there to
Inverleith. And it was just a youngster! There are about half a dozen species of yew in
the northern hemisphere, all of which are very variable. *T. baccata* alone has some 45
named cultivars, varying in habit, foliage and berry colour. Best-known is
'Fastigiata', the upright Irish yew of churchyards which originated in two plants
found in County Fermanagh in 1780. This and many others can be seen throughout
the Arboretum, with a suitably compact form ('Procumbens') being planted on
the Rock Garden. The only other species to be seen at Inverleith is the Japanese yew
(*T. cuspidata*).

Yews are generally classed as conifers, though they belong to the order Taxales, a
closely related and much smaller group which bears single seeds enclosed in a fleshy
aril, rather than seeds within cones. Close relatives of the yews can be seen in the
conifer area near the West Gate. These include the Chinese plum yew (*Cephalotaxus
fortunei*), a large broad shrub with outsize yew-like foliage and greenish-brown
fruits - which resemble olives more than plums - and its Japanese counterpart, *C.
harringtonia*. Most interesting of all is Prince Albert's yew (*Saxegothea conspicua*), a
monotypic genus found in southern Chile and nearby areas of Argentina. Though
close to the yews, it also shows clear affinities to the conifers, with globular scaly
cones which become fleshy when ripe and whorls of irregularly shaped leaves at the
ends of the shoots.

Yews and conifers of all persuasions play a dominant role in the landscaping of the
garden, providing focal points and shelter upon which other plants - including other
conifers - depend. Given the fact that the Edinburgh garden is anathema to many
conifers, with its dryish climate, thin poor soil and urban setting, the backbone of
these plantings is provided by species which thrive under duress. They include the
yews, junipers (*Juniperus*) which grow on almost any kind of site and are especially
well-represented on the Rock Garden, and various pines (*Pinus*) such as the shore
pine (*P. contorta* subsp. *contorta*), a colonising species that copes with high winds
and poor soil. Yet alongside these tolerant species grows a great variety of specimen
conifers, many of which have reached impressive proportions.

The Royal Botanic Garden's main collection of conifers is at Benmore, with many
fine and interesting examples too at Dawyck, and selected, more tender species at
Logan. Nevertheless, Inverleith has plenty to interest even the most discerning
visitor. A number of 'champion trees' - the tallest or stoutest of their kind in the
country - can be found here. These include a specimen of *Pinus coulteri*, a species
from California and Mexico which is renowned for the heaviest cones of any pine,
weighing up to 5lb. It has reached over 80ft in Edinburgh, though it is rarely more
than half this height in the wild. Also noteworthy are specimens of the Chinese red
pine (*P. tabuliformis*), grown from Ernest Wilson's original seed, and of *Picea
balfouriana*, named after Sir Isaac Bayley Balfour, which both now exceed 60ft.

The grove of Sierra redwoods (*Sequoiadendron giganteum*) in the Woodland
Garden has been found by many visitors to be an especially relaxing place to sit, or,
with one's back against one of the fibrous red-brown trunks, one of the best places to
shelter from a sudden downpour. Though it cannot compare in stature or grandeur
with the avenue of redwoods at Benmore, the grove has the same cathedral quality.
The trees themselves were planted in the early 1920s and in autumn 1990 the grove

Top. The Chinese holly, *Ilex pernyi*, has smaller,
flatter leaves than the common holly and fewer
spines. The leaves are arranged in neat rows down
either side of each branch, giving it a rather
dignified appearance.

Bottom. Many of the most popular hollies are
forms of the hybrid *Ilex* x *altaclarensis*.
'Camelliifolia Variegata' is one of the most
colourful - and least prickly.

There are about 45 cultivars of the common yew, *Taxus baccata*. The Westfelton yew, *T. baccata* 'Dovastoniana' forms a broad, spreading tree with tiers of long, drooping branchlets. It originated in a specimen found at Westfelton in Shropshire in 1777. Edinburgh's venerable specimen can be seen near the Pond.

was dedicated to John Muir (1836-1914), the pioneering American conservationist and founder of the national parks system, who was born in Dunbar, near Edinburgh. Inverleith's conifers include many other interesting species, such as the foxtail pine (*Pinus balfouriana*) which is found wild only in the Klamath Mountains of northern California. It has a distinctive higgledy-piggledy habit, the upswept branches bearing short needles that last for 10 to 20 years - far exceeding the usual three- to four-year lifespan of conifer foliage. The bristlecone pine (*Pinus longaeva*) is renowned as the Earth's longest-living organism, specimens of which have existed for over 4000 years in the arid mountains of the southwestern United States. Located on the Rock Garden, this is one of the rarest conifers at Inverleith.

Interesting conifers from Asia are in evidence too. The Likiang spruce (*Picea likiangensis*), an outstandingly handsome species, covers whole hillsides in Yunnan, southwest Sichuan and dry areas of southeast Tibet. It has blue foliage and produces bright red young female cones at an early age. The Royal Botanic Garden's trees were grown from seed collected by George Forrest. Another attractive species is the morinda spruce (*P. smithiana*) from the western Himalayas. The drooping habit, long needles and large light brown cones give it a majestic appearance.

The Fossil Garden

While on the subject of intriguing trees, mention must be made of the Fossil Garden, situated in the courtyard between the Palm, Orchid and Cycad, and Fern Houses, which was established in 1991. The Royal Botanic Garden has in its possession two of five fossilised Pitys trees which were uncovered in the Craigleith Quarry, Edinburgh, between 1835 and 1865. At 35ft long, one is Scotland's largest fossil, and at 320 million years old, they are certainly the oldest specimens in the Garden! The purpose of the Fossil Garden, supported by the adjacent living fern and cycad collections, is to demonstrate the evolution of Scotland's vegetation in the context of its geological history. Plantings around the fossil trees are of species which belong to ancient groups of extant plants. These include ferns, horsetails and clubmosses, as well as living relatives of plants known from fossil records. The finest examples of such living fossils are the dawn redwoods (*Metasequoia glyptostroboides*), which together with monkey puzzle trees (*Araucaria araucana*) are planted in the corners of the site. Also present are chusan palms (*Trachycarpus fortunei*), a remarkably hardy

Left. The grove of Sierra redwoods, *Sequoiadendron giganteum,* was recently dedicated to John Muir.

Below. The Fossil Garden was established in 1991. The centrepiece is one of Scotland's largest fossils, a 35ft Pitys tree, surrounded by examples of 'living fossils', such as the monkey puzzle, *Araucaria araucana.*

species found at 8000ft (2400m) in China, the ancestors of which once grew wild in Scotland.

The Alpine House and Rock Garden in winter

Most true alpines are out of season in winter, having sensibly assumed complete dormancy when in the wild they would be buried under snow. Nothing much peeps above the surface in the Rock Garden until late winter when the snowdrops (*Galanthus*) and *Iris reticulata* appear. Depending on the weather, the Algerian iris (*I. unguicularis*) makes a show on the Rock Garden and beside the Alpine House at any time from November to February. Its scented flowers are generally lilac in colour with a feathering of yellow on the falls, though there are variants with white (var. *alba*), deep violet ('Mary Barnard') and pale lavender ('Walter Butt') flowers.

As for the Alpine House, the first signs of life come in January when plants from more genial climates - such as lower altitudes or Mediterranean regions - sense that the days are lengthening and it is time to flower. The early birds include the rare *Crocus baytopiorum*, a Turkish species with pale lilac flowers, and *Pleione humilis* from Nepal, which produces its exotic 2½in mauve orchids when still leafless. Earliest of the hoop-petticoat daffodils is *Narcissus romieuxii* from the Atlas Mountains in Morocco. The citrus-scented flowers are produced for weeks on end in the New Year.

Cyclamen of one kind or another are in flower throughout the autumn and winter. Grown in pans, *C. graecum* is kept dry and exposed to full sun during the summer in order to ripen the corms. New growth is under way by September, rapidly followed by pale to deep pink flowers which continue into the winter. *C. cyprium* also flowers from autumn to winter. But the mainstay is *C. coum* in its almost infinite variety of leaf markings and flower colour. As might be expected, the reason for this variability is its very wide distribution, from eastern Europe to the Caucasus and through central and northern Turkey into Iran, Syria and the Lebanon. The various forms are, however, consistent in having squat little flowers with a dark pink spot at the mouth, which are produced throughout the winter. Though perfectly hardy, as are a number of plants displayed in the Alpine House, this diminutive species can be better enjoyed by visitors when grown in pans here, rather than on the Rock Garden.

The bulbous irises make a valuable contribution to the Alpine House display in winter. First to flower is *Iris histrioides* 'Major', followed by *I. danfordiae*, with its

Above. The exquisite blooms of the Algerian iris, *Iris unguicularis*, grace the Rock Garden and beds near the Alpine House in the dullest months of the year.

Right. Conspicuous in winter in the Heath garden is a young golden Scots pine (*Pinus sylvestris* 'Aurea') which stands in startling contrast above the pink heaths.

delightful lemon-yellow, green-spotted flowers which smell of honey. This species is found wild in the mountains of Turkey at up to 9000ft (3000m). The ever-popular *I. reticulata* follows on in February, flowering in almost every shade of blue and purple. Closely related to *I. reticulata* and with clear sky-blue flowers is the little-known *I. hyrcani*, a native of northern Iran and areas to the west of the Caspian Sea.

Winter in the garden is unthinkable without snowdrops. *Galanthus* is a genus of some 15 species which are centred upon the eastern Mediterranean, where the Royal Botanic Garden has long had research interests. That all the species are very similar is no fault in the eyes of snowdrop lovers, but part of their fascination. The Garden's collection of snowdrops is especially strong, with about a dozen species and numerous forms and cultivars. The majority are grown on the Rock Garden and elsewhere in borders, but pans of the autumn- to winter-flowering *G. reginae-olgae* can be seen in the Alpine House after being treated to a dry sunny summer. Cultivars of the common European snowdrop, *G. nivalis*, include the unusual donkey's ear snowdrop, 'Scharlockii', which has long spathes projecting like ears above the flowers, and 'Virescens', an entirely green snowdrop. These can be spotted by the keen-eyed on the Rock Garden in February.

The Winter Garden

Just as the Mediterranean or Silver Garden is designed for maximum enjoyment in summer, with its aromatic and grey-leaved plants, so the adjoining Winter Garden has been planted with all kinds of shrubs, bulbs and herbaceous perennials that are of interest in winter. The path through the Winter Garden is flanked by shrubs such as *Mahonia bealei* and *Lonicera standishii*. The former is a great stand-by in winter, its tiers of prickly evergreen leaves surmounted by erect racemes of fragrant yellow bells; the latter a shrubby honeysuckle with sweetly scented tiny cream flowers in mid-winter.

Beside the path are bold plantings of a wide range of plants that give colour between Christmas and March. They include bright yellow winter aconites (*Eranthis hyemalis*); lime-green *Hacquetia epipactis* an unusual little umbellifer from eastern Europe; lilac-blue anemones (*Hepatica transsilvanica*); pink *Cardamine pentaphyllos*; and a range of hellebores. Fine foliage is a feature too, with broad slabs of *Bergenia* and mosaics of patterned *Cyclamen* and *Arum italicum* 'Pictum'.

Above. The fresh colours of *Hacquetia epipactis* signal that spring is on its way. Its floral display consists of dense umbels of minute yellow flowers, surrounded by lime green bracts.

Left. The Winter Garden is planted with a variety of shrubs, bulbs and herbaceous perennials which are of interest in winter and early spring.

The Great Escape: winter in the Glasshouses

In the most inclement winter weather, or even as a respite from cold on a fine day, visitors can continue their botanical explorations by heading for the glasshouses. Stepping inside the warmth, humidity, lush greenery and scent of earth and flowers, has more impact in winter than at any other time of the year, awakening the senses and giving rise to exclamations of relief and excitement.

The Cactus and Succulent House is the coolest of the sections, but even here the difference between outdoors and under glass is marked. It is a dry and stony world, but one that shares the temperate winter's leaflessness. That plants from harsh northern regions and from hot deserts have devised the same strategy might seem

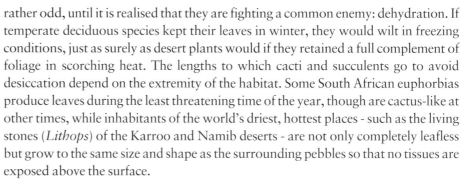

Left. Plants in the Cactus and Succulent House withstand surprisingly low temperatures in winter, provided they are kept dry.

Right. Lush greenery and the sound of running water can be enjoyed in the Fern House when the outside world is leafless and frozen.

rather odd, until it is realised that they are fighting a common enemy: dehydration. If temperate deciduous species kept their leaves in winter, they would wilt in freezing conditions, just as surely as desert plants would if they retained a full complement of foliage in scorching heat. The lengths to which cacti and succulents go to avoid desiccation depend on the extremity of the habitat. Some South African euphorbias produce leaves during the least threatening time of the year, though are cactus-like at other times, while inhabitants of the world's driest, hottest places - such as the living stones (*Lithops*) of the Karroo and Namib deserts - are not only completely leafless but grow to the same size and shape as the surrounding pebbles so that no tissues are exposed above the surface.

At the other extreme - and at the opposite end of the main glasshouse range - is the Fern House, where plants which enjoy constant moisture are displayed. The setting is a grove of tree ferns, beneath which - and on the trunks of which - grow mosses, liverworts and other ferns. Through the centre of the house runs a stream which both benefits the plants and provides an added dimension of interest, engaging both the ears and the eyes in this evocation of a natural landscape. The trunks of tree ferns are composed of densely matted roots rather than bark-covered wood. Most of the 300 species of tree ferns are denizens of the upper slopes of tropical mountains but some occur in temperate regions of Australia, New Zealand and South Africa. Among the hardier species is *Dicksonia antarctica* which thrives and produces sporelings outdoors at Logan Botanic Garden.

The Fern House is not restricted to ferns and fern-like plants. It also contains some of the Royal Botanic Garden's collection of conifers which are a doubtful proposition outdoors. These include the Malaysian celery pine (*Phyllocladus hypophyllus*) which grows at up to 13,000ft (4000m) in the mountains of the Philippines, Indonesia and New Guinea, and the rare *Acmopyle pancheri*, a primitive conifer from New Caledonia which was collected during research into the endangered conifers of this Pacific island.

The Orchid and Cycad House has both foliage and flowering plants that are of interest in winter. The centrepiece of the house is a splendid specimen of the common screw pine (*Pandanus utilis*), complete with prop roots, Spanish moss (*Tillandsia usneoides*) and epiphytic orchids. Nearby is *Euphorbia punicea*, a shrub from the West Indies which bears complex but insignificant flowers surrounded by bright red petal-like bracts. *Euphorbia* is a genus of about 2000 species within the 8000-strong

Euphorbia punicea (*Left*) and *Pandanus utilus* (*Right*) both attract attention in the Orchid and Cycad House.

spurge family (Euphorbiaceae). One of the most diverse families of plants, it includes a number of hardy perennials grown outdoors in the Botanic Garden, together with cactus-like African species (which can be seen in the Cactus and Succulent House) and Christmas poinsettias (*Euphorbia pulcherrima*), as well as such well-known species as the rubber tree (*Hevea brasiliensis*), cassava (*Manihot esculenta*) and the ornamental foliage plant, *Codiaeum variegatum*, all of which are grown in the Tropical Aquatic House.

As most tropical orchids bloom when dormant or just as new growth begins, there is a constant succession of flowers through the winter. Of special interest is the star-of-Bethlehem or comet orchid (*Angraecum sesquipedale*) whose waxy ivory flowers, which measure 5-7in across, often open around Christmas. Growing at ground level are the slipper orchids: *Paphiopedilum* from tropical Asia and *Phragmipedium* from the American tropics. Their bizarre flowers with conspicuous pouches and patterns of spots and stripes, mostly in greens and maroons, are quite distinctive among orchids. Scent, if present, tends to be unpleasant, as these terrestrial orchids are pollinated by flies or beetles - the pouches serving to trap the insects until the task of pollination is performed.

The Tropical Palm House is linked to the Orchid and Cycad House by a covered path. Its dark and steamy interior, centred around the 200-year-old West Indian fan palm (*Sabal bermudana*), is kept at a minimum night temperature of 65°F (18°C), giving a good approximation of conditions in a tropical rain forest. Here can be found such plants as a southeast Asian rattan or climbing palm (*Calamus*) and the wine palm (*Caryota urens*) which dies after its one and only, but spectacular, flowering, while at ground level may be seen the intensely fragrant, narrow-petalled *Crinum amabile* from Sumatra.

Among the palms in the adjoining Temperate Palm House are some familiar species, more commonly seen as pot plants: the curly palm (*Howea belmoreana*) and the kentia palm (*H. fosteriana*), the only two species of a genus confined to Lord Howe Island in the South Pacific; and the cabbage palm (*Livistona australis*) from eastern Australia, a species with fan-shaped leaves. This House also has its share of southern hemisphere conifers, including both species of papuacedar (*Papuacedrus papuana* and *P. arfakensis*), which are found only in New Guinea, and a large Australian kauri pine (*Agathis brownii*) from the rain forests of Queensland. Currently the tallest plant under glass at the Royal Botanic Garden is *Cinnamomum camphora*, which has reached 52½ft - a good size, even for wild Chinese and Japanese specimens. An aromatic evergreen, it is prized as the source of camphor, an oil extracted from the wood of mature trees.

Meanwhile in the Peat House, the Vireya rhododendrons are beginning to flower. The Royal Botanic Garden's collection of these tender rhododendrons from southwest Asia is of international importance, containing about 100 wild-collected species, many of which are new to cultivation. As one might expect in the tropics, a number of the red- and orange-flowered species are pollinated by birds, while the highly scented white ones attract moths. There is also a wide range of foliage, which

Left. The exotic flowers of *Crinum amabile* gleam in the undergrowth of the Tropical Palm House.

Right. A bird's-eye view of vegetation in the Temperate Palm House.

when developing is coated in a protective layer of scales that give the young leaves a strikingly different coloration. In *R. rugosum*, a bird-pollinated species with pink flowers, the new leaves are clad in bright ginger scurf which is an attractive feature in itself. Many Vireya rhododendrons grow as epiphytes in moist forests, perched high up in trees. Though requiring cool conservatory conditions in Britain, they are becoming popular garden plants in warmer parts of the world.

No matter how hard the winter, Edinburgh's Vireyas bloom as if it were spring. They are all extravagantly beautiful, none more so than *R. polyanthemum* from northern Sarawak, whose sumptuous orange-red flowers have the added bonus of perfume. This species was collected by the Royal Botanic Garden in 1978 and flowered for the first time in cultivation four years later. Though not as showy, the white-flowered species are very attractive, with their clusters of long-tubed scented flowers. They include *R. loranthiflorum* from Polynesia and *R. suaveolens* which occurs on Mount Kinabalu, Sabah. The various habits of Vireya rhododendrons can be seen from the representative selection grown in the Peat House, from large, often sprawling shrubs to miniatures. Some are surprisingly unlike rhododendrons in appearance, with foliage so narrow that they resemble heaths or conifers when not in flower. In more ways than one, the Vireyas are an eye-opener which most visitors acknowledge as a highlight, not just in winter, but throughout the year at the Royal Botanic Garden.

Left. Rhododendron polyanthemum, one of the remarkable range of Vireya rhododendrons grown at Edinburgh.

Top right. Rhododendron loranthiflorum has long-tubed, scented white flowers which attract moths.

Bottom right. Rhododendron macgregoriae blooms on and off throughout the year, a feature valued in breeding Vireya rhododendrons for the horticultural trade.

enmore - as the Younger Botanic Garden is usually known - lies on the Cowal peninsula in Argyllshire, between Holy Loch and Loch Eck. It occupies part of the valley of the River Eachaig and its tributary the River Massan, together with the lower slopes of the Cruach which rises between them - some 120 acres (48.5 ha) in all. The highest point of the garden is the Wright Smith Memorial Shelter at the View Point on Benmore Hill, a shoulder of the Cruach, 450ft (137m) above sea level, from which there are panoramic views of the surrounding mountains and Holy Loch. The situation thus combines many different aspects: a valley on boulder clay; riverside; steep hillsides of schistite rocks and thin acidic soils; and a mild oceanic climate. In addition, it is blessed with abundant rain, the yearly total ranging from 80-120in (2000-3000mm), much of which falls between September and December. All this adds up to near perfect growing conditions for those trees and shrubs which enjoy moist lime-free soil and high humidity. Benmore is therefore the garden *par excellence* for rhododendrons and conifers, especially those which come from oceanic regions, such as the Pacific coast of North America, or high rainfall areas, such as the Himalayan foothills.

Opposite. The Younger Botanic Garden Benmore, lies between Holy Loch and Loch Eck in Argyllshire, in a dramatic landscape of river valleys and mountains.

Benmore's moist lime-free soil makes it ideal for rhododendrons and conifers.

HISTORY

The Founding of The Younger Botanic Garden

The Younger Botanic Garden was the first specialist garden acquired by the Royal Botanic Garden Edinburgh. It was established in response to the enormous number of plants that entered cultivation at the turn of the century, largely in the wake of George Forrest's explorations of western China. Regius Keeper Isaac Bayley Balfour recognised that Inverleith was bursting at the seams and was in any case too urban and eastern a setting for rhododendrons and conifers which need high humidity and clean air. He therefore conceived the idea of a west coast garden and began discussions with the Forestry Commission for a site within the Glenbranter Reserve, which lies at the northern end of Loch Eck. He died before negotiations were finalised, leaving his successor, William Wright Smith, to complete the agreement. The arguments used in favour of establishing the new west coast garden (which at one time was to have been named the Balfour Memorial Garden) were that many of the new introductions might prove of economic value in forestry and horticulture if given suitable conditions. There was no plan for either an arboretum or a trial ground as such; it would be a forest area in which the new plants would be established and then left to their own devices, with minimal maintenance.

Planting had begun along these lines in the allotted 50 acres (20ha) of Glenbranter when in 1925 there came a dramatic change of circumstances. It happened as a result of the Forestry Commission's ongoing negotiations with Harry George Younger for the purchase of part of his estate which bordered on Glenbranter. In a moment of inspiration, Younger decided to gift a large part of his estate, from Bernice on Loch Eck to Gairletter on Loch Long, to the nation via the Forestry Commission. The area amounted to 11,000 acres (4452ha) and included 1,100 acres (445ha) of forest, Benmore House and a number of estate buildings and farms. One condition of the

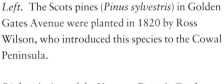

Left. The Scots pines (*Pinus sylvestris*) in Golden Gates Avenue were planted in 1820 by Ross Wilson, who introduced this species to the Cowal Peninsula.

Right. A view of the Younger Botanic Garden from across Loch Eck.

gift was that the area surrounding Benmore House - about 90 acres (30.5ha) - should be used for education and research. More importantly, Younger's interest in the fledgling garden in Glenbranter prompted him to suggest that his estate might offer a better site. In particular, the grounds of Benmore House offered distinct advantages, being already developed as a garden and readily accessible from the ferry harbours at Dunoon. There were also well-established specimen trees which would give an air of maturity to the collection, enabling it to be opened to the public almost immediately. All parties were agreeable, and in 1929 Harry Younger handed over the estate and set up a trust fund, managed by the Younger (Benmore) Trust, to help run the new venture which was duly named the Younger Botanic Garden. The arrangement was that Benmore House would serve the Forestry Commission as a training school for foresters, while the grounds were managed - though not owned - by the Royal Botanic Garden Edinburgh.

The Garden thus found itself, by a stroke of greatest good fortune, with a remarkable site which was ideal for growing rhododendrons and conifers, and well situated as a local amenity and tourist attraction. Moreover, Harry Younger's stipulation concerning research and education suited the Botanic Garden's purposes admirably. The young rhododendrons and conifers raised in Edinburgh from the collections of the great plant hunters were destined for a garden that already had an illustrious history.

Benmore's early days

Prior to 1870, the estate of Benmore was known as Inisninruisg ('vale of the fleeces'), in reference to its long history of sheep farming. For half a century it belonged to Ross Wilson who planted about 55 acres (22ha) with the first Scots pines and other conifers on the Cowal Peninsula - an area of southwestern Scotland never reached by the Caledonian Scots pine forests which came to dominate much of Scotland after the ice ages. Several of these pioneering pines, which date back to 1820, remain between Benmore House and the Golden Gates.

In 1862 the estate was purchased by an American, Piers Patrick, who built the baronial tower to Benmore House and constructed new estate buildings, including the Courtyard. More importantly, in 1863 he planted the avenue of Sierra redwoods (*Sequoiadendron giganteum*) which was to become the garden's most outstanding feature. Now nearing 165ft and still growing, Patrick's trees were mere saplings when the property changed hands again in 1870, passing into the ownership of James Duncan, a sugar refiner from Greenock. Duncan also bought Kilmun to the south and Bernice to the north, forming a single estate which extended from the Firth of Clyde to the north end of Loch Eck, and which he renamed Benmore.

James Duncan set about applying the energy and drive which had brought him success in industry to the rather different skills of farming and forestry. He obviously took a dim view of the impoverished moorlands, to which most of Scotland had been reduced when its natural forests were destroyed, and had a passion for trees, which he shrewdly regarded as a great resource. In the words of his forester, Donald Stalker:

> 'Moorlands, the most sterile and uninteresting, when planted, rapidly become a source of great beauty, attraction and wealth . . . it increases their revenues and greatly improves the soil for pasturing purposes, as well as the climate.'

The crusade began in 1871 with the division of the estate into 31 enclosures which were then systematically reafforested over the next decade. In all, 6,488,000 trees

James Duncan, a sugar refiner from Greenock, carried out major planting and building programmes during his ownership of the estate. These included an extension to Benmore House in 1874.

were planted over an area of 1622 acres (656ha). These included nearly three million larch, over two million Scots pines, in excess of a million spruce, some 126,000 ornamental conifers and 20,000 assorted hardwoods.

A riverside pinetum along the Eachaig and an arboretum on the banks of the Massan were also established. Trees remaining from this period still stand out clearly and, at between 130 and 165ft are among the most majestic in the garden. They include western hemlocks (*Tsuga heterophylla*), Douglas firs (*Pseudotsuga menziesii*), noble firs (*Abies procera*) and Sitka spruces (*Picea sitchensis*). When first planted, they were new to cultivation, having been recently discovered or introduced by David Douglas.

Among Duncan's other developments were a heated fernery in a rock face in Glen Massan, a sugar refinery near the Courtyard and an acclaimed Picture Gallery beside the House 'embowered with crotons, palms, ferns and other graceful foliage plants' which housed many notable works of art. An extension to Benmore House was constructed too, along with extensive glasshouses and a winter garden that stood on what is now the Formal Garden. All that remains of these structures is a small greenhouse against the north wall of the Formal Garden and the Fernery, now in ruins and awaiting restoration.

In 1889 the estate was purchased by Henry Younger, owner of the Edinburgh brewery. He carried on planting trees, as did his son, Harry Younger, who inherited the estate when his father died. During this period, the gardens were further developed and groves of the recently introduced Japanese larches (*Larix kaempferi*) and western red cedars (*Thuja plicata*) were planted on the ridge above Golden Gates Avenue. Though experimental at the time, these plantings endured to become an important feature of the garden. The last major scheme carried out by Harry Younger was a shrubbery to the south of Redwood Avenue, commemorating the Silver Jubilee of 1916 - an area now known as the Younger Memorial Walk.

The Golden Gates bear the initials of James Duncan. He brought them back from the Paris International Exhibition in 1878, and they have been an ornamental feature of Benmore ever since.

A new era of planting

When the Royal Botanic Garden Edinburgh took over in 1929, there was a shift of emphasis in the plantings. Whereas Patrick, Duncan and the Youngers were experimenting mainly with conifers recently collected in North America, most of the Botanic Garden's new plants were Sino-Himalayan rhododendrons. Transferring these from the nursery in Edinburgh to Benmore occupied much of the 1930s, the highlight of which was the commemorative planting near the Golden Gates for the coronation of King George VI in 1937. Regrettably, from 1939 until the early 1950s, there were such severe shortages of staff and resources that much of the garden became a wilderness, overrun by the rampant weed *Rhododendron ponticum*.

By 1953 life was returning to normal and clearing operations began in earnest, starting from the garden entrance and moving towards Benmore House. The commemorative plantings were extended to honour the coronation of Queen Elizabeth II and included the handkerchief tree (*Davidia involucrata*) near the viewpoint on Benmore Hill, which flowered for the first time in 1990.

In 1956 Richard Shaw transferred from Edinburgh to run the garden at Benmore. Under his direction, the garden re-emerged; overgrowth was cleared to reveal the surviving specimen trees and shrubs, and new rhododendrons were planted out in groups according to Balfour's preliminary classification. However, one major obstacle remained. Many of the Victorian conifers were now sizeable trees which in many areas were so densely planted that nothing could grow underneath them. Judicious thinning and clearing was necessary to create space and light for new plantings, but the Forestry Commission (who still actually owned Benmore), were reluctant to give permission. This meant that new plantings were few and of limited success during this period.

In 1968, three years after Arthur Hall succeeded Richard Shaw as Assistant Curator, Benmore was ripped apart by the hurricane that struck central Scotland with gusts of 134 miles per hour. On the night of January 15th countless trees were blown down or smashed, more than 500 of which exceeded 120ft, and the last of the Formal Garden's major glasshouses was flattened. Fortunately, Sierra redwoods are extremely stable trees and only one - the weakest - was lost from the Avenue. It took four years to clear the damage, during which time the Forestry Commission inevitably relaxed its approach to the garden's management of the woodland canopy. In retrospect therefore, the disaster literally opened up new horizons for Benmore. Inspired by the potential, Botanic Garden staff formulated a policy for planting trees, especially conifers, and set about making space for new collections.

Recent developments

The Younger Botanic Garden took another major step forward in 1974 when ownership was transferred from the Forestry Commission to the Royal Botanic Garden Edinburgh. At the same time an additional 60 acres, comprising land in Glen Massan and on Benmore Hill, was acquired by the Garden, affording even greater scope for new plantings. From the mid-1970s to the present, the story of Younger Botanic Garden has been one of clearance, drainage, the cutting of new roads and paths, and the planting of collections of rhododendrons and conifers which now rank among the most comprehensive in the world.

Though mainly concerned with the cultivation of plants to support the research, conservation and education programmes, the garden and its infrastructure are also maintained to the highest standards for the benefit of visitors. All of this is undertaken with a ground staff of 10, about one-fifth of the number employed for a much smaller area in the garden's Victorian heyday. Facilities for visitors, whose

The cutting of new roads and paths began in the 1970s and still continues as Benmore is restored and extended.

Above. The William Wright Smith Memorial Shelter stands high up on Benmore Hill, with magnificent views over Holy Loch. The original wooden structure was replaced in 1989 by a building constructed of stone taken from the demolished Golden Gates cottage.

Below. The courtyard and clock tower, which underwent restoration in the 1980s, are outstanding architectural features of the Younger Botanic Garden.

numbers exceeded more than 40,000 in 1990, include a tea room and shop. Between 1982 and 1989 the Courtyard underwent a major restoration and now provides offices, staff rooms, tractor and equipment sheds, and a sawmill. Set around a cobbled courtyard whose focal point is a fine clock tower, this restoration has received a Civic Trust award.

There are a number of attractive features in the garden which honour those who contributed much to its development. Sir William Wright Smith is commemorated in the garden by a Memorial Shelter at the viewpoint on Benmore Hill. An original wooden structure was replaced in 1989 by a stone building, designed appropriately by the grandson of Robert Lorimer who had been responsible for Puck's Hut, the Bayley Balfour Memorial. It was during the reign of Wright Smith's successor, Harold Fletcher, that the garden once again began to flourish. Fletcher is commemorated by an armillary sphere set in the heart of the Formal Garden.

Perhaps the single most dramatic change to the appearance of the garden came in 1973 when the main drive to Benmore House was re-routed. The drive originally ran through the avenue of redwoods, a scheme dating back a century when there were but a few horse-drawn vehicles rumbling along each day. However, in recent years - especially since 1965 when Benmore House became an Outdoor Education Centre for schools of the Lothian Region - the volume of traffic increased considerably both in weight and numbers. So from a busy thoroughfare Redwood Avenue was transformed by a carpet of grass into a green cathedral, where visitors find inspiration and where the trees can continue their monumental growth.

SPRING

The Younger Botanic Garden at Benmore has been called 'a living textbook of the genus *Rhododendron*'. Sheltered by the accompanying - and equally impressive - collection of conifers, it has amassed one of the world's finest collections of rhododendrons, numbering about 250 species, 100 subspecies and varieties, and over 300 cultivars. The collection is arranged botanically, groups of closely related species being planted together. This makes it easier to compare characteristics but is often of ornamental value too, as members of certain groups tend to flower at the same time, thus giving a better display. Whether scientifically minded or not, everyone enjoys seeing the different manifestations of *Rhododendron cinnabarinum* and its close allies flowering together, or a mass planting of azaleas.

The climatic conditions and soil at Benmore suit these predominantly montane plants down to the ground. Natural regeneration is in fact quite a problem at Benmore, for rhododendron seedlings come up so thickly that without periodic weeding the plants would soon be swamped by their own progeny. The real enemy, however, is the 'wild' rhododendron, *R. ponticum*. This familiar mauve-flowered species is native to the Caucasus and Armenia, whence it was introduced to Britain in 1763 and widely planted as game cover. Since then it has taken over vast tracts of countryside, gaining hybrid vigour in the process by crossing with other cultivated rhododendrons. The dangers of introducing alien species are now well known but were not appreciated in the 18th century - though the poet William Wordsworth saw it as a blot on the landscape. Even today, intrepid visitors will encounter areas in the far west of the garden which are yet to be cleared; these are still ponticum territory and virtually impenetrable.

Maintaining Benmore's magnificent collection can pose problems, especially in a terrain and climate which may be ideal for the plants (and the midges!) but can be challenging for human beings. The flowering season is, however, an annual reward for those involved and a source of great delight and interest to the thousands of visitors. Though the rhododendrons including the cursed *R. ponticum* when in flower! - are what most visitors come to see in spring, there is a wide range of other flowering trees and shrubs which provide a contrast to the rhododendrons' evergreen mounds and flamboyant blooms. Many of these are deciduous, giving a display of blossom on bare branches or opening delicate new leaves along with their flowers. There are also some fine expanses of spring-flowering bulbs.

Earliest and tallest: Rhododendron arboreum and its kin

By the time the garden officially opens its gates to visitors in March, the rhododendrons have already started flowering. Such early flowering is a gamble with the vagaries of the climate - often successful but sometimes cut short by frost that turns the flowers brown overnight. As its scientific name suggests, *Rhododendron arboreum* is a species that can reach tree-like proportions. Many of the older specimens in the garden are over 20ft tall. Introduced in 1820, it was the first Himalayan species to reach these shores. Subsequent introductions have shown that it is a widespread and very variable species, with globular heads of flowers that usually open in January and may be anything from white to deep red - the red forms (subsp. *delavayi*) from western China and Burma being the least hardy. Now more commonly seen by tourists trekking in the Himalayan foothills than in cultivation (for it abounds in the wild but is too large for most gardens), this majestic species is well-represented at the Younger Botanic Garden in the main Arborea planting to the southeast of Benmore House and elsewhere as a legacy from Victorian times.

For *Rhododendron arboreum* March is almost the end of its flowering period, which generally begins in January but in mild seasons may be as early as December.

Above and Below left. The vivid red blooms of *Rhododendron barbatum* are an almost unbelievable sight in a Scottish glen in February.

Below right. The red-flowered *Rhododendron thomsonii* has attractive peeling gold and blue-green bark.

R. arboreum was used extensively in breeding during the 19th century, one of the first hybrids being *R.* x *nobleanum*, a cross with *R. caucasicum*. Though not outstanding in terms of its flowers, which range from white to bright pink, *R.* x *nobleanum* is unusual in flowering intermittently at any time from October to March. The white form 'Album' can be seen on the Wild Bank above the Formal Garden. Other *R. arboreum* hybrids are conspicuous in early spring on account of their size, the largest of all being a red-flowered specimen on Golden Gates Avenue that reaches about 80ft, though its stature is rather obscured by the surrounding trees.

Red rhododendrons

Even at the height of spring, red-flowered rhododendrons look somewhat unreal in a Scottish glen, but in February they are an almost unbelievable sight. *R. barbatum* is a most attractive plant, forming a rounded shrub or small tree with plum-coloured flaking bark, bristly stalks and dense heads of brilliant red flowers. It grows wild in the western and central Himalayas and is slightly tender, needing sheltered woodland conditions. Best seen in rain, which further enriches its intense colours, this species does well beneath large conifers on the lower slopes of Benmore Hill. Growing nearby is *R. strigillosum* which also has red flowers and bristly leaf stalks but is recognisable by the in-rolled leaf margins and more open, flatter trusses of flowers. Restricted to Sichuan in western China, the Royal Botanic Garden's plants of this species were raised from seed brought back by E H Wilson in 1904.

Both *R. barbatum* and *R. strigillosum* have been crossed with another splendid red-flowered species, *R. thomsonii*, which can be seen in the main Thomsonia planting between the lower Benmore Hill road and fernery road, and along Golden Gates Avenue. Quite different in appearance from the red-flowered species already mentioned, *R. thomsonii* has peeling gold and sea-green bark, rounded oval leaves which are glaucous when young, and loose heads of large deep red flowers with persistent pale green or red-flushed calyces.

Stars, stripes and scents among rhododendrons

There are certain species of *Rhododendron* which are so striking that they hold the attention for longer than the merely beautiful. *R. morii*, for example, is a star performer - one of the most floriferous of all rhododendron species and quint-essential in its beauty, with buds flushed deep pink and bell-shaped flowers that open pink to white. Found wild only in Taiwan, *R. morii* belongs to subsection Maculifera which is planted beside the big-leaf rhododendrons on fernery road.

Rather more eccentric in appeal are the bicolored *R. cerasinum* and *R. floccigerum*. The latter has narrow, waxy flowers which may be either a uniform scarlet to crimson or yellowish with red stripes and rims. Two different collections of this species, made by George Forrest and Joseph Rock in the Sino-Himalayas, can be seen in March and April at the top of Benmore Hill in the area devoted to subsection Neriiflora.

With such luxuriant blooms, scent may seem superfluous to rhododendrons, but many are as perfumed as they are beautiful. The azaleas *R. luteum*, *R. occidentale*, *R. atlanticum* and *R. viscosum* - and most of their hybrids - have a sweet spicy scent to match their delightful flowers. Among the larger evergreens, the prize must go to *R. fortunei*. Its white to pale lilac-pink flowers have a delightful fruity scent and measure 3in across; they appear in May. *R. fortunei* has passed on its rich fragrance to the lily-like flowers of *R. x loderi*, one of the finest of all rhododendron hybrids, which was raised in 1901 by Sir Edmund Loder. The other parent was *R. griffithianum*, also scented and possessed of enormous white flowers. Members of subsection Fortunea, these species and their hybrid have been planted mainly on the hillside above the Formal Garden and Redwood Avenue, around the upper and lower hill paths.

Aromatic foliage is another bonus in rhododendrons, which comes as something of a surprise to the uninitiated. The smallish ovate leaves of the Sino-Himalayan *R. rubiginosum* have a lemony scent and a scaly rust-brown indumentum (hairy covering) on the undersides. The flowers are unscented but abundantly produced from March to May and are generally pink to mauve with brownish spots on the uppermost petal. Specimens of this large shrub can be found in many places in the garden, but the main area for subsection Heliolepida, to which it belongs, is along the upper hill path.

Foliage rhododendrons

Even the best rhododendrons only flower for a few weeks of the year. For the rest of the time, they provide year-round evergreen interest - with the exception of the deciduous azaleas which flare into gorgeous autumn colours before assuming winter dormancy. Indeed, many rhododendrons are worth growing for their foliage alone - a saving grace in the case of shy-flowerers, and a great bonus for those that are also regularly well-endowed with blooms.

If small is beautiful, then we should start with two very different rhododendrons which have shape and texture, if not size, to recommend them. *R. orbiculare* immediately appeals, possessing silky matt leaves which are very nearly round, with heart-shaped bases and glaucous undersides. One of E H Wilson's introductions from Sichuan, it may be seen above the Formal Garden in the northernmost corner of Benmore Hill. Conspicuously hairy leaves - at least when young - are a feature of the Himalayan *R. wallichii* which is closely related to *R. campanulatum*, differing only in terms of indumentum. Specimens in the Eachaig Arboretum and in the new subsection Campanulata planting at the far end of fernery road are a splendid sight in spring when flush with new growths.

Above. Rhododendron floccigerum is a variable Sino-Himalayan species. Its waxy flowers may be a uniform scarlet to crimson, or interestingly bicoloured.

Below. The sweetly scented *Rhododendron occidentale* from western North America is the parent of many hybrid azaleas.

Subsection Taliensia includes some of the aristocrats among foliage rhododendrons and should be visited in late spring when the new growths are well-
developed. Best of all is *R. bureavii*, another of E H Wilson's introductions from
Yunnan. One can give or take the flowers, which are white to pale pink with a
sprinkling of crimson spots, but the leaves and stems, with their rich brown woolly
indumentum, are quite irresistible. *R. roxieanum* has woolly foliage too, but its main
attraction lies in the leaf shape, which is exceptionally narrow. It has very fine
flowers too in April and May - blush-white, dotted with dark red inside - which are
held in tightly rounded trusses. The Garden's specimens of both these
Sino-Himalayan species derive from collections made by George Forrest and later by
Joseph Rock.

Left. The new leaves of *Rhododendron wallichii*
are conspicuously hairy, providing interest after
the bell-shaped lilac flowers have faded.

Right. Rhododendron bureavii is at its best in
spring, the fur coats of the upstanding new leaves
turning into a golden halo when backlit by the
sun.

Moving on to grander things brings us to the big-leaf rhododendrons. These majestic
plants are concentrated in three main areas of the garden: in the Eachaig Arboretum;
between Golden Gates Avenue and fernery road; and on the slopes of Benmore Hill
above the House. Greatest of them all is *R. sinogrande*, discovered and introduced by
George Forrest in 1913 and subsequently described by Isaac Bayley Balfour and
William Wright Smith. The excitement generated by the discovery of this plant lives
on as visitors wonder at its lustrous dark green leaves which in optimum conditions
reach 3ft long. As might be expected, it is a massive shrub altogether, attaining 30ft
in height when mature. The young leaves with their metallic sheen are a feature
too, as are the huge trusses of up to 50 large cream flowers, each defined by a
crimson centre.

Big-leaf rhododendrons are a fine sight at any time but are at their most spectacular
when streaming with rain. Visitors that arrive in these conditions - which are not
unknown at Benmore! - are advised to head for the boardwalk through the main
collection of subsections Grandia and Falconera to enjoy this phenomenon. At their
best in a real downpour, the huge ribbed leaves shine as if newly painted and resound
with the patter of rain drops on their leathery surfaces. The occasional gust of wind
adds to the effect, upturning the foliage momentarily so that the silvery indumentum
shows like the white of an eye.

In April and May, and perhaps in more clement weather, the flowers of these grand
masters can be enjoyed too - though flowering does not occur in young specimens of
these long-lived species. Compared with the leaves, the flower trusses look small, and
some adjustment of perspective is needed to appreciate that they too are of ample

proportions. *R. falconeri*, for example, produces large domed trusses of 20 or more 2 inch creamy-yellow bells.

Deciduous rhododendrons and evergreen azaleas

The majority of deciduous rhododendrons belong to subsection Azalea. However, not all deciduous rhododendrons are azaleas and not all azaleas are deciduous! This conundrum can be understood by looking at some of the species in question.

First to flower are two rhododendrons which are deciduous but are definitely not azaleas, belonging instead to subsection Rhodorastra (formerly Dauricum). *R. dauricum* and *R. mucronulatum* are in fact very similar, both being East Asian, very

Top left. Kurume azaleas are evergreen, late-flowering, and slightly tender.

Top right. Big-leaf rhododendrons, such as *Rhododendron hodgsonii*, are most spectacular in a downpour.

Bottom. The familiar yellow azalea, *Rhododendron luteum*, though common in gardens, is now very rare in its Caucasian homelands.

hardy and pink-flowered. The two can be compared in the border near the pond and along the Younger Memorial Walk, where they open their shallow funnel-shaped flowers from January onward. Also beside the Younger Memorial Walk can be seen a number of threatened azaleas: *R. vaseyi*, found wild only in North Carolina; and *R. schlippenbachii* which is native to Korea and Manchuria. Though different in character, both coincidentally have pink flowers and are deciduous, with brilliant autumn colour. Banks of the sweetly scented *R. luteum* - Europe's only native azalea and now very scarce in the wild - can be found in most of the older areas of the garden, enlivening shrubberies in May.

The Younger Botanic Garden also has a collection of evergreen azaleas, both species and Kurume hybrids, which are spectacular in May and June. Kurume hybrids were bred mainly from the Japanese *R. kaempferi* and *R. kiusianum*. They have tiny glossy leaves and a profusion of small, predominantly pink to salmon or magenta flowers. Evergreen azaleas are more tender than most of the deciduous species and generally need sheltered sunny sites to flower well.

Other spring flowers

Against the dark evergreen background of the conifer and rhododendron collections, there is a succession of ephemeral blossoms and delicate new leaves in spring as other kinds of trees and shrubs stir from winter hibernation. A number of these are lime-hating species which thrive in the acid soils of Benmore. First to flower are the witch hazels (*Hamamelis*) beside the Younger Memorial Walk. Closely related to the witch hazels is *Fothergilla major* from the Allegheny Mountains in the

Top left. Pieris japonica is one of several species grown at Benmore. These relatives of the rhododendrons produce colourful new growths, as well as delightful flowers, in spring, and enjoy the same conditions.

Top right. Nothofagus menziesii, a southern beech from New Zealand, has tiny rounded leaves with finely scalloped margins.

Bottom. Osmanthus delavayi, a Chinese member of the olive family, Oleaceae. This handsome shrub has tiny evergreen leaves, neatly toothed round the margins, and scented white flowers, rather like a miniature jasmine, in April.

eastern United States. Its spring offering takes the form of white bottle-brush flowers that show up well against a dark background. The main area of camellias behind Benmore House comes alive as winter turns into spring. Here can be found *Camellia saluenensis* from western China and the Japanese *C. sasanqua*, along with a range of cultivars and hybrids.

Pieris is a distant relative of *Rhododendron*, distributed in both North America and Asia. Though spring-flowering, the buds form in the previous autumn, giving one the false impression that spring is already on the way. *P. formosa* has large glossy leaves, copper-coloured when young, and the characteristic flowers in May. Not surprisingly, it was George Forrest who found the subspecies *forrestii* on his travels in southwest China and Upper Burma, and from whose collections the garden's plants have been raised. *P. formosa* subsp. *forrestii* is widely regarded as one of the finest shrubs for acid soils, with stunning bright red new growths - which from a distance look like exotic blooms - and large scented flowers in April. *Pieris* of all kinds can be found in the older parts of the garden, especially in the shrubbery near Puck's Hut and on the Wild Bank.

Most of the magnolia collection is concentrated in the eastern half of the garden between the Viewpoint and the Golden Gates. The flowering season starts as early as February with the sumptuous blooms of the giant Himalayan tulip tree, *Magnolia campbellii* and its white form *alba*. April sees a gathering of momentum, with various specimens of the resilient *M. kobus* aflutter with countless white blooms, followed by the pink waterlilies of *M. sargentiana*. Less conspicuous but worth looking for beside Benmore House Road is *M. liliiflora* which produces upright slender flowers, purple-flushed on the outside, intermittently from late April until June.

There are some splendid specimens of beeches (*Fagus*) and southern beeches (*Nothofagus*) at Benmore, mostly in the lower part of the garden. Southern beeches dominate forests in the southern hemisphere, just as Eurasian beeches are an important element in northern broad-leaved woodlands. They may be deciduous or evergreen according to the species, and generally have smaller leaves than European beeches. At the eastern end of the Younger Memorial Walk is a 1916 planting of Chilean raouls (*N. procera*) and roblé beeches (*N. obliqua*) beneath which can invariably be found some hybrid seedlings. The garden's collection of southern beeches features virtually all the hardy species, including the silver beech (*N. menziesii*), and the black or mountain beech (*N. solandri*). Their delicate appearance belies the fact that in their native New Zealand they form stands so dense that little else can grow beneath them - as is the case with beech woodland in Europe.

SUMMER

Summer begins imperceptibly at Benmore with late-flowering rhododendrons, azaleas and magnolias coming into bloom as if it were still spring. At the same time, the dark greens of the conifers are enlivened by tufts and fringes of apple-green new needles, and by the presence of both male and female flowers. By midsummer the sense of newness has faded but there are highlights to come, such as the flowering of Benmore's magnificent eucryphias and desfontaineas against a landscape of purple-heathered mountains.

Summer-flowering rhododendrons

There are rhododendrons in flower at Benmore right through until August. The turning of spring into summer is spanned by many of the azaleas already mentioned and by several other major groups. These include Yak and Hobbie hybrids which are planted near the earlier flowering Loderi hybrids beside Benmore House Road. Yak hybrids are characterised by a compact dwarf habit, handsome foliage and extravagant numbers of colourful, often well-marked flowers which mostly appear in May and June. The Hobbie hybrids were developed in Germany in the 1940s and 50s by Dietrich Hobbie who anticipated the demand for dwarf hardy rhododendrons to suit small gardens. He took some of the best dwarf hybrids then available (such as the red flowered 'Britannia' and 'Essex') and crossed them with two of the finest compact species: *R. williamsianum* and *R. forrestu* var. *repens*. His programme was supported by the Royal Botanic Garden Edinburgh who supplied pollen for the crosses. In return, the Garden was given some of the most successful hybrids which were planted below the crag in 1958. After more than 30 years of exuberant growth, the Hobbies are now being propagated and replanted.

Not far from these hybrids are some superb summer-flowering species. *R. auriculatum* must be one of the loveliest rhododendrons, producing enormous trusses of large, highly scented, white flowers in July and August. As it flowers only at the tops of the branches, and not before it has reached quite a size, some of Benmore's plants are positioned below paths to give an overhead view. *R. brachyanthum* is a neat shrub with small aromatic leaves, peeling bark and a host of little deep yellow bells from late May to July, during which time it attracts every bee in the neighbourhood. The specimen near frog pond can be located by the buzzing of bees! Native to Yunnan and southeast Tibet, this appealing plant was introduced into cultivation as the result of efforts by two of the most accomplished plant hunters of all time: the Abbé Delavay, a French missionary who discovered over 1500 new species during his extensive travels in China, including this one in 1884; and George Forrest, who brought back seed of *R. brachyanthum* in 1906.

A visit to subsection Cinnabarina on the lower hill path behind Benmore House is a must in May and June. *R. cinnabarinum* itself is a quite distinctive but immensely variable Himalayan species which is now divided into several subspecies and variants. All have waxy tubular flowers which are more or less pendent, and small elliptic leaves that in some forms are glaucous when young. Similar but less showy is the related *R. keysii* from Bhutan which in June produces bicoloured red flowers with yellow tips, but in this case they are so narrow as to be scarcely recognisable as a rhododendron.

Unfortunately, these lovely plants are very susceptible to powdery mildew, a fungal disease which has recently caused devastation in collections throughout Britain, the United States and Australia. The symptoms are a yellowing of the upper leaf surface and greyish patches beneath, leading to defoliation which may kill the plant. The implications are serious in that, if untreated, certain species might well disappear

Rhododendron cinnabarinum is a variable species. The Benmore collection includes subsp. *cinnabarinum*, whose crimson flowers have a plum-like bloom (*Top*) ; and subsp. *tamaense* which is semi-deciduous and has flowers in shades of lilac-pink (*Bottom*).

The view of Benmore House in early summer is dominated by a gigantic specimen of *R.* x *russellianum*. Planted in about 1890, it has now reached some 50ft tall and around 250ft across. Its late-flowering and thicket-forming habit are derived from *R. catawbiense*, a native of the Allegheny Mountains in the southeast United States. The other parent is *R. arboreum*, from which it presumably inherited the red colouring.

from cultivation. Susceptible plants in the garden are sprayed regularly with a preventative fungicide but as yet there is no cure. The Royal Botanic Garden Edinburgh is at the forefront of mycological research and is now studying the mildew organism itself, on the basis that understanding its life cycle may provide the vital clue in controlling the disease.

No one visiting the garden in June can fail to notice two of the most splendid red-flowered rhododendrons: *R. griersonianum* and *R.* x *russellianum*. The former is a Chinese species collected by George Forrest in 1917. Unique in the genus for its summertime display of scarlet flowers, it constantly surprises visitors at this time of the year, being one of the first things they see at the start of Redwood Avenue.

Other summer-flowering trees and shrubs

Benmore's list of summer-flowering trees and shrubs is extensive. It includes such interesting species as the yellow-flowered Himalayan *Jasminum humile*, New Zealand hoherias, American snowdrop trees (*Halesia*), oriental snowbells (*Styrax*) and the related epaulette tree (*Pterostyrax hispida*) which combines the foliage of *Halesia* with the fragrant white bells of *Styrax*. Benmore Hill is a good place to enjoy many of these. Here too are collections of Australasian eucalypts, bottlebrushes (*Callistemon*) and leptospermums. Summer-flowering magnolias are well-represented, the most conspicuous being *M. wilsonii* from western China. The American *M. macrophylla* and its rare relative, *M. fraseri*, are especially interesting on account of their large leaves, which in *M. macrophylla* reach 24in and are accompanied by huge fragrant off-white flowers.

Several members of the genus *Clethra* are grown at Benmore. Though little-known, these are lovely shrubs for moist lime-free soil in sheltered conditions. All flower in July and August, producing long racemes of fragrant white flowers. The Younger Memorial Walk is the place to see the so-called white alder (*C. acuminata*) and the sweet pepper bush (*C. alnifolia*) from the eastern United States, while the Chinese *C. delavayi* can be tracked down near the fernery road. But best of all is the splendid specimen of the Japanese *C. barbinervis* on Golden Gates Avenue which puts on a most elegant floral display when little else is flowering.

Visitors reaching the Wright Smith Memorial Shelter at the top of Benmore Hill in early summer will have as a reward not only a superlative view across Strath Eck to Holy Loch but also the sight of a handkerchief tree (*Davidia involucrata*) in full flower. The same time of year also sees the flowering of the Chilean lantern bushes (*Crinodendron hookerianum*) which do exceptionally well in Benmore's mild climate and lime-free soil. The waxy red lanterns, which hang like jewels along the branches in May and June, turn green after pollination but persist, splitting open in August to release numerous pearly seeds.

After rhododendrons and conifers, the Younger Botanic Garden's greatest *pièce de résistance* are the eucryphias which appear like white fountains among the greenery from July to September. A range of species is grown: *Eucryphia cordifolia*, *E. lucida*, the deciduous *E. glutinosa* and its double form 'Plena', and the hybrids *E. x intermedia* 'Rostrevor' and *E. x nymansensis* 'Nymansay'. The first eucryphias to come into view are in the car park, so little effort is needed to enjoy their cascades of white multi-stamened flowers. However, the largest grow on Benmore Hill where they are set against the spectacular scenery.

Top. Davidia involucrata, another of Ernest Wilson's introductions from China, is one of the most spectacular trees in the world, especially on windy days when the huge white bracts are in constant motion.

Bottom left. The Chilean lantern bush, *Crinodendron hookerianum*, thrives at Benmore, flowering prolifically in May and June.

Bottom right. The summer-flowering *Magnolia wilsonii* was collected in western China by Ernest Wilson in 1908.

Left. Eucryphias on the Wild Bank frame a view across the Formal Garden to the heather-clad mountains beyond.

Right. *Eucryphia* x *nymansensis* 'Nymansay' is a fast-growing columnar tree, which is smothered with large white hypericum-like flowers in late summer.

Pines and firs

It should be borne in mind when visiting the Younger Botanic Garden that the areas between the main entrance and the Golden Gates, which include the Pond, Formal Garden and the grounds immediately surrounding Benmore House, have been cultivated since the 19th century for ornamental purposes. They therefore contain a mixture of species, including the oldest and largest specimens, among which certain elements of the scientific collection have been planted as space - and aesthetics - permits. Beyond this is woodland on mountainous terrain which was created largely as an afforestation experiment by James Duncan. It is this much larger area of 'wild wood' that the Botanic Garden has been developing for major scientific collections, especially of conifers and rhododendrons, since the 1970s. Here the visitor will notice a complete change of scene, from historical garden to silviculture on a grand scale. New roads and paths are still being built, and hundreds of young trees and shrubs are carefully planted each year on the steep rough hillsides. Areas are seldom clear-felled; instead, selected mature trees are left to provide shelter for the new plantings which in years to come will form what is in essence a national Pinetum for Scotland.

Much of Benmore Hill was devastated by the hurricane of 1968, giving the Botanic Garden a free hand to develop areas for special plant groups. The main collection of firs (*Abies*) was sited on the northeastern part of Benmore Hill, interspersed with *Sorbus* species. Asian firs are encountered first as one climbs up the zigzag path toward the Wright Smith Memorial Shelter, the most conspicuous species being *A. koreana*. Higher up are the North American firs. Of great interest is the grand fir (*A. grandis*), tallest of all, exceeding 250ft in western North America, and the noble fir (*A. procera*) from Oregon and Washington, whose blue-grey foliage makes it easily recognisable at a distance. Both of these were introduced by David Douglas in 1830 and immediately caught the imagination of landowners. As a result, large specimens of grand and noble firs are frequently encountered in the older parts of Benmore. Further west across Benmore Hill is the pine collection. It includes the graceful blue pine (*Pinus wallichiana*), which was introduced from the Himalayas in about 1823 and re-collected in 1979 by botanists from the Garden while working on the Flora of Bhutan. An even greater find for this team was the Bhutan pine (*P. bhutanica*), a new species described in 1980, which is being established in sheltered positions.

Top left. The cork fir, *Abies lasiocarpa* var. *arizonica*, flanked by young noble firs (*A. procera*) in the main collection of firs on Benmore Hill.

Top right. *Abies koreana* produces its dark purple cones from a very early age - often when under 3ft tall.

Large areas of Benmore are still being reclaimed from old plantations which became overgrown with wild rhododendron during the war years (*Middle*). Clear-felling is seldom carried out, mature trees being left to provide shelter for new plantings (*Bottom*) which form the basis of a national Pinetum.

Chinese firs, junipers and incense cedars

Near the new plantings of pines and spruces is one of Chinese firs (*Cunninghamia*). The genus has only two species - *C. lanceolata*, which is found in most parts of China, and the less hardy *C. konishii* which is confined to Taiwan. They are distinctive trees, somewhere between a monkey puzzle and a yew in terms of foliage.

Below the pines, spruces and Chinese firs, Benmore Hill plunges dramatically over a 200ft cliff into Glen Massan. On the rim and terraces of the cliff are several new plantings, including one of Chinese junipers. Several species have become important in horticulture since the 19th century. *Juniperus chinensis* is very popular as an ornamental and can be seen in many of its guises in the Formal Garden.

Another recent planting is of incense cedars (*Calocedrus decurrens*), which are also important ornamentals on account of their narrow habit and resistance to honey fungus. They are also used commercially in the manufacture of pencils. A noticeable scent surrounds mature trees which in the wild - western North America - reach over 200ft. The young grove of incense cedars is near the edge of the cliff, from which there is a fine view of the Massan Hills.

The Chinese fir, *Cunninghamia lanceolata*.

The hiba cedar and Japanese umbrella pine

Two of the garden's most important conservation collections can be seen on Benmore Hill. They are both of Japanese conifers which, like many of Japan's endemic species, are severely threatened in the wild. The hiba cedars (*Thujopsis dolobrata*) have been planted in the shelter of the Japanese larches above Golden Gates Avenue. Just as rare and even more distinctive is the Japanese umbrella pine (*Sciadopitys verticillata*) which is found wild only in central Honshu. The bright green glossy leaves are linear in shape and up to 5in long, arranged in whorls at the ends of the shoots - rather like the spokes of an umbrella. Sadly, this lovely tree is now reduced to a single small colony in Japan. As part of the Royal Botanic Garden's international Conifer Conservation Programme, seed has been collected from almost every remaining wild tree as the basis for this new collection. The plants should do well, as umbrella pines enjoy moist lime-free conditions. Older specimens can be seen elsewhere in the garden, notably on the Younger Memorial Walk.

Tasmanian ridge

Above the old Fernery is a ridge on which a collection of unusual Tasmanian conifers has recently been established. The island of Tasmania has, like Japan, a number of endemic species which are being progressively diminished through deforestation. The collection includes the shrubby *Diselma archeri* and *Microcachrys tetragona* which are both restricted to western Tasmania, and Tasmanian cedars (species of *Athrotaxis*), which are small, slow-growing trees with whipcord foliage. Other shrubs and trees have been added to this geographical planting, such as the Tasmanian waratah (*Telopea truncata*), an evergreen which produces red flowers in June, and the Tasmanian southern beech (*Nothofagus cunninghamii*).

The Bhutanese Glade

A geographical theme was also the inspiration for the Bhutanese Glade at the western end of Glen Massan. The Glade occupies the south-facing cliff at the base of

The Tasmanian cedar, *Athrotaxis laxifolia*.

Benmore Hill. Inspired by an expedition for the Flora of Bhutan project, a planting scheme has been devised to reflect the various zones encountered in the Bhutanese ranges of the Himalayas. The five zones range from: the valley bottom, planted with species such as *Tetracentron sinense* and *Populus ciliata*; a pine zone, dominated by *Pinus wallichiana*; a larch zone, mainly with *Larix griffithiana*; a fir zone, consisting largely of Sikkim firs (*Abies densa*) and rhododendrons; and lastly a juniper scrub of *Juniperus pseudo-sabina* and *J. recurva*, which in Bhutan would be at about 13,780ft (4200m). Underplantings include species from genera which are familiar to any gardener - *Rosa, Berberis, Lonicera, Cotoneaster, Ribes* and *Spiraea* - all of which abound in this botanical paradise. The Bhutanese Glade was planted in 1988. For a number of years to come, there will be little to see but young trees and shrubs, and a vision of what such a forest ecosystem will look like when mature - a planting for future generations which is very much in the spirit of Benmore.

Top. The arching red-berried boughs of *Cotoneaster frigidus* are set among white mounds of the late-flowering *Hydrangea paniculata* and the dark greens and golds of conifers.

Bottom left. Photinia villosa resembles the hawthorn, but prefers lime-free soil. In autumn the leaves turn such a vivid scarlet and gold that the bright red fruits are scarcely noticeable.

Bottom right The Younger Memorial Walk is especially colourful in autumn, providing an experience which can be enjoyed within a short distance from the car park.

AUTUMN AND WINTER

Late autumn and winter are times when inclement weather is most likely at Benmore. Visitors braving the elements will, however, find much of interest, for the flare of autumn colour is followed by the delicate blooms of precocious rhododendrons, magnolias and cherries. But best of all in the depths of winter are the more permanent features of trees and shrubs - structure, details of bark, and an infinite variety of evergreen foliage. There is the scenery too, of which the trees are such an important part, which changes suddenly according to the weather - misty one moment and as clear as a bell the next, briefly covered in snow (which rarely lies long at Benmore) or lashed by storms.

Autumn colour at Benmore

The main areas to enjoy autumn colour are the Younger Memorial Walk, approaches to Benmore House, and borders around the pond and Formal Garden where the deciduous azaleas are especially effective, showing every autumnal shade imagineable. The witch hazel family (Hamamelidaceae) makes a valuable

contribution too, the witch hazels themselves mostly turning yellow, while the fothergillas are more adventurous, adding bright red and gold. The Persian ironwood (*Parrotia persica*) - a witch hazel relative despite its beech-like leaves - excels, with deep reds predominating.

Equally brilliant are *Photinia* and *Enkianthus*, of which Benmore has some fine examples. *Photinia* belongs to the rose family (Rosaceae), as might be expected from its hawthorn-like flowers and fruits. Best for autumn colour is *P. villosa* which grows wild in China, Japan and Korea. Specimens of the ericaceous *Enkianthus campanulatus* and *E. perulatus* are widely planted at Benmore, giving much pleasure in May when hung with diminutive bell-shaped flowers, and again in autumn as the foliage flames into reds and yellows. Both these shrubs are Japanese in origin and have been in cultivation here since the late 19th century. Benmore also has a fine collection of cotoneasters, with about 25 species and a range of different forms. Many of the low-growing kinds give colour to the Formal Garden in the autumn, but it is the tall ones, such as the splendid specimen of *Cotoneaster frigidus* on the Wild Bank behind the Formal Garden which, seen against a blue sky, bring visitors to an admiring halt.

A particularly good view of autumn colour may be had by walking up to the frog pond on the upper hill path. From the crag on the corner there is a panorama of the Formal Garden and, to the right, a view in the direction of the Pond through magnificent conifers underplanted with deciduous azaleas and Japanese maples. The most spectacular autumn colour is given by *Acer japonicum* and *A. palmatum*, with cultivars such as *A. palmatum* 'Osakazuki' turning a uniform vivid red. Other maples tend to be more subtle and repay careful examination.

The Pond itself is worth a closer look, for in addition to azaleas and Japanese maples it has as its centrepiece a Japanese katsura tree (*Cercidiphyllum japonicum*). This is an unusually lovely species in autumn, its rounded leaves turning a warm biscuit colour and filling the air with an intriguing smell of caramel. Bending as it does over the Pond, the attractive leaves continue to delight long after they have fallen, floating on the surface and glistening with rain drops. Also guaranteed to catch the eye near the Pond is the golden larch (*Pseudolarix amabilis*) which, like the true larches (*Larix*), is deciduous - a characteristic shared by only a handful of conifers - and turns a lovely golden colour in autumn.

Top right. A Japanese maple, *Acer palmatum* var. *atropurpureum*, beside the Pond turns a magnificent red in October.

Top left. *Sorbus hupehensis* is a distinctive rowan with blue-grey foliage and white, often pink-flushed fruits.

Bottom. The white fruits of *Sorbus prattii* last well into the winter, being relatively unattractive to birds.

Rowans of the World

The rowans (*Sorbus*) are characteristic of uplands throughout the northern hemisphere. Our native rowan or mountain ash (*S. aucuparia*) has the distinction of being found at 3280ft (1000m), higher than any other tree in Scotland. How fitting, therefore, that the Younger Botanic Garden displays this and many other members of the genus on Benmore's mountainous flanks. Many of the rowans in the collection will be familiar to the keen gardener: the white-fruited *S. cashmiriana*, *S. prattii* and *S. koehneana*; *S. hupehensis* with pink-flushed fruits; *S.* 'Joseph Rock' whose cream fruits turn amber as they age; and the various red-fruited species such as *S. sargentiana*, *S. decora* and *S. commixta*. Anyone interested in this genus will also want to find some of the more unusual species - such as *S. himalaica*, introduced from Nepal only in 1986, which has bright pink fruits. In the rough ground to the southwest of the View Point is the only surviving specimen of George Forrest's type collection of *S. pteridophylla*, a white-fruited species with fern-like leaves.

The *Sorbus* species with leaves divided into leaflets are generally known as rowans, while those with entire leaves are referred to as whitebeams. Benmore has two whitebeams of great interest. The first is a specimen of the Japanese *S. alnifolia* on the Younger Memorial Walk which at over 55ft is the largest in Britain. However, size is not its only virtue, as its rich autumn colours testify. The second is the Himalayan whitebeam (*S. thibetica*), grown from seed collected by Frank Kingdon Ward, which can be seen en route from the View Point to the main collection of big-leaf rhododendrons. Though not particularly colourful, it is a spectacular species, with broad leaves up to 10in long which have silvery undersides and turn inward, revealing this feature, before they fall in autumn.

Big trees

Benmore's most impressive trees are the conifers of oceanic regions which thrive in areas of high humidity. Most memorable of all are the Sierra redwoods or wellingtonias (*Sequoiadendron giganteum*), 50 of which were planted in 1863 to form the great Avenue. The Sierra redwood is the largest tree in the world, though not the tallest - a distinction held by the coast redwood (*Sequoia sempervirens*). Sierra redwoods, which in the wild are confined to the western slopes of the Sierra Nevada in California, may live 3500 years, reach about 300ft and weigh 6000 tons. Their longevity owes something to the massive buttressing of the trunks, which improves stability, and to the red-brown bark, which is up to 2ft thick. This spongy, deeply furrowed layer resists not only insect damage and fungal infections but also, most importantly, forest fires.

The coast redwoods (*Sequoia sempervirens*) are taller, more slender - reaching a phenomenal 370ft or more - and are found wild from southwest Oregon to the Santa Lucia Mountains of California. Another difference is that the foliage of the coast redwood is yew-like, while in the Sierra redwood it is cord-like. Both trees however share the need for ample moisture and humidity. Benmore's coastal situation and generous rainfall create some of the best growing conditions in Britain for redwoods. Though not yet the largest in the country, its tallest coast redwood measures over 120ft and the best of the avenue's Sierra redwoods exceed 160ft. When standing

A human's eye view of big trees at Benmore: Sierra redwoods (*Sequoiadendron giganteum*), Douglas firs (*Pseudotsuga menziesii*) and monkey puzzles (*Araucaria araucana*).

beneath these tremendous trees, it is awe-inspiring to realise that they are still only half the height of their wild relatives!

The redwoods capture the imagination, but they are not the only big trees on the Pacific coast of North America. Further north, from Oregon to Alaska are pockets of temperate rainforest receiving over 12ft of rain a year where other giant conifers abound. Species such as Sitka spruce (*Picea sitchensis*), western red cedar (*Thuja plicata*), western hemlock (*Tsuga heterophylla*) and Douglas fir (*Pseudotsuga menziesii*), which commonly exceed 250ft tall, reach their greatest proportions in such lush growing conditions. Many of Benmore's tallest trees belong to these oceanic species and are found in the oldest parts of the garden, especially in the Eachaig Arboretum, around Benmore House and in Glen Massan. All of them were introduced in the first half of the 19th century, mostly as a result of David Douglas's explorations, and were first planted at Benmore by James Duncan.

While admiring these oceanic conifers, a number of other splendid trees will be encountered in the old parts of the garden. There are magnificent monkey puzzles (*Araucaria araucana*) on Benmore House lawn, clothed with branches of dagger-sharp leaves right down to the ground. The area of Chinese Firs has some interesting specimens too: the only mature Sikkim fir (*Abies densa*) in Britain and the largest Faber fir (*A. fabri*), which measures 92ft in height. Not all record-breaking trees in the garden are conifers. Benmore also has very large specimens of the Chilean *Nothofagus betuloides* and New Zealand's black beech (*N. solandri*), both above the upper hill path, a deodar (*Cedrus deodara*) on Cedar Walk which at 125ft is possibly the largest in Britain, and two huge birches on the Younger Memorial Walk - a paperbark birch (*Betula papyrifera*) measuring 65½ft and a 62ft Chinese birch (*B. szechuanica*).

Glen Massan

The Glen Massan Arboretum combines the old with the new, with trees dating back to the turn of the century alongside some of the garden's most recent plantings. They do however have something in common, both being by nature experimental. James

Right. The western hemlock, *Tsuga heterophylla*, is the dominant species of temperate rain forest on America's northwest Pacific coast. This graceful conifer can be recognised by its drooping leader, spreading branches and fans of tiny dark green needles (*Left*). Western hemlocks are thoroughly at home in the Younger Botanic Garden, regenerating freely on 'nurse logs' - fallen trees or trunks that provide the necessary boost of nutrients for the seedlings.

Above. The Japanese cedar, *Cryptomeria japonica*, is a fast-growing handsome tree with soft, widely spaced juvenile leaves and densely braided adult foliage. The fibrous red-brown bark is also attractive, flaking in young specimens and peeling away in strips on old trees.

Below. Cultivars of the very variable Lawson cypress, *Chamaecyparis lawsoniana*, border part of the Formal Garden.

Duncan tried out exotic new introductions from North America in the late 19th century and Harry Younger devised a trial 'companion planting' of Japanese larch and western red cedars in 1916 with the aim of reducing the number of branches in the larches and thereby the frequency of knots in the timber. Today, the Younger Botanic Garden is planting southern hemisphere conifers for the first time, establishing unique breeding groups of threatened species and trying to recreate plant communities from different geographical zones.

Glen Massan itself is a narrow valley through which runs the River Massan, adding the sound of running water to that of wind in the trees. The walk into Glen Massan begins at the Golden Gates and proceeds along the southern boundary, where many of the garden's grandest conifers are to be found. Huge specimens of noble fir (*Abies procera*), Colorado white fir (*A. concolor*), Pacific fir (*A. concolor* var. *lowiana*), western hemlock (*Tsuga heterophylla*) and Sitka spruce (*Picea sitchensis*) lead to an amphitheatre dominated by the garden's tallest Douglas fir (*Pseudotsuga menziesii*), which in 1991 measured 177ft. An uninterrupted view of the mighty trunks enables visitors to appreciate the very different bark textures of each species.

The steep hillside and crags on the north side of Glen Massan support the recently established Bhutanese Glade and a scenic Cryptomeria Glade in which a planting of Japanese cedars (*Cryptomeria japonica*) ascends the hill in the company of various spruces (*Picea*), punctuated by a handsome copper beech (*Fagus sylvatica* forma *purpurea*). The track in Glen Massan terminates in the amphitheatre at present, but the Younger Botanic Garden goes on, both in terms of land and endeavour. Straight ahead is untamed forest overgrown with *Rhododendron ponticum* - a reminder to visitors of how large areas of the garden looked before the great hurricane opened up swathes and initiated a new era of planting.

The Formal Garden

The Formal Garden has been redeveloped since 1965 to display ornamental garden conifers. It stands on the site of the former walled garden which was once flanked by James Duncan's magnificent conservatories. Many ornamental conifers are dwarf in stature and, having both aesthetic and practical appeal, enjoy immense popularity as garden plants. Though many cultivars have been developed through breeding or are sports which occur in cultivation, some - such as the prostrate Canadian juniper (*Juniperus communis* var. *depressa*) - are distinctive forms found in the wild.

The conifer with the greatest number of cultivars is the Lawson cypress (*Chamaecyparis lawsoniana*). There are well over 200, ranging from diminutive forms suitable for rock gardens and containers, to tall trees, in a variety of habit and foliage forms and a range of greens, blues, greys and yellows. The Formal Garden is bordered on the south and east by examples of the larger forms which include the golden 'Hillieri', 'Pembury Blue' - the brightest of the blue-greys - and 'Green Pillar', a narrow bright green cultivar which is excellent for hedging. In the wild, Lawson cypresses are found only in the forests of northwest California and southwest Oregon. Despite their narrow range, they are very variable - hence the enormous number of cultivars - but all have aromatic foliage and in April are dotted with tiny but decorative red male cones and slate-blue female cones. Lawson cypresses were introduced from the United States in 1854 by seed sent to Lawson's nursery in Edinburgh. With this Scottish connection, it is fitting that the Botanic Garden has such a fine collection of the world's most widely grown conifer.

The development of the Formal Garden was a stroke of genius, being on the one hand a unique reference collection of conifer variants, while on the other hand creating a spectacular contrast with the surrounding countryside. To appreciate the

Formal Garden fully requires two very different approaches. The first is to wander through or sit in it, taking in the remarkable variability and colourfulness of these conifers; the second is to climb Benmore Hill and look down on it from a height, from where its geometry, neatness and verdure appear as an oasis of cultivation among the rugged mountains and apparently impenetrable forests, thus symbolising Benmore itself - a unique balance between garden and wild landscape.

The Formal Garden stands on the site of the old walled garden (*Top*) which once contained James Duncan's magnificent glasshouses. It now displays a remarkable collection of ornamental garden conifers (*Bottom*).

*L*ogan Botanic Garden is situated a short distance from Scotland's most southern point, in the Rhinns, the narrow peninsula that runs from Stranraer to the Mull of Galloway. This peninsula is only about 2 miles (4km) wide at Logan, the garden lying midway between Luce Bay to the east and the Irish Sea to the west. It is surrounded by the sea on three sides, at about 100ft (30m) above sea level, and basks in a subtropical climate created by the influence of the Gulf Stream. Logan Botanic Garden's 24 acres (10ha) constitute one of the most favoured sites on the west coast, comparable in horticultural terms to the Scilly Isles. As a consequence, the Royal Botanic Garden's collections from the southern hemisphere - from southern South America, southern Africa and Australasia - are located principally at Logan. Here many species that need greenhouse protection elsewhere can be grown outdoors and - in the case of trees and shrubs - reach their full potential.

Opposite. Logan Botanic Garden basks in a subtropical climate. Surrounded by sea on three sides, it is situated on the Mull of Galloway, near Scotland's southernmost point. The cabbage palms, *Cordyline australis*, overlooking the Water Garden are characteristic of Logan.

An aerial view across Logan Botanic Garden towards Luce Bay. The main house and surrounding grounds are privately owned; the Walled Garden dominates the lower half of the picture.

The exceptionally mild climate is complemented by soil which is a slightly acid sandy loam - ideal for lime-hating subjects such as rhododendrons, camellias and many montane species which naturally grow in moist peaty conditions. Rainfall averages 40in (1016mm), fairly well distributed throughout the year, with no month consistently the wettest. Logan's situation is not, however, without drawbacks. Being so close to the sea, the prevailing southwest winds, which frequently reach gale force, whip across the peninsula in a fury of salt spray. Many plants tolerate salt on their foliage but others - especially if evergreen - may be irreparably damaged, as if scorched by fire. For this reason, some of the most important plantings at Logan are the shelter belts.

Originally these shelter belts consisted of native hardwoods which were subsequently interplanted with Sitka spruce (*Picea sitchensis*) and Monterey and Corsican pines (*Pinus radiata* and *P. nigra* var. *maritima*). Today, wherever possible, wild-collected southern hemisphere species are being planted as windbreaks. The thickets of *Pittosporum, Griselinia, Olearia* and *Phormium* give not only protection but add to the character of the garden and support its scientific interest.

HISTORY

The land at Logan has been inhabited since at least medieval times. Records show that John Baliol, Lord of Galloway, granted Lougan to Dougal McDouall in 1295. The McDoualls lived in the castle of Balzieland which was burnt down in 1500 when Patrick McDouall held sway. Its ruins can still be seen in the West Wall above the Terrace and give a dramatic accent to the Walled Garden.

From the 16th century onward the estate passed from father to son, a tradition which was broken only in 1945 when Kenneth McDouall left Logan to his cousin, Sir Ninian Buchan-Hepburn. In 1949 it passed into the ownership of Mr R Olaf Hambro, whose trustees gave part of the estate to the nation in 1969. The Queen Anne house and policies were then re-acquired by Sir Ninian. The Walled Garden, originally the fruit and vegetable garden, and surroundings became Logan Botanic Garden, the second specialist garden of the Royal Botanic Garden Edinburgh.

There is evidence that a garden has been in existence at Logan since about 1200 but it was in only 1869, when James McDouall married Agnes Buchan Hepburn (Sir Ninian's great aunt) that the present development began. Agnes McDouall was a keen gardener and brought lilies, roses and other shrubs with her from the East

Left. The ruined Castle of Balzieland forms part of the West Wall above the Terrace. It was burnt down in 1500, when it was the residence of Patrick McDouall. The plant in the foreground is an asphodel, *Asphodeline ramosus.*

Right. Kenneth McDouall (1870-1945) and his brother Douglas (1872-1942) inherited their gardening expertise and love of plants from their mother, Agnes. The present-day garden at Logan began in their time.

Lothian garden of her childhood at Smeaton. She also planted the first eucalyptuses. Her sons, Kenneth (1870-1945) and Douglas (1872-1942), inherited their mother's love of gardening and knowledge of plants, so much so that with her encouragement they travelled widely in warm temperate regions to collect new species. They also obtained seed from the leading plant hunters of the day - George Forrest, Reginald Farrer, Frank Kingdon Ward and Ernest Wilson. Virtually all rhododendrons dating back to this time were raised from collections made in China by Forrest and Farrer, as were many other plants new to cultivation on these shores. Originally Kenneth McDouall sowed seeds of Wilson's *Primula japonica* from an upturned umbrella but they soon seeded themselves and became so well established that the path from the garden to the sea (which runs between Logan Botanic Garden and the Fish Pond at Port Logan Bay) has since been known as Primula Walk or Ladies' Walk.

Over the years, the McDouall brothers turned the fruit and vegetable garden at Logan into a cornucopia of rare and exotic plants. In 1909 they planted an avenue of 62 seedling cabbage palms (*Cordyline australis*) from home-grown seed. Described in the first guide book to Logan Botanic Garden as a feature of 'pagan splendour', the original avenue was severely damaged by the winters of 1962-3 and 1978-9 and was replanted in 1980, again with plants raised from seed produced at Logan. A few of the original cabbage palms, now over 80 years old, remain elsewhere, notably beside the pond. The McDoualls were also responsible for the rows of Chusan palms (*Trachycarpus fortunei*) on either side of the stream which flows from Deer Hill through the Gunnera Bog to the entrance. This remarkable species is virtually the only palm which is hardy in the British Isles. The short avenue of Chusan palms is a key feature of the garden, being close to the entrance and the first exciting glimpse of subtropical vegetation that greets visitors as they approach from the car park. The tree ferns (*Dicksonia antarctica*), the oldest of which were planted over 70 years ago, are also a striking feature of the Walled Garden.

The McDouall brothers are best remembered for their development of peat wall gardens. Constructed from terraces of peat blocks infilled with peaty soil, peat walls are now the standard technique for growing dwarf lime-hating plants from alpine regions. Their innovation was prompted by the introduction of plants from the Himalayas and western China which grow wild on steep slopes and meadows in high mountains. Needing constant moisture and humidity but free drainage and acid conditions, they proved impossible to cultivate in the conventional rock garden,

Left. The original peat wall garden developed by the McDouall brothers and (*Right*) as it is today.

The Chilean coral plant, *Berberidopsis corallina*, is one of the many plants at Logan which requires a very mild climate and lime-free soil.

which was too dry and alkaline. Their experiment proved a success and was a considerable step forward in the cultivation of the more difficult species of *Primula*, *Meconopsis*, *Nomocharis* and dwarf rhododendrons, to mention but a few of the plants for which Logan, and later the Royal Botanic Garden Edinburgh, became famous.

The energy and dedication of Agnes McDouall and her sons were continued by Hambro who greatly restored the garden. Tragically, parts of the garden have been decimated by some of the severe winters experienced at Logan. At the start of 1963 frost was recorded on 48 of the first 60 days. Indeed, temperatures plumetted below -13°C, the harshest conditions at Logan for half a century. A succession of gales also took their toll, especially of the shelter belts. As a result, many of the tender plants were killed outright or so badly damaged that they had to be removed. When the Royal Botanic Garden took over in 1969 it was yet again in need of major restoration. Much of this work was undertaken by Martin Colledge, who had trained at the Royal Botanic Garden in Edinburgh and was Head Gardener when Logan changed hands, becoming Assistant Curator of the newly established Botanic Garden.

Now well and truly restored, Logan continues to develop both in terms of its scientific collections and as an outstanding amenity for visitors to Dumfries and Galloway.

SPRING

Exotic rhododendrons, magnolias and camellias

The first sight to greet visitors to Logan in spring is the colony of daffodils beneath the avenue of Chusan palms (*Trachycarpus fortunei*), typifying the blend of familiar and exotic which is the garden's hallmark. Vying for attention next are the rhododendrons and magnolias which have an arresting presence during their flowering period.

Many of the rhododendrons grown at Logan are too tender for the majority of gardens and can rarely be seen thriving outdoors anywhere in Britain. These include the Himalayan *Rhododendron maddenii*, a variable species with scented white to pink flowers in late spring to early summer, and 'Fragrantissimum', best-known of Maddenia hybrids and also later-flowering. The large blush-white flowers of the latter are a feature of the shrubbery between the Tree Fern Lawn and the Centre Wall, being so fragrant that the surrounding air is sweetly scented. This hybrid was made in the 19th century by crossing *R. edgeworthii*, a fragrant pink-flowered species with the similarly fragrant *R. formosum*. Both the parents are also grown at Logan. Flowering earlier but unscented is the Himalayan *R. ciliatum*, one of the hardiest Maddenia species. It has a neat habit and flowers freely when young, making a good plant for sheltered mixed borders.

Left. A colony of daffodils beneath chusan palms, *Trachycarpus fortunei* - a combination of the familiar and exotic which gives Logan its unique character.

Right. Rhododendron 'Fragrantissimum', a Maddenia hybrid which is generally treated as a conservatory plant, blooms in May outdoors at Logan, filling the air with its sweet perfume.

The most outstanding spring-flowering magnolia at Logan is *Magnolia sprengeri* which occupies pride of place in the Lower Walled Garden. This old and shapely tree is a delight in April when the bare branches exult in fragrant tulip-like pink flowers. The species was introduced to cultivation by E H Wilson from central China in 1901. Similar but with even larger flowers is the giant Himalayan tulip tree, *M. campbellii*, a rather tender species which reached the west in 1865. In the wild it is very variable, usually with white but often with pale or deep pink flowers. However, a pink-flowered plant was the first to be scientifically described and therefore became the type. Later, when the commoner white-flowered plants were discovered, they then had to be described as the variety *alba*. Pink-flowered plants have always been the most highly prized, being even lovelier than the white against an early spring sky, but

Top. *Magnolia sprengeri* var. *diva* holds centre stage in the Lower Walled Garden in April when the bare branches are weighed down with fragrant pink goblets.

Left. Among the world's largest ferns is the Tasmanian tree fern, *Dicksonia antarctica*. It develops a fibrous trunk up to 20ft tall topped with 6ft fronds.

Right. Banks of camellias flower from earliest spring beneath the cabbage palms.

they are unfortunately the least hardy. In 1920 Frank Kingdon Ward introduced the hardier pink-flowered variety *mollicomata*, which grows wild in southeast Tibet and Yunnan. Both *M. campbellii* var. *mollicomata* and the beautiful hybrid 'Charles Raffill' are resplendent in the South Woodland in March and April.

Flowering in late winter and spring are the camellias which are concentrated on the north side of the Centre Wall and in the shrubbery to the south. As camellias are easily damaged by frost when flowering, most of the Botanic Garden's collection is held at Logan. Here one can see the key species *C. japonica*, *C. reticulata* and *C. saluenensis*, together with a wide range of their cultivars and hybrids. Also grown are less common species such as *C. cuspidata* from southern China, which has coppery young foliage and diminutive cream flowers, and *C. oleifera*, an East Asian species with toothed leaves and small fragrant white flowers.

Logan's giant plants

Though flowers come first among the joys of spring, new leaves and growth can be almost as thrilling. At the end of the winter, especially if it has been a hard one, the leaves of the tree fern (*Dicksonia antarctica*) in the Walled Garden and in the shelter of the South Woodland look rather brown and tattered. The fresh green fronds unfurl from tight felted crooks, expanding with supreme grace to reach up to 6ft in length. The mighty *Gunnera manicata* from Brazil holds the record for producing the largest leaves of any plant that can be grown outdoors in Britain. At Logan it excels itself, forming a vast impenetrable colony, known as the Gunnera Bog. Completely dormant during the winter, this giant awakens in April with gargantuan young leaves, accompanied by cone-shaped spiky panicles of insignificant green flowers which reach 3ft long before shedding pollen in May and June. The development of *Echium pininana*, a Canary Islands endemic, is impressive too. The plants sow themselves randomly throughout the garden and those in suitable positions are left to establish for two to three years. In the spring of their third or fourth year they elongate at a meteoric rate to a towering 18ft or more, bearing a pillar of blue flowers from May onwards. After flowering these monocarpic plants die, but not before setting seed and founding another dynasty.

Top left. Gunnera manicata produces massive spiny leaves up to 10ft across. Logan's Gunnera Bog makes even adults feel like Alice-in-Wonderland!

Top right. Echium pininana from the Canary Islands produces a spectacular 10-18ft spike of flowers.

Bottom. The South African water hawthorn, *Aponogeton distachyus*.

The Water Garden in spring

The Water Garden comes alive in spring with skunk cabbages: the western North American *Lysichiton americanus* with bright yellow spathes and its East Asian counterpart, *L. camtschatcensis*, with slightly smaller and later pure white inflorescences. These are followed by their more elegant relatives, the South African arum lilies (*Zantedeschia aethiopica*) with bright green arrowhead leaves and white-spathed inflorescences. Skunk cabbages and arum lilies are marginal aquatics, enjoying rich mud and wet conditions. Among the true aquatics is the water hawthorn, *Aponogeton distachyus*, a subtropical South African species with slender ovate leaves which float flat on the surface. It blooms for most of the year, starting in about February, producing forked clusters of black-anthered white flowers whose heavy scent is noticeable on the approach to the pool.

The flamboyant, fragile and fragrant

Bright blue flowers never fail to attract attention. Visible from afar are the Himalayan poppies (*Meconopsis grandis*) whose brilliant sky blue contrasts vividly with the lemon yellow of the smaller Welsh poppy (*M. cambrica*). The first of these fragile flowers open toward the end of May. Rather earlier is the endangered New Zealand forget-me-not (*Myosotidium hortensia*) which is endemic to the wet and windy Chatham Islands in the South Pacific. Notoriously difficult to cultivate in Britain, this striking maritime plant needs a mild humid climate and rich moist soil. Traditionally mulched with seaweed and rotting fish in an attempt to mimic its natural habitat close to the high tide mark, it grows with enthusiasm only in gardens such as Logan which can supply the requisite warmth, dampness and tender loving care.

Blues of various shades, from powder blue to azure and indigo, are produced by the Californian lilacs (*Ceanothus*). The flowering time depends on the species or variety, ranging from spring to autumn, but the intense blue of *C. thyrsiflorus* is a feature of the garden during May. The buddlejas have a lengthy flowering period too, beginning with the South African sage wood, *Buddleja salvifolia*. Last is *B. nivea* in

Right. Meconopsis from two continents - sky blue Himalayan poppies (*Meconopsis grandis*) and yellow Welsh poppies (*M. cambrica*) - grow side-by-side in Logan's moist acid soil.

Below. Chilean fire bushes (*Embothrium*) are aflame near the Centre Wall in May.

August, though its drooping spikes of sparse purple flowers are of less interest than the white-felted foliage.

Bright red flowers are equally memorable. Rather hidden away on the West Wall is the connoisseur's flowering currant, *Ribes speciosum*, which in April and May produces red fuchsia-like flowers in pendulous clusters beneath the shiny foliage. The flowering currants seen in almost every suburban garden are varieties of *R. sanguineum*, a species which is widely distributed in western North America. *R. speciosum* is found wild only in California, making it far less hardy. Both are pollinated by humming birds as they migrate north after spending the winter in Central and South America. Red also but very different in shape are the flowers of the Chilean lantern bushes (*Crinodendron hookerianum*) which are to be found in the woodland areas of the Garden. In May the dark evergreen foliage is illuminated with rows of pendulous fat red lanterns. Chilean fire bushes (*Embothrium*) also come in for a great deal of comment from visitors in May when their brilliant scarlet flowers flicker like flames against the sky. Three kinds are grown: *E. coccineum*, *E. coccineum longifolium* and *E. lanceolatum*, all of which are semi-evergreen. Some of the largest fire bushes are in the shrubbery on the north side of the Centre Wall where they sow themselves freely. *Embothrium* belongs to the protea family (Proteaceae). So too does *Grevillea rosmarinifolia*, an antipodean shrub with needle-like leaves and short bottle brushes of spiky curved flowers in late spring and early summer which, like many bird-pollinated flowers, are bright red. Grevilleas are usually considered greenhouse subjects in Britain but this species thrives in the warmth and shelter of Logan's east-facing Terrace.

Quite different from *Embothrium*, but just as flamboyant in its way, is *Abutilon vitifolium*, another Chilean shrub which is touch-and-go as regards hardiness. A fast-growing species, it obviously revels in conditions at Logan, sowing itself around the garden and reaching 8ft in no time at all. In cold areas, young plants make handsome pot plants for the conservatory or patio, and in the open ground often survive the winter if planted against a sunny wall.

The flowers of *Jovellana violacea* are also pale mauve, but there the resemblance ends. This Chilean sub-shrub belongs to the foxglove family (Scrophularicaeae) and in late spring is smothered in $^1\!/_2$in bell-shaped flowers which are marked with yellow and purple-spotted inside. *J. violacea* is too tender to be grown outdoors in most gardens but its small size, twiggy habit and neat foliage make it a good subject for pots under glass. At Logan it forms a hedge against the retaining wall which

surrounds the raised ponds at the foot of the Centre Wall. Also with its back to this low wall is a large lemon verbena (*Aloysia triphylla*, formerly *Lippia citriodora*) - another shrub which is much more commonly seen as a pot plant. It is grown for its aromatic foliage which has a strong lemon fragrance and is used whole in pot pourri and herb teas or distilled for its essential oil. Being deciduous, the leaves are at their best in late spring and early summer. The white to pale lilac flowers, which appear in late summer, are insignificant.

Most of the spring-flowering shrubs described so far are grown for their appearance rather than their fragrance, but in the largely Chilean genus *Azara* it is perfume which is the main attraction. *A. microphylla* can be found on the upper Terrace where it blooms in late winter and early spring. The flowers are so small as to be barely noticeable, but their vanilla scent is sufficiently powerful to bring visitors to a halt in an attempt to locate the source.

Euphorbia is a large and diverse genus of over 2000 species, ranging from annuals to sub-shrubs and cactus-like succulents, worldwide in distribution but mostly tropical. Rather tender and rarely seen in gardens is *E. mellifera* from Madeira, a spreading shrub which has reached about 6ft in the centre bed of the Lower Walled Garden's main lawn. Its name means 'honey-bearing', which refers both to the abundant nectar and the honey-like scent of its greenish-yellow flowers. In the same bed as *E. mellifera* is another spring-flowering shrub that merits a closer look. *Corokia* x *virgata* is covered in small yellow flowers in May and subsequently bears numerous tiny orange fruits. *Corokia*, native to New Zealand, is the most far-flung genus of the dogwood family (Cornaceae) which is mainly north-temperate in distribution.

A spring-flowering shrub that has every virtue - handsome evergreen foliage, pretty

Left. Euphorbia mellifera is an unusual shrub from Madeira, seldom seen outdoors in Britain.

Below. Abutilon vitifolium is a rather tender, fast-growing Chilean shrub. Insubstantially tall and slender, it looks like a pale mauve cloud when in bloom. The hibiscus-like flowers are 2in across and borne in large clusters, obscuring the downy palmate leaves.

flowers and a delightful scent - is Winter's bark (*Drimys winteri*), a South American species which was named after its discoverer, Captain Winter of the *Golden Hind* in which Sir Francis Drake made his epic round-the-world voyage. The peppery aromatic leaves and bark of this and other *Drimys* species have medicinal applications and were once used by sailors to prevent scurvy. The small family Winteraceae has seven or eight genera and about 120 species of trees and shrubs which occur mainly in temperate rainforests and tropical montane forests within the southern Pacific region. It is of great evolutionary interest, being among the most primitive of flowering plants.

Winter's bark, *Drimys winteri*, is a handsome South American evergreen. Its jasmine-scented flowers resemble small starry magnolias and are borne in loose clusters that hang downward against the simple leathery leaves. They appear in May and are one of the highlights of the garden at that time.

No account of spring-flowering southern hemisphere plants would be complete without mentioning the wattles or mimosas (*Acacia*) whose acid yellow flowers herald spring in the Australian bush. The majority are cool greenhouse subjects in Britain but a few, such as *A. pravissima* and *A. melanoxylon*, succeed outdoors in favoured gardens such as Logan, bearing the typical yellow pompom flowers in late winter and early spring. *Acacia* belongs to the pea family (Leguminosae) and so too does the New Zealand lobster claw or parrot's bill, *Clianthus puniceus*, some fine specimens of which grow on the east gable end of the cottage at the entrance to the Walled Garden. Its spectacular curved red flowers are produced in pendent racemes during late winter and spring among the attractive pinnate leaves. Though trained against the wall it is not a climber but a slender shrub which in the open has an arching or sprawling habit.

SUMMER

A botanical blaze of colour

On a fine summer day at Logan, when the exotic foliage of the tree ferns and cabbage palms reaches into a blue sky and flowers of astonishing brilliance open in the shelter of its walls, it is hard to believe that this is a Scottish garden and not somewhere in the Mediterranean. Logan's subtropical character is at its most exuberant from June to September with shrubberies of fuchsias, hebes and hydrangeas, and borders that achieve the customary 'blaze of colour' using mostly wild species rather than

hybrids. That Logan is the most colourful of the four gardens at this time of year reflects its specialisation in plants from the southern hemisphere.

In this part of the world many plants are pollinated by butterflies, birds and small mammals which are attracted to primary colours, especially reds, and to certain flower shapes, such as tubular or spiky. These include the salvias, fuchsias, bottle brushes (*Callistemon*) and *Metrosideros* which have predominantly red or pink flowers. Also well-represented are daisies - the 'day's eyes' - which open flat in bright sunshine and perhaps more than any other flower symbolise the joy of summertime warmth and light. Daisies from Africa and the Canary Islands - a galaxy of *Osteospermum*, *Gazania* and *Argyranthemum frutescens* - in a variety of pastel shades, dazzling white and intense yellows, beam their simple rayed flowers toward the sun, attracting gregarious smaller insects to the floral feast of pollen and nectar in their centres.

Left. Logan is renowned for its summer bedding. None of the familiar hybrid bedding plants are grown; instead the effect is produced by wild flowers from dry subtropical regions of southern Africa, South America and Australasia.

Right. The white daisies of *Argyranthemum frutescens* among pink *Diascia rigescens*, yellow *Bidens ferulaefolia* and *Malva sylvestris* 'Primley Blue'.

Below left. The curry plant, *Helichrysum angustifolium*, provides a foil for *Salvia patens* 'Cambridge Blue'.

Below right. African kingfisher daisies, *Felicia pappei*, and South American *Verbena chamaedrifolia*.

The focal point for this summer display is the Water Garden, presided over by rows of New Zealand cabbage palms (*Cordyline australis*). Looking like neither cabbages nor palms, these subtropical trees are in fact related to agaves, which is evident from the dense head of sword-shaped leaves that tops each branch. In June and July the older trees produce conspicuous panicles of heavily scented cream flowers. These are followed by pea-sized white berries which in the autumn can be found scattered around the garden by the activities of birds. The seeds germinate readily - so much so that without vigilant weeding there would be thickets rather than rows of these commanding plants.

While the cabbage palms are a key architectural element in creating the subtropical effect, it is the flower beds in the Walled Garden that provide the all-important

Above left. Cape marigolds, *Osteospermum jucundum*.

Above right. Angels' fishing rods or African harebells, *Dierama pulcherrimum*, overhang the pond in summer. The Royal Botanic Garden has an outstanding collection of dieramas but nowhere are they as effectively displayed as at Logan.

dazzling colours. The scene is set with beds of *Salvia* species (red *S. gesnerifolia*, pink *S. neurepia* and blue *S. semiatrata* and *S. ambigens*), interplanted with yellow *Calceolaria integrifolia* and pinkish-mauve *Antirrhinum australe*. The eye is then drawn to the lawn and avenue of cabbage palms where beds of half-hardy perennials are planted out each summer in the traditional manner, using mostly species and cultivars instead of the usual hybrids. The result is of greater botanical interest and gives a quite different range of colours. Some six to seven thousand plants are raised annually by the horticultural staff at Logan for this purpose. Though the display is varied from year to year, it generally includes the soft pinks of South African diascias (notably *D. rigescens*, *D. barberae* and *D. vigilis*), clear blue kingfisher daisies (*Felicia*) - also from southern Africa - and *Salvia patens* from Mexico. Among these stand out the unbeatable bright red of *Verbena chamaedrifolia*, and scarlet double nasturtiums (*Tropaeolum majus* 'Hermione Grashoff') which contrast with white and mauve Cape marigolds (*Osteospermum jucundum*).

Around the pool itself are larger-growing perennials. Very large, but of exquisite delicacy are the African harebells or angels' fishing rods (*Dierama pulcherrimum*), whose pink flowers are attached by thread-like stalks to wiry stems that arch gracefully under their weight. Dieramas belong to the iris family (Iridaceae) and grow from corms. They enjoy rich, moist, well-drained soil and in most parts of Britain are not sufficiently hardy to be left in the ground through the winter. There are about 25 species, mostly with pink flowers of various shades in summer. Several can be seen at Logan, including *D. pendulum* which is half the size of *D. pulcherrimum*.

Alongside the dieramas are bold clumps of another southern African member of the iris family, *Crocosmia* x *crocosmiiflora*. Commonly known as montbretia, this hybrid was first made about a century ago by crossing *C. aurea* and *C. pottsii*. Hardier and more prolific than either of its parents, montbretia soon made its escape from gardens and became widely naturalised. Its favourite haunts are waste ground and cliffs, presumably where it was first tipped from wheelbarrows after being weeded out from borders. Interestingly, it is especially common in the coastal areas of southwest Scotland around Logan, flourishing right down to the sea. Though attractive in its own right with upright one-sided spikes of orange flowers, rather like a miniature gladiolus, it has largely been superceded as a garden plant by varieties such as the vivid red 'Lucifer'. The latter is at least twice the size of the original hybrid and makes a magnificent summer border plant. Various other kinds of *Crocosmia* can be seen elsewhere in the garden, including *C. masonorum* whose flower spikes curve forward.

Fringing the pool border is the handsome banana-like foliage of *Cautleya spicata*, a Himalayan ginger whose tubular yellow flowers are held in dark red calyces. Though usually needing greenhouse conditions, this species grows outdoors at Logan and spreads vigorously, flowering from summer to early autumn. *Cautleya* is a small genus of just five species. Only one other - *C. gracilis* - is common in cultivation and this too is grown at Logan. Another hardy ginger from the Himalayas is *Roscoea auriculata* which has orchid-like flowers of a rich purple. It likes cool moist soil and is grown in the Peat Garden at Logan where it flowers in midsummer.

Through the row of cabbage palms that line the north side of the pool can be seen a large stand of blue African lilies (*Agapanthus*). These are mostly 'Headbourne Hybrids' which are generally hardier than the species. The umbels of flowers, which range from deep violet-blue to pale azure or white, are borne on erect stems over 2ft tall. Elsewhere in the garden is *A. africanus* with larger umbels of narrower pale blue flowers. Pleasing from an aesthetic point of view, but troublesome to the horticultural staff, is the colony of silkweed (*Asclepias syriaca*) from eastern North America which inexorably advances on the hybrid agapanthus. Very different but belonging to the same family, Asclepiadaceae, is *Marsdenia oreophila* from southwest China. This rare twining climber has leathery oval leaves and clusters of sweetly scented ivory flowers in late summer, which can be seen on the wall above the gate leading from the Terrace to the Castle Woodland.

Climbers and wall shrubs

The wall behind the agapanthus is colourful in summer with the red-and-yellow lanterns of *Abutilon megapotamicum* from Brazil, the red bottle brush (*Callistemon rigidus*) which is found wild in Australia, and the large pink daisies of the so-called climbing gazania, *Mutisia ilicifolia*. Abutilons and callistemons are normally grown

Top. Crocosmia is a southern African genus of the iris family. One of the most widely grown crocosmias is 'Lucifer', which at Logan is planted alongside angels' fishing rods and *Nepeta govaniana*.

Bottom. Cautleya spicata, a Himalayan member of the ginger family (Zingiberaceae), in which the Royal Botanic Garden has a special interest.

Above left. Blue African lilies, *Agapanthus*, occupy a large bed near the Centre Wall. At one end, they jostle for space with a silkweed, *Asclepias syriaca*, whose heavily scented, beige-pink flowers attract all manner of insects.

Above right. A red bottle brush, *Callistemon rigidus*, is one of several rather tender shrubs which are trained against the Centre Wall.

in cool greenhouses and conservatories. *Mutisia* is less well-known but just as striking, being one of the few members of the huge daisy family (Compositae) that climb. The genus *Mutisia* has about 60 species, all evergreen climbers native to South America, mainly in Chile, but are only hardy in warm gardens such as Logan.

Further along the wall are more tender summer-flowering climbers: a purple passion flower (*Passiflora umbilicata*) from Bolivia; *Trachelospermum asiaticum* from Japan and Korea; and the Chinese *T. jasminoides* which in July and August is covered in sweetly scented white flowers, shaped like propellers and resembling those of a periwinkle (*Vinca*), to which they are related. On the north side of the wall are climbing hydrangeas and an old specimen of the Chilean coral plant, *Berberidopsis corallina* (illustrated on page 156) which produces pendent racemes of little red bells in late summer.

Dahlias at Logan include the largest of all, *Dahlia imperialis*, which is chiefly grown for its tiers of dark grey-green foliage, and *D. merckii* which reaches 3ft and produces small flowers of palest lilac. Also grown is 'Bishop of Llandaff', an old variety but still one of the best, with dark bronze foliage and single deep red flowers.

Right. A climbing gazania, *Mutisia ilicifolia*, from Chile flowers against the West Wall throughout the summer and early autumn.

Above left. Passiflora umbilicata is an unusual purple passionflower from Bolivia.

Above right. Trachelospermum asiaticum, a climber native to Japan and Korea, produces scented jasmine-like flowers in summer.

Exotic herbaceous borders

Similar to a dahlia is *Cosmos atrosanguineus* which has almost black leaves and dark maroon flowers. Dramatic this may be, but it is the chocolate scent of the flowers that are the plant's main attraction. It too is grown from tubers that are lifted in the autumn and kept frost-free when dormant.

Other interesting herbaceous plants include *Geranium maderense* from Madeira, a half-hardy cranesbill with large, deeply cut palmate leaves and numerous magenta-pink flowers which appear in late spring and early summer. Nestling at the foot of the West Wall, it survives happily outdoors at Logan and reliably self-sows. The flowers of *Blumenbachia acanthifolia* are a true orange and reveal a surprising complexity at close quarters. However, approaching this plant too closely is inadvisable for, like all members of the family Loasaceae, it is covered in bristly, often stinging hairs.

In recent years half-hardy salvias or sages have become increasingly popular as conservatory and summer border plants. Their appeal lies in the aromatic attractive

Left. Cosmos atrosanguineus is a relative of the dahlias with dramatically dark foliage and chocolate-scented flowers.

Top. The complex flowers of *Blumenbachia acanthifolia* deserve a closer look - but not too close as, like all members of the family Loasaceae, the plant is covered in stinging hairs.

Bottom. *Salvia aurea* is one of many tender sages grown at Logan which have become popular in recent years for their aromatic foliage and colourful flowers.

Right. The half-hardy African genus *Phygelius* is well-represented at Logan. *P.* x *rectus* 'Salmon Leap' is seen here behind x *Venidio-arctotis* 'China Rose'.

foliage and the small but often brilliantly coloured flowers that are produced throughout the summer and autumn. The genus *Salvia* belongs to the mint family (Labiatae) and contains over 700 species. The essential oils from a number of species, including common sage (*Salvia officinalis*), clary (*S. clarea*) and pineapple sage (*S. rutilans*), are extracted for use in medicine and perfumery, or contribute their flavour to foods. Although salvias with flowers of red (such as *S. elegans* and *S. dombeyi*) or blue (*S. patens* and *S. cacaliifolia*, for example) are the most eye-catching, there is almost every other colour to be found in the genus. Among the more unusual of the 30 or more ornamental salvias grown at Logan are: *S. discolor* whose near-black flowers are in marked contrast to the downy white stems and foliage; the sticky-leaved *S. glutinosa* with pale yellow flowers; and the Mexican sage bush, *S. leucantha*, which late in the season produces white flowers from bright purple woolly calyces. Logan's borders are also noted for *Phygelius* and *Penstemon*. Both genera belong to

the Scrophulariaceae - the family which also includes foxgloves (*Digitalis*) and monkey flowers (*Mimulus*), as can be seen by their rather similar tubular, open-mouthed flowers. *Phygelius* is South African and *Penstemon* is native to various parts of the United States and Mexico. The colour range is different too, *Phygelius* having brick reds and greenish-yellows, while *Penstemon* has warmer reds, pinks, purples and mauves. All are excellent border plants, flowering for several months of the summer. They are, however, slightly tender and need sheltered conditions to survive the winter.

Other outstanding border plants include *Lobelia tupa* from Chile and two bastard jasmines, *Cestrum fasciculatum* from Mexico and *C. parqui* from western South America. The latter are usually grown as greenhouse shrubs in Britain. In the case of *C. fasciculatum* the flowers are tubular and maroon, while those of *C. parqui* are yellow and night-scented to attract moths, giving it the common name of lady-of-the-night. *Lobelia tupa* is a striking plant up to 5ft or more, with hairy foliage and large dark red flowers. Like many lobelias, it is extremely toxic and even smelling it may cause poisoning. The poisonous compounds in lobelias may, however, be put to good use, as several species are important medicinal plants. *L. syphilitica*, a blue-flowered species which can be found near the pool, was named after its use in the treatment of venereal disease.

Tender summer-flowering shrubs

Most visitors begin their exploration of Logan by entering the walled garden. At the entrance and along the neighbouring borders are many interesting fuchsias. The genus *Fuchsia* has around 100 species all told in Central and South America and just four in New Zealand. About 35 of these and easily as many varieties and hybrids are in the Royal Botanic Garden's collection, most of which are grown outdoors at Logan. The typical tubular shape of the flowers in bright reds, oranges and yellows indicate that many are pollinated by birds. Hardiest of all is *F. magellanica* which grows wild in Mexico, Peru, Chile and the Falkland Islands - and, one might add, in Cornwall, Eire and Logan, where it self-seeds and reaches 10ft or more. There are numerous cultivars, varying in flower and leaf colour and size: the pale pink 'Molinae' and 'Versicolor' with foliage variegated in grey-green, pink and cream being among the most noticeable.

The flowers of *F. magellanica* are what everyone thinks of as fuchsias but there is considerable variation within the genus. In several Mexican species - *F. microphylla* and *F. ravenii*, for example - the flowers are so small that the characteristic shape is barely distinguishable. Three New Zealand species can be seen at Logan. *F. excorticata* is a venerable old tree-like shrub in the south border which flowers from late winter onwards, rather than summer. Its unusual greenish flowers are borne singly directly from the trunk and main branches, and are followed by edible black berries. *F. perscandens* forms mounds of wiry stems and rounded leaves beside the path that runs along the south border. It is particularly difficult to recognise as a fuchsia, as the flowers are borne close to ground level beneath the foliage and are cryptically coloured green and purple. *F. procumbens* is of special interest to conservationists, surviving in the wild on only one or two coastal banks in the North Cape area of North Island, though widely cultivated for its intricately marked upright flowers and comparatively large pink berries.

Though very different in appearance, the genus *Eucryphia* has a similarly odd distribution in South America and Australasia. There are just five species, all of which thrive at Logan: the Tasmanian *E. lucida* and *E. milliganii*; *E. moorei* from New South Wales; and *E. cordifolia* and *E. glutinosa* which are native to Chile.

Top. The striking *Lobelia tupa* .

Bottom. *Fuchsia arborescens* forma *parva* produces minute upright flowers on magenta stalks, well clear of the foliage. Black fruits develop as the flowering period progresses, giving further interest to the display.

E. lucida flowers in July, with small fragrant pink-anthered flowers. The miniature of the genus is *E. milliganii*, a neat little shrub with sticky buds and flowers less than an inch across. At the other extreme is *E. cordifolia*, an 80ft tree in the wild which in late summer is a mass of much larger brown-anthered white flowers.

Logan also has fine collections of New Zealand hebes and parahebes, and daisy bushes (*Olearia*), many of which are of doubtful hardiness in most parts of Britain. With such a range of species and varieties, the flowering season is long, with something of interest throughout spring, summer and autumn. The season begins with *Olearia cheesemanii* and *O. arborescens* which stand out in the South Woodland when covered in their brilliant white daisies. Outstanding among summer flowerers is *O. semidentata* from the Chatham Islands, which has grey-

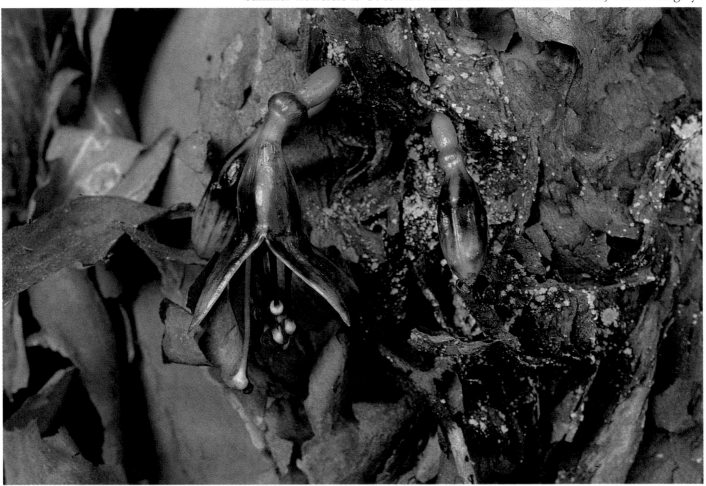

Fuchsia excorticata is one of the few fuchsias native to New Zealand. Its cryptic flowers sprout directly from the bark of the main trunk and branches.

green silver-backed foliage and loose clusters of lilac daisies from June to August. In late summer it is the turn of some of the less spectacular but delightfully scented species: *O. odorata* with wiry stems of minute spidery flowers; and *O. solandri*, a heath-like shrub with tiny fragrant white daisies. Thriving in mild coastal areas but often difficult to cultivate elsewhere is the evergreen South American genus *Escallonia*. One of the largest specimens at Logan is the *E.* 'Iveyi' in the Castle Woodland - a shrub 20ft or more which in August is completely covered in white flowers. This vigorous hybrid was made by crossing *E. bifida*, a white-flowered Brazilian species, with the blush-pink *E.* x *exoniensis*, itself a cross between the white-flowered *E. rosea* from Patagonia and the deep pink *E. rubra* from Chile.

The myrtle family (Myrtaceae), which includes eucalyptuses and bottle brushes as well as the myrtles themselves, is well-represented at Logan. This large family of about 100 genera and 3000 species of trees and shrubs occurs in almost all tropical and subtropical regions but is concentrated in South America and Australia. Several of Logan's specimens of *Eucalyptus coccifera* flower reliably each summer as does the closely related *Metrosideros*. Most spectacular is the New Zealand Christmas tree (*M. umbellata*), a winter-flowering species in its homelands but here flowering in late July or early August. The neat glossy leaves provide a perfect background for the radiant spiky red flowers. The huge specimen on the lawn behind the Centre Wall is of considerable age. From Chile comes *Myrtus luma*, a shrubby tree with attractive peeling bark, pretty white flowers and sweet, edible black and red fruits. Several old specimens can be found between the Tree Fern Lawn and the Centre Wall, where they flower in August. The antipodean tea trees (*Leptospermum*) belong to the myrtle family too. More commonly seen as greenhouse shrubs, at Logan they reach

Top. Among Logan's many daisy bushes is *Olearia semidentata*.

Bottom. The spectacular red flowers of the New Zealand Christmas tree, *Metrosideros umbellata*, appear in late Summer. When in bloom, the massive specimen in the Middle Walled Garden is a sight not to be missed.

20ft or more in height and bloom profusely in the summer with white or pink flowers that resemble miniature rock roses.

Other interesting families at Logan include the mallows (Malvaceae), among which are several outstandingly attractive but rather tender summer-flowering shrubs. An example is the genus *Hoheria* from New Zealand. Three of its five species (*H. glabrata*, *H. lyallii* and *H. sexstylosa*) are grown at Logan, all of which have white apple-blossom flowers. They form large leafy shrubs about 10ft tall and bloom freely in July and early August. Quite different is the African violet family (Gesneriaceae), best known for its house plants. One of its more unusual members, the Chilean mitre flower (*Mitraria coccinea*), flourishes at Logan. It forms a low spreading evergreen shrub which, given the chance, will climb up a wall or tree trunk and in late spring and throughout the summer produces bright orange-red velvety flowers.

AUTUMN AND WINTER

Late flowers

As Logan Botanic Garden specialises in southern hemisphere plants, it is not noted for 'autumn colour' - a phenomenon associated with deciduous trees and shrubs of northern temperate regions. There is, however, plenty of other colour and, as always, a rich diversity of plants to be seen which are scarce or unknown elsewhere in British gardens. Some of the late colour is provided by plants such as fuchsias and hebes which are, strictly speaking, summer flowering but, given an absence of frosts, continue well into November. There are also a number of genuinely late-flowering plants, such as nerines and gentians, that are in their prime as the days shorten and colder weather sets in. Interest is not confined to flowers though. Autumn is the

Left. The flowering season for crinums spans late summer and early autumn. These tender southern African bulbs include *Crinum moorei.*

Right. The trumpet creeper, *Campsis radicans,* is a rather tender plant grown in greenhouses and outdoors in sheltered places in the United Kingdom, but is an invasive alien in many parts of the United States.

season of berries and seed pods, and a time when evergreens and bark may be keenly appreciated.

Loveliest among autumn flowers are the lily-like blooms of three South African genera which are actually related to daffodils: *Crinum, Amaryllis* and *Nerine.* The crinums are the largest and earliest, beginning in August and continuing into October. Pink to white flowers are borne in umbels on stout stalks above disgracefully untidy strap-shaped leaves, for which they are generally forgiven on account of their late and lovely display. By comparison, nerines are impeccable, their neatly crisped flowers appearing before the leaves which in any case are tidy and unobtrusive. Nerines flower from September to November, producing stems of bright pink, narrow-petalled flowers. The hardiest and therefore most widely grown species is *N. bowdenii,* of which 'Fenwick's Variety' is the tallest and deepest in colour. Somewhere between a crinum and nerine in size is the sweetly scented *Amaryllis belladonna* which also flowers when leafless. Again the flowers are pink, fading to white in the throat, and strongly resemble lilies in appearance.

Something of interest can be found on Logan's extensive area of walls at any time of the year. One climber which should not be missed in autumn is the trumpet vine, *Campsis radicans,* a member of the family Bignoniaceae which consists mostly of tropical lianas. This self-clinging deciduous species from the southeastern United States bears handsome pinnate leaves and glorious two-tone orange and scarlet trumpet-shaped flowers. The flowers are produced on the current year's growth, appearing from September onward. Smaller in every respect but otherwise similar is the closely related Chilean glory flower, *Eccremocarpus scaber*, a short-lived evergreen tendril climber that is hardy in mild British gardens but usually dies back in the winter or self-sows and behaves like an annual, making at least 16ft of growth in a season. The tubular flowers are carried in racemes throughout the summer and autumn.

Also with tropical affinities is *Fascicularia bicolor*, a half-hardy relative of the pineapples (Bromeliaceae). Most of the family are epiphytes that perch up in trees in tropical American rainforests, but *Fascicularia* comes from cooler parts of Chile and is ground-dwelling (terrestrial). Some of Logan's clumps of *Fascicularia* are 3ft or more in height, indicating plants of considerable age. These can be seen in the borders near the main pond.

A number of shrubs flower in winter, with stray flowers in autumn or early spring. Logan shares most of these - viburnums, sarcococcas, daphnes etc. - with the other three gardens. Unique to Logan as outdoor winter-flowering shrubs are several species of *Correa* which are native to Australia and Tasmania. All are small to medium-sized compact evergreens, with elongated waxy bell-shaped flowers. In *C. backhousiana* they are greenish-white; crimson with green tips in *C. decumbens*; and, perhaps loveliest of all, are rose-pink in *C. pulchellum*. Specimens can be found on the Terrace and against the Centre Wall.

Logan's benificent climate enables the Royal Botanic Garden to grow many half-hardy trees outdoors where they reach proportions which could never be achieved under glass. Eucalyptus trees are an obvious example - over 20 species being grown at Logan, with specimens sufficiently large and numerous to be an important feature of the garden. The eucalypts are archetypal southern hemisphere trees, dominating the sclerophyll ('hard-leaf') forests of Australasia. There are about 500 species, varying considerably in hardiness but mostly needing ample moisture, warmth and a deep friable soil. Belonging to the myrtle family, they are well-represented at Logan, particularly in the woodland areas. Eucalypts are characterised by open crowns and waxy, often grey-green leaves, which hang downward to prevent overheating of the foliage. This habit creates a light and airy woodland with a rich understorey of shrubs and herbs in which forest fires are an integral part of the ecosystem. In order to resist damage by fire, eucalypts tend to shed their bark. The grey leaves are another

Left. *Fascicularia bicolor* forms dense rosettes of narrow spiny leaves, the outer ones of which reach 18in or more in length. The inner leaves are shorter and bright red, drawing the eye to a central cluster of silvery bracts from which pale blue flowers emerge in the autumn.

Right. *Correa* is a genus of tender winter-flowering shrubs from Australasia, which generally have neat evergreen foliage and bell-shaped flowers. Several species thrive outdoors at Logan, including the white-flowered *C. alba*.

attraction which in many species change shape, and sometimes also colour, as the tree matures. Generally rounded in young specimens and sickle-shaped when adult, the foliage in most species is aromatic, containing eucalyptus oil which has valuable medicinal properties. Eucalyptus fruits are woody capsules, known in Australia as gum nuts, which may be anything from minute to 2 inches in diameter and variously shaped - like flat-topped bowls or strangely sculpted. These fruits can easily be seen on specimens of *E. coccifera* in the South Woodland during the autumn.

Left. The Mount Wellington peppermint, *Eucalyptus coccifera*, sheds its bark in patches, leaving a smooth but mottled surface, whereas in some eucalypts it comes off in shreds. The shedding of bark helps them resist fire, which flickers quickly through the peeling sections, leaving the inner bark undamaged.

Right. Another of Logan's plants with interesting bark is *Polylepis australis*, a member of the rose family (Rosaceae) from Argentina. Though undistinguished in flower and foliage, it has the most extraordinary red-brown papery bark that peels away in scrolls.

Grasses and flaxes

Grasses and spiky-leaved plants are another element in the planting at Logan that gives it a subtropical air. Simple strap-shaped foliage is found in plants of widely differing habitats, but whether naturally waterside species or native to wide open plains or arid land, in cultivation they are most successful in punctuating more complex shapes and provide year-long interest in several areas of the garden. Close to the entrance, beside the avenue of Chusan palms, is a magnificent stand of giant grasses, dominated by *Cortaderia richardii*, an elegant pampas grass. Also from New Zealand and producing large plumes that last well into the winter is the Hunangemoho grass (*Chionocloa conspicua*).

The New Zealand flax, *Phormium tenax*, is an architectural plant with sword-shaped leaves that reach anything from 3ft to an impressive 10ft in length. Mature plants produce mighty branched panicles, about 15ft high, of dark red flowers in late summer which remain a feature for many months. The species has dull green leaves but there are variants with bronze or variegated foliage. The smaller *P. cookianum* has thinner, more flexible leaves and 3ft spikes of yellowish flowers. New Zealand flaxes are of commercial importance for their strong durable fibres which are used in matting and cordage. They are more or less hardy but do particularly well in mild coastal gardens such as Logan, where their high tolerance of salt spray makes them exceedingly useful as shelter plants.

Evergreens can be enjoyed at any time of the year but tend to be overlooked during the floriferous months of spring and summer. In autumn and winter, when gales are frequent, Logan's evergreens are appreciated in more ways than one as many are planted in shelter belts to break the force of the Irish Sea's salt-laden winds. The more recently planted wind breaks include some of the larger species of *Olearia*, such as *O. paniculata*, *O. traversii*, *O. macrodonta* and the Maori holly, *O. ilicifolia*, together with *Pittosporum tenuifolium* and *Griselinia littoralis*, New Zealand trees with dense foliage which is resistant to maritime winds. These are attractive foliage plants in their own right and are widely planted in mild areas as ornamentals.

Left. The New Zealand flax, *Phormium tenax*, has been planted throughout the garden but is especially attractive in the bed beneath *Eucalyptus pauciflora*. Here it is accompanied by grasses and other plants with grass-like foliage such as *Carex trifida* and *Helichrysum hookeri*.

Right. Logan has some very unusual conifers. One of the rarest is *Taiwania cryptomerioides* which grows wild only on the western slopes of Mount Morrison in Taiwan, from where it was introduced in 1920.

Tender evergreens

Anyone interested in conifers will appreciate that Logan has some very unusual species, mostly rather tender and from those parts of the world in which the garden has a special interest. On the lawn of the Middle Walled Garden can be found *Pilgerodendron uviferum* from the southern Andes of Chile and western Argentina, a very upright slow-growing species. Beside it grows a blue celery pine or toatoa, *Phyllocladus glaucus*, which is indigenous to the northern part of New Zealand's North Island. Celery pines are unusual in having flattened shoots instead of true leaves, giving the foliage an appearance midway between celery and oak - certainly not what we expect in a conifer! *Phyllocladus* is a genus of the podocarp family (Podocarpaceae), a group of conifers which is largely confined to the southern hemisphere. One of the dominant podocarps in New Zealand forests is the rimu, *Dacrydium cupressinum*, which has long pendulous branchlets of rather spiky whipcord foliage. A young specimen of this graceful tree has been established in the South Woodland. Other interesting conifers at Logan include the Prince Albert yew (*Saxegothaea conspicua*), a yew-like podocarp from southern Chile and adjoining parts of Argentina, and the smooth Tasmanian cedar, *Athrotaxis cupressoides* which is one of three species in a genus restricted to the western mountains of Tasmania.

From southern hemisphere conifers to Himalayan gingers - even this brief survey reveals Logan as a plantsman's paradise where, in any season, the visitor gets the chance to encounter exotic species which are grown nowhere else in Scotland.

DAWYCK BOTANIC GARDEN

*D*awyck became Edinburgh's third specialist garden in 1978 when Lt Col A N Balfour gifted 60 acres (24ha) of the family's historic arboretum to the nation. The estate of Dawyck is situated 28 miles (45km) south of Edinburgh and about 8 miles (13km) southwest of Peebles, in a range of hills which give rise to both the Clyde and Tweed rivers. It lies on Silurian formations, consisting of glacial drift which gives a porous shallow soil, stony in texture and acidic, with areas of rich peaty humus along the stream that bisects the arboretum from south to north. The garden rises from 750ft (230m) beside Dawyck House, which is privately owned, to 900ft (280m) in the southwest corner on the slope of Scrape Hill. The relatively high altitude and inland location make Dawyck one of the coldest parts of Britain with average winter temperatures of −6.7°C (20°F). In contrast, the annual rainfall averages only 35-45in (890-1140mm) and is fairly evenly distributed throughout the year. This cold dry climate - a far cry from subtropical Logan and oceanic Benmore - may be described as continental, making Dawyck a good site for trees and shrubs originating from areas with harsher climates. These would not thrive in the more genial regimes of Logan or Benmore and for reasons of space, cannot be accommodated in Edinburgh.

Opposite. Dawyck House seen from above the Azalea Walk. The House remains in private ownership.

Aerial view of the estate of Dawyck.

Top. Dawyck is renowned as the home of the Dawyck beech (*Fagus sylvatica* 'Dawyck'). This columnar form of the common beech was discovered as a seedling by Sir John Naesmyth, who planted vast numbers of native and exotic trees at Dawyck in the second half of the 19th century.

Bottom. Dawyck's oldest Douglas firs were raised from the original seed sent by David Douglas from Oregon in the 1820s. This specimen grows beside a giant fir (*Abies grandis*) in Scrape Glen.

HISTORY

Three families over three centuries have shaped the development of Dawyck as one of Scotland's greatest gardens. The first of these was the Veitch family which hailed from Jedburgh and in 1491 exchanged the Mains of Syntoun (near Jedburgh) for Easter Dawyck. Later to become an illustrious name in British horticulture, they founded the famous nursery of John Veitch & Sons at Exeter and subsequently in Chelsea. The Veitches made history by introducing the first exotic tree species into Scotland. Through the Veitches' endeavours, the native oak, hazel, birch and Scots pine were joined in the 1650s by the horse chestnut (*Aesculus hippocastanum*), an extremely hardy and attractive species from eastern Europe. The last of the original horse chestnuts survived until the storm of 17 December 1932. In 1680 the European silver firs (*Abies alba*), which dominate mountainous regions of France, Germany and Switzerland, were planted among the sessile oak (*Quercus petraea*) in Heron Wood. Some of the original silver firs stand here to this day, though most succumbed to the hurricane which swept across central Scotland in 1968.

The Naesmyths at Dawyck

In 1691 the estate of Dawyck passed from the Veitch family to James Naesmyth of Posso, who carried out major improvements to both the house and garden. On his death in 1720, the property and baronetcy (he was knighted in 1706) were inherited by his son, the second Sir James Naesmyth. In his hands, Dawyck continued to develop, the family interest in horticulture being furthered by his professional status as a botanist who had trained under Linnaeus. In 1725 Sir James Naesmyth, accompanied, so the story goes, by the great Linnaeus himself, planted European larches (*Larix decidua*) at Dawyck which were among the first in Scotland. Five years later, in 1730, he planted a lime avenue which stretched for three quarters of a mile to the east of the house. He also introduced, for the first time in Scotland, the maritime pine (*Pinus pinaster*) in 1742. Though Mediterranean in origin, this species is hardy as far north as Edinburgh and thrives in dry situations. Other first introductions included North American conifers, such as the balsam fir (*Abies balsamea*) in 1743 and the white spruce (*Picea glauca*) in 1759. Broadleaved species were introduced too, notably the North American sugar maple (*Acer saccharum*) in 1754 and the Lombardy poplar (*Populus nigra* var. *italica*) in 1765.

It was the fourth Baronet, Sir John Murray Naesmyth, who transformed the estate, creating almost 2000 acres (809ha) of mixed woodlands. He commissioned a new house to be built after the original mansion was destroyed by fire in 1830. Dawyck House was designed by William Burn and completed in 1832. His love of trees and interest in new species coincided with the age of the great plant hunters. He obtained seeds from James Veitch's nurseries in Exeter and Chelsea which were then financing plant-hunting expeditions to eastern Asia and North America. Among Veitch's collectors was Thomas Lobb who in 1853 sent back seed of the giant Sierra redwood (*Sequoiadendron giganteum*) from California. In the same era, the Horticultural Society (later the Royal Horticultural Society) sent David Douglas to Oregon in western North America. His expeditions of 1824 and 1829, to which the Naesmyths subscribed, resulted in the introduction of many magnificent trees - the best-known being the Douglas fir (*Pseudotsuga menziesii*). Some of Dawyck's largest conifers - notably the mighty Douglas firs in Scrape Glen - were raised from Douglas's original seed collections.

Sir John Naesmyth also purchased plants from Lawson's nursery in Edinburgh, an establishment which pioneered the introduction of several outstanding conifers, notably the Lawson cypress (*Chamaecyparis lawsoniana*). Particularly successful was the black or Austrian pine (*Pinus nigra*), the original specimen of which was planted by Sir John Naesmyth in 1840 and by 1990, at 138ft, was the tallest in Britain. Sir John's interest in trees was not, however, confined to the new and exotic. He also planted a large number of Scots pines, raised from seed from the native pine woods of Braemar. This planting can be seen on the hill to the east of Scrape Glen. Landscaping was another of his concerns and he employed Italian artisans to create the terraces, steps, bridges and pillared urns that continue to give interest and structure to the garden.

But Sir John Naesmyth's most original contribution to Dawyck was his discovery of a beech seedling with a remarkably upright habit. He was so taken with this find that he had it transplanted from the wood near Dawyck Mill to the immediate grounds of the house where he could keep an eye on its development. Sure enough, it retained the distinctive conical shape and became known as the Dawyck beech (*Fagus sylvatica* 'Dawyck'). The original tree is now 95ft, and specimens propagated from it can be seen at the entrance and elsewhere in the garden.

The Balfour era

The estate changed hands in 1897, passing to Mrs Alexander Balfour, widow of a businessman from Leven in Fife who had made his fortune in Liverpool. The Balfours - who were not related to the Royal Botanic Garden's two Regius Keepers of that name - had a son, Frederick Robert Stephen, who was 24 when Dawyck was acquired. Working in California he saw, in the glory of their natural surroundings, trees remembered from Dawyck. Inspired, he started collecting seeds and plants to swell Dawyck's arboretum. After settling once again in Britain, he returned on several occasions to make further collections. In the course of these explorations, F R S Balfour - Fred to his friends - became an authority on the plants and history of plant collecting in western North America, publishing accounts and photographs of his findings in various journals, from *Country Life* to *Proceedings of the Linnean Society*.

Over the years, Balfour established a comprehensive collection of new introductions which were judged to have horticultural merit and likely to thrive at Dawyck. He

Top. F R S Balfour was an avid collector and authority on trees and shrubs. This photograph, taken in 1931, shows him beside *Rhododendron vernicosum*, a species from northwest China.

Bottom left. Sir John Naesmyth commissioned Italian craftsmen to create the pillared urns, steps and bridges which remain a striking feature of the garden.

Bottom right. Brewer's weeping spruce was introduced by F R S Balfour in 1911 from Oregon's Siskiyou Mountains.

The North American salmonberry (*Rubus spectabilis*). Though attractive in flower in spring (*Top*) and autumn (*Bottom*), it became Dawyck's worst weed, spreading over much of the garden as an impenetrable thicket of thorny 10ft stems, now substantially cleared.

carried out large-scale trials of conifers which had potential in forestry, comparing, for instance, the European larch (*Larix decidua*) with the hybrid, Japanese and Siberian larches (*L.* x *eurolepis*, *L. kaempferi* and *L. gmelinii*), respectively. Awarded the Victoria Medal of Honour in 1927 'for his active part in forestry and arboriculture for many years passed', he had established contacts worldwide in order to obtain new species of trees and shrubs. A large number of acquisitions resulted from collections made by Ernest Wilson in the Far East on behalf of both Messrs Veitch and the Arnold Arboretum in Boston, Massachusetts. For example, Balfour raised 370 plants of *Prunus sargentii* from seed sent in 1911 by Professor Sargent of the Arnold Arboretum from Wilson's Japanese collections.

F R S Balfour was a prodigious planter of rhododendrons, many of which originated from Wilson's expeditions to China. In the Naesmyth's time, there were just 20 species; by 1930 Balfour had increased this to 120, plus numerous hybrids - some of which he had raised himself.

Balfour's most memorable introduction was Brewer's weeping spruce (*Picea breweriana*), a species endemic to Oregon's Siskiyou Mountains which had been discovered in 1884 and named after an eminent Californian botanist. In August of 1907 Balfour and his wife tracked down two small colonies of this rarity at 7000ft (2133m) and arranged for a local contact to dig up some young plants at a more suitable time of the year and nurture them in his own garden until Balfour's next visit. In 1911 Balfour returned to carry off his prize - 14 healthy saplings packed in a wooden box, 11 of which survived. Brewer's weeping spruce grows at high altitudes in dry conditions - a recipe for success at Dawyck where it has become as closely identified with the garden as the Dawyck beech.

Memorable for different reasons was his introduction of the salmonberry (*Rubus spectabilis*), whose bright pink flowers attract hummingbirds in the moist forests of the Pacific northwest and bear orange-yellow, occasionally purple, raspberry-like fruits. First planted by Balfour in 1908 as game cover, it adapted to Dawyck's very different conditions and served the purpose well. Then, after the devastating hurricane of 1968 toppled an estimated 50,000 trees at Dawyck, it spread unchecked to cover half the garden with thorny canes 10ft tall. Despite its attractive flowers and fruits, delightful autumn tints and value as game cover, the salmonberry was to become the garden's worst weed.

F R S Balfour died in 1945, leaving Dawyck in the hands of his son, Lt Col A N Balfour, who had the joyless responsibility of clearing the mountains of debris left by the hurricane. Aware of the garden's great historical importance, the Balfour family began negotiations with the Royal Botanic Garden and handed the arboretum over to the nation in 1978.

For the first decade, work at the renamed Dawyck Botanic Garden was taken up with clearing the arboretum of dead and dangerous trees, waging war on the salmonberry, and with the provision of roads and essential garden buildings. In addition to clearing operations and the erection of boundary and deer fences, windbreaks were replanted with thousands of young pines, and progressively paths and vistas were opened up for the enjoyment of visitors. Most significantly, after a gap of some 35 years, the planting of new trees and shrubs - largely from wild sources - recommenced. Scientific collections of genera such as *Acer*, *Berberis*, *Betula*, *Cotoneaster*, *Metasequoia*, *Sorbus* and *Spiraea* are being established. These new plantings and the continuing development of the infrastructure are re-establishing Dawyck as one of the country's finest arboreta. Dawyck Botanic Garden is becoming both a vital part of the Royal Botanic Garden Edinburgh's research, conservation and education programmes and an outstanding amenity for visitors to the Scottish Borders.

SPRING

Spring comes late to Dawyck, its hosts of daffodils still in bud when in many parts of the country they are fading. Far from being a disadvantage, this is often a bonus for visitors during the Easter holidays, enabling those from other areas to enjoy the spring flowers all over again. And the daffodils at Dawyck are a sight worth seeing, their lively yellow lining the drive and transfiguring large areas of grass, which for the rest of the year is but a green foreground for the garden's trees and shrubs. Less conspicuous are the cowslips and other diminutive wild flowers that stud the grassy approaches to the chapel and elsewhere - a reminder that the native ground flora and other wildlife thrives in the relatively undisturbed setting of an arboretum.

Top left. Expanses of daffodils fill grassy areas of Dawyck in the spring. The planting of daffodils was started by F R S Balfour who acquired a ton of bulbs every year for 20 years from Tresco in the Scilly Isles.

Top right. Wild flowers abound at Dawyck. Beneath a mighty western hemlock (*Tsuga heterophylla*) is a mass of greater stitchwort (*Stellaria holostea*) and Welsh poppies (*Meconopsis cambrica*).

Bottom. Cherry blossom is a delightful feature of Dawyck in spring. Rather different from most are the cylindrical clusters of almond-scented flowers produced by the bird cherry (*Prunus padus*).

Cherries, Oemleria and crab apples

The daffodils, and later the bluebells, are accompanied by a flurry of cherry blossom from more than a dozen different species. First to greet visitors are several specimens of *Prunus* x *dawyckensis* near the entrance, which open their pale pink flowers in April. Something of a mystery, this cherry appeared in the garden following a number of introductions from Ernest Wilson's expeditions to China.

The main collection of cherries is on Chapel Bank. Here among the many species which produce typical blossom are some that instead have racemes (cylindrical clusters) of flowers. These include the bird cherry (*P. padus*) which grows wild across northern Asia and Europe, from Japan to the British Isles. Its almond-scented white flowers are quite delightful in late spring. Closely related, but from eastern North America, is the choke cherry (*P. virginiana*), a large shrub or small tree which bears pendent white spikes of blossom, followed by dangling clusters of small sour cherries that from a distance look like redcurrants. The similar but smaller western choke cherry, *P. virginiana* var. *demissa*, which F R S Balfour came across *en route* for the Brewer's weeping spruces, can be seen near the entrance.

Closely related to *Prunus* but quite unlike any cherry in appearance is *Oemleria cerasiformis*, a suckering shrub from California which has a rather graceful arching habit. Commonly known as the oso berry or Indian plum on account of its use by

North American Indians as a food, it resembles a flowering currant when in bloom, with pendent clusters of tiny fragrant white bells which appear in early spring. Male and female flowers are borne on different plants, making it necessary to have both in close proximity if the purple plum-like berries are to be produced. There are oso berries near the entrance and the lower reaches of the stream.

Among the cherries and around the chapel are a number of crab apples (*Malus*) which add to the floral display in spring. Standing out are two Chinese species, *M. halliana* and *M. spectabilis*, which both have deep pink buds, opening to pale pink. Though similar when in flower, their fruits are quite different - those of the former being small and purple, while the latter bears yellow crab apples.

Rugged rhododendrons

F R S Balfour tried out virtually every new rhododendron that came his way, determining by trial and error which could withstand the garden's cold winters and relatively low rainfall. Today, the requirements of most species are known and in general only the hardiest and those most tolerant of dry conditions are planted at Dawyck. In fact, Dawyck's rhododendron collection of some 80 species serves as a guide to the toughest, most resilient plants which, given the right soil and level of light, will thrive in the coldest of British gardens. The peak flowering season is from April to June. In addition to those on Rhododendron Walk, there are rhododendrons along Scrape Glen and near the entrance.

Some of the early introductions did indeed prove hardy. The yellow-flowered *R. lacteum* was originally raised from seed sent back by George Forrest from the Sino-Himalaya in 1910. Though perfectly hardy, it is quite demanding in other respects,

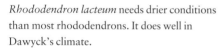

Rhododendron lacteum needs drier conditions than most rhododendrons. It does well in Dawyck's climate.

apparently needing well-drained, decidedly acid soil and actually preferring the relatively cool dry climate which is Dawyck's forte. Among Ernest Wilson's collections, the most successful at Dawyck were *R. oreodoxa* var. *fargesii*, a floriferous pink-flowered species with smooth oval leaves that curl up in cold (or hot) weather but remain undamaged, and *R. calophytum*, the hardiest of all large-leaved species, whose trusses of maroon-centred near-white flowers are beautifully poised above the downward-pointing foliage in early spring. Rather earlier and not quite so tough, though still successful at Dawyck is the closely related *R. argyrophyllum*, which is distinguished largely by its taller habit and longer silver-backed leaves.

Well-suited to drier, even slightly alkaline soils and cold situations - at least in its hardier forms from high altitudes - is the lovely *R. decorum*, which in late spring produces tight trusses of wide-open flowers which are apple-blossom-pink and fragrant. F R S Balfour remarked in *The Rhododendron Society Notes* that this species flowered reliably every year, even after 41° of frost! Also doing best in the drier eastern parts of Britain is *R. souliei*, another species from Sichuan. Its almost flat pink to white flowers, which appear in May and June, are complemented by rounded leaves which are attractively glaucous when young.

Dawyck's Azalea Walk is one of the garden's most colourful features when flowering in May and June. It is also an excellent vantage point for viewing the house against the background of hills. Many of the plants are Ghent, Exbury and Knap Hill hybrids but among them is the summer-flowering *R. occidentale* from western North America, which produces its deliciously scented pink-flushed white flowers in June. This species was among half a dozen or so wild-lifted American azaleas that F R S Balfour tried at Dawyck, but it excelled them all, flowering freely every year.

The Azalea Walk is a highlight of Dawyck in late spring and early summer.

New leaves

Over half of Dawyck Botanic Garden consists of semi-natural woodland in which beech (*Fagus sylvatica*) predominates. The woodland walks are always enjoyable but never more so than in late spring when the new beech leaves unfurl. From the bursting of the buds to full expansion takes about two weeks, during which time they are an almost luminous acid green that draws one's gaze upward to admire their mosaic against the sky. Once the foliage has developed, it darkens in colour and sheds its silken coat. Flowering occurs in May as the leaves expand; the inconspicuous female flowers being upright, with a bulbous base topped by a three-lobed style; and the males consisting of a bobble of cream stamens that dangles on a long stalk.

Although beech trees are so plentiful at Dawyck and in its environs, they are not native to this part of the country. Most of Scotland's beeches were planted as ornamentals on estates during the 18th century, from where they seeded to form large stands in the surrounding countryside - a process aided by both red and grey squirrels. The Beech Walk at Dawyck was planted in the 1790s. It is a fine avenue, the grass drive towered over on one side by a steep bank of ancient beeches, with an equally steep drop on the other side which places the visitor on a level with the treetops below. As a landscape it is most successful, giving space and perspective in an otherwise densely planted area.

Left. The new leaves of beech unfold in May and are covered with silvery-white hairs which protect them against cold and ultraviolet radiation.

Right. The Beech Walk dates back to the 1790s. Cut into a steep hillside, it provides many interesting vistas.

Variants of the common beech are equally attractive when in new leaf. Dawyck has fine copper beeches (forma *purpurea*) on the Chapel Bank and the unusual 'Tricolor' on the bank above the Swiss Bridge. There is a fern-leaved beech ('Asplenifolia') too. This can be seen near the entrance, where there is also a rare cut-leaved hazel (*Corylus avellana* 'Heterophylla') which has extremely pretty foliage. The latter is an outstanding specimen and the only example in the Royal Botanic Garden's Living Collection.

Among the other trees that stand out in spring are the maples (*Acer*) with their ornamental lobed leaves and chains of flowers which, though in themselves inconspicuous, are an attractive yellow-green or wine red *en masse*, especially in species that flower before the new leaves open, such as the Norway maple (*A. platanoides*). On closer inspection, the familiar 'keys' can be seen in their earliest stages of development. The Japanese maples (*A. palmatum*) in Scrape Glen, whose new leaves are delicate shades of green and pink, are perhaps the most easily recognised. The red Norway maple (*A. platanoides* 'Schwedleri') on Policy Bank also draws attention in spring, with its glossy copper-coloured foliage. Vine-leaved maples (*A. circinatum*) occur here and there along the stream. These denizens of western North America's temperate rain forests have adapted quite well to Dawyck's colder and drier regime. Forming shrubs rather than trees, they are attractive in spring, with their rounded leaves and modest floral display in its muted shades of red and white.

Left. Foliage of the red Norway maple in spring.

Right. An urn stands beside the trunk of a Sierra redwood; adjacent rhododendrons provide late spring colour.

Fastigiates

An upright or fastigiate habit, in which the branches grow almost vertically, is characteristic of many conifers but is unusual among deciduous species. When it does occur in a species that would normally have spreading branches, the clone in question is commonly named 'Fastigiata'. This freak of nature rarely comes true from seed, so it must be propagated vegetatively - usually by grafting. Fastigiates combine the best of both worlds - a columnar, conifer-like shape with seasonal changes in foliage and, in certain cases, the attractions of blossom and fruits. They are therefore of great interest to horticulture for situations which do not permit overhanging branches, such as streets and car parks, and in positions where space is limited.

Dawyck is renowned as the home of the fastigiate beech, *Fagus sylvatica* 'Dawyck', which was a chance discovery made by Sir John Naesmyth and diligently propagated until its fame spread far and wide. The original Dawyck beech is in the grounds of Dawyck House which is not open to the public. However, there are fine specimens beside the Botanic Garden car park and on the bank above the Swiss Bridge.

Among other interesting fastigiate trees growing, though not originating at Dawyck, are several hornbeams (*Carpinus betulus* 'Fastigiata') found near the entrance and on Policy Bank. There are also some exceptionally narrow specimens of the so-called cypress oak (*Quercus robur* 'Fastigiata') - an interesting rather than handsome tree. One of the most remarkable is beside the lower reaches of the stream, which though 75ft tall, is only 4ft wide. It is also a good example of the dilemmas faced by Botanic Garden staff in maintaining Dawyck's historic trees, as it was planted right beside a Nootka cypress (*Chamaecyparis nootkatensis*) when the eventual dimensions of these trees were unknown. Though encroaching on each other (much to the detriment of the oak which needs to stand clear if it is to be fully appreciated), both specimens are healthy and of importance, but one day it may be necessary to decide which has to be removed.

Left. One of the most striking fastigiate trees in the collection at Dawyck is the exceptionally narrow cypress oak.

Right. The oso berry (*Oemleria cerasiformis*) is a graceful Californian shrub. It resembles a flowering currant (*Ribes*) when in bloom, but in fact is closely related to cherries.

SUMMER

Dawyck's cold climate, with its frosty winters and late springs, suits many montane trees and shrubs, even if it sounds somewhat inhospitable to potential visitors. However, this continental weather pattern also affords summer conditions that are as warm as and often drier than many other parts of Scotland.

Late spring and early summer are in fact some of the loveliest times of the year to visit Dawyck, with all the new leaves unfurled but still fresh and herbaceous perennials at their best. The planting of perennials on the banks of the stream and also as an understorey for the trees and shrubs began in 1987 and continues as new areas are cleared. These plantings consist mainly of species with bold foliage - astilbes, bergenias, hostas, rodgersias and herbaceous saxifrages - providing a contrast to the woody plants and large expanses of grass. Hardy ferns are well-represented too, notably along Rhododendron Walk where there are some fine colonies of the oak fern (*Gymnocarpium dryopteris*) - an attractive species which is quite common in Scotland. There are also spectacular beds of the Himalayan blue poppy (*Meconopsis* x *sheldonii*) which form pools of sky blue beside the stream and beneath the trees.

The fabled Himalayan poppy grows to perfection in Dawyck's cool acid conditions. Among the finest is the hybrid *Meconopsis x sheldonii*.

Summer-flowering shrubs

Though the peak flowering time for trees and shrubs is in the spring, a number wait until summer. These include rhododendrons such as *R. brachyanthum* and *R. maximum*, as well as the azalea *R. occidentale*, whose spring-like blooms often come as a surprise to visitors in July. More familar as summer-flowering subjects are the cotoneasters which in most cases produce their tiny but numerous white or pink-flushed flowers in June, and the spiraeas which vary in their flowering time from late spring to September, according to the species. Again, the predominant colour is white to pink but the effect much more showy. Of special interest is *Spiraea veitchii* which is believed to have been raised from seed collected in China by Ernest Wilson. It is the tallest of the spiraeas, a worthwhile distinction in June and July when its arching 12ft branches are wreathed in white blossom. Both *Cotoneaster* and *Spiraea* belong to the rose family (Rosaceae) but the former is more varied in terms of habit, from tree-sized bushes to completely prostrate shrubs. The cotoneaster collection is therefore spread over a number of locations, according to habit, while the spiraeas are mainly in Scrape Glen.

Opposite. Blue Himalayan poppies flourish beside the conifers of Scrape Glen.

Left. The magnificent larch on the lawn beside Dawyck House is possibly the first specimen to be planted in Scotland, although it has suffered the ravages of storms in recent years.

Below. Large colonies of the oak fern can be found along Rhododendron Walk. One of the loveliest of native ferns, it is quite common in Scotland and northern parts of England and Wales, but rare elsewhere.

Great conifers of Dawyck

The great majority of conifers are of course evergreen, which makes them more constant in appearance from one season to the next than deciduous trees. Arguably at their loveliest when covered in snow, they are nevertheless at their most interesting in the summer when fringed with new needles and bearing a new crop of cones. Conifers are Dawyck's crowning glory, with a number of outstanding specimens in terms of size, history and rarity which few other gardens in Britain can rival. The measuring of trees is an age-old preoccupation of arboriculturists, landowners and historians alike. One of Dawyck's original larches was known simply as the Tall Larch and was so impressive at the time, being 80ft when 108 years old, that it was described in Loudon's *Arboretum et Fruticum* (1838). Techniques for measuring and ageing trees are rather more sophisticated now than in the 19th century - F R S Balfour's method was to send a boy up with a fishing rod and long tape! - and the statistics gathered are generally used for more scientific purposes. There is nevertheless always an element of straightforward curiosity over which is the biggest or oldest, as anyone visiting Dawyck will discover when they stand before its mightiest specimens.

Top. Foliage of the European silver fir (*Abies alba*).

Bottom. Sierra redwoods are native to the Pacific coast of North America and despite Dawyck's drier climate, there are a number of magnificent specimens.

Japanese and European firs

Dawyck's champion conifers include two Japanese species. One is a Nikko fir (*Abies homolepis* var. *umbellata*), raised from Wilson's seed, which has now reached 79ft. This tough adaptable species has distinctive violet-blue cones which, unusually for a conifer, are in good years borne at every level of the tree, rather than only in the uppermost branches. The other is a Maries fir (*A. mariesii*), a subalpine conifer from Honshu, which is an outstanding 75.5ft - most specimens of this species reaching little more than 50ft. Britain's largest specimen of the Austrian black pine (*Pinus nigra*), which measures 131ft, can be seen near the path leading up Policy Bank to Shaw Brae. The oldest trees at Dawyck are some of the European silver firs (*Abies alba*) planted in Heron Wood by the Veitches in 1680. When these pioneers reached

maturity they were, at over 130ft, the tallest conifers then growing in the British Isles.

North American giants

Some of the tallest trees at Dawyck are North American conifers, a good selection of which can be seen on Policy Bank and lower down along the stream. These include over a dozen magnificent Sierra redwoods (*Sequoiadendron giganteum*). The largest Douglas firs were planted in 1835, having been raised from seed sent back by David Douglas in 1827. They are among the most majestic of conifers, reaching over 300ft in the wild and exceeding 200ft in British conditions. The Douglas fir's scientific name, *Pseudotsuga menziesii*, pays tribute to Archibald Menzies, Scottish botanist and student of John Hope, who went on Captain Vancouver's expedition of 1792 and wrote the first description of this species which David Douglas was later to introduce. Fast-growing and with strong attractive timber (known as Oregon or British Columbian pine), the Douglas fir transformed forestry worldwide and is now grown on a vast scale in virtually all temperate regions. Sadly, it is still being cleared from virgin forests in Canada and the United States, so that giant wild specimens are now few and far between.

Another of Archibald Menzies' discoveries was the Nootka cypress (*Chamaecyparis nootkatensis*), which occurs in the wild from Alaska to Oregon. This perfectly conical tree bears sprays of flattened foliage which are held in drooping vertical plates, giving the effect of a verdant waterfall. There are several fine specimens at Dawyck dating from 1859, the oldest in Britain, which are easily spotted near the lower stream and beside the path leading to the chapel. Western hemlocks (*Tsuga heterophylla*) come from the same part of the world as Douglas firs and are important both for timber and as a source of tannin for the leather industry. There are several splendid western hemlocks at Dawyck which provide an imposing backdrop to Rhododendron Walk.

There are few conifers more impressive than the giant (or grand) and noble firs (*Abies grandis* and *A. procera*), for which we again have to thank David Douglas. The noble fir may be a mite smaller than the giant fir but wins outright in terms of beauty, with upward curving blue-grey needles on antler-shaped branches and huge cylindrical cones. Dawyck has about a dozen fine specimens of the noble fir, the tallest planted in 1855 being 120ft.

Top. The noble fir is easily recognised by its blue-grey foliage (*left*) and antler-shaped branches.

Bottom. The oldest Nootka cypresses in Britain can be seen at Dawyck.

Weeping, Serbian and Balfour spruces

Quite different from any other western North American species is Brewer's weeping spruce (*Picea breweriana*). All mature trees of this species at Dawyck were lifted from the Siskiyou Mountains (which bridge northern California and southern Oregon) by F R S Balfour in 1908 and were the first to reach Britain. Brewer's weeping spruce is not closely related to any other spruce and has a very limited distribution, with a total population of about 5000, confined to a few small areas in this one range of mountains.

The Serbian spruce (*P. omorika*) is not dissimilar to the Brewer's weeping spruce in habit, but makes a tight spire of slightly upturned branches. Again with a restricted distribution, the limestone valley of the Drina in Yugoslavia, its habit also readily sheds snow. Interestingly, wild trees vary in their degree of narrowness, being broadest in the valley bottom and extremely tapered at high altitudes where snowfalls are heavier. Dawyck's specimens can be seen at opposite ends of the garden, to the south near Dynamo Pond (a 1988 planting) and in the extreme east, planted in 1910.

The Balfour spruce (*P. balfouriana*) was named in honour of F R S Balfour. Originally regarded as a variety of the Likiang spruce (*P. likiangensis* var. *balfouriana*), it was first grown at Dawyck from seed sent by Ernest Wilson. It grows wild in very dry areas and is therefore well-suited to Dawyck's conditions. There are several specimens in the extreme north of the garden, where they can be recognised by their glaucous foliage and purple cones. These include Britain's tallest which tops 100ft.

The dawn redwood story

The discovery of the dawn redwood (*Metasequoia glyptostroboides*) is one of the most famous stories in botanical history. The species was first described and named by the Japanese palaeontologist S Miki in 1941 from material 20 million years old. Then, by extraordinary coincidence, living specimens of this fossil species were seen in southern China, on the border of western Hubei and northeastern Sichuan. Within a few years the identification had been verified and seeds were collected, the first to enter Britain being sent by the Arnold Arboretum, from which Edinburgh's first specimens were raised. In no time at all, this attractive and uniquely interesting tree could be seen in virtually every botanic garden and arboretum in the temperate world.

Right. A grove of young Chinese dawn redwoods (*Metasequoia glyptostroboides*) was planted beside the stream in 1987 as part of the Royal Botanic Garden Edinburgh's Conifer Conservation Project.

Below. The flaky fir (*Abies squamata*) is extremely rare in cultivation, and in the wild, where it is restricted to high mountains between China and Tibet. Dawyck's solitary specimen is probably the finest in Britain.

The dawn redwood is a fast-growing deciduous conifer, conical in shape with a deeply fluted, often buttressed trunk and fibrous red-brown bark that peels away in shaggy strips. The short, light green needles are soft in texture and arranged in flat rows down either side of short branchlets, giving a feathery effect. In the autumn they change colour through pinky-fawn to russett. Mature trees in the wild apparently reach 130ft.

The flaky fir

Dawyck's rarest conifer is the flaky fir (*Abies squamata*) which was introduced from China by Ernest Wilson in 1910. For one reason or another very few of Wilson's seedlings reached maturity. Until recently Dawyck was probably unique among gardens in having two specimens. One of these was blown down in a gale in 1983, leaving a solitary - though splendid - remaining flaky fir in the Royal Botanic Garden's collection. Experimental propagation using scions of the fallen tree were successfully grafted on to rootstocks of Korean and Caucasian firs (*A. koreana* and *A. nordmanniana*). In due course, these will be planted out at Dawyck to increase the perilously low numbers of cultivated flaky firs, which in the whole of Britain number less than ten.

The flaky fir is not just rare in cultivation but, like Brewer's weeping spruce, is also restricted to a very small area in the wild, to the west of Tatien-Lu in western Sichuan, on the border with Tibet. It also has the distinction of growing in extremely dry conditions at higher altitudes than any other tree, forming forests at 12,000-15,420ft (3657-4700m). The common name derives from its mahoghany-coloured bark that is shed in thin papery flakes from the age of about five years.

A Caledonian forest

At the end of the Ice Age most of Scotland was covered in tundra - vegetation consisting largely of mosses, lichens and sedges, with relict populations of birch. As the climate improved, the pioneering birch trees expanded their range, in turn paving the way for the Scots pines which eventually became dominant in what is known as Caledonian forest. In an area of woodland in the south of the garden a representative sample of Caledonian forest is being nurtured, using Scots pines which were raised from seed collected in Caledonian forest in Braemar about 150 years ago, along with a natural ground flora. This project ties in with the Royal Botanic Garden's programme of research into Scotland's distinctive flora and vegetation. In addition, Dawyck is also undertaking the cultivation of selected

Mature Scots pine on the hill slopes at Dawyck are being underplanted with associated native ground flora.

Scottish wild plants in order to promote interest in Scotland's heritage and provide resources for study. Dawyck is ideal for this purpose, with its extensive semi-natural areas and climatic conditions that suit many of Scotland's upland species. Before long, visitors to Dawyck in the summer will not only enjoy walking through Caledonian forest but may also have a taste of the Highlands as Dawyck's steep banks turn purple with heather.

AUTUMN AND WINTER

Dawyck is a haven of peace in which to appreciate the rich colours and golden light of autumn, and throughout the winter is virtually undisturbed. Occasional snowfalls transform Dawyck, the monochrome effect of the snow highlighting the stream as it runs darkly between white banks, outlining the bare deciduous trees and etching the details of conifer foliage so that the character of each species is instantly revealed. And when the snow melts, up come the snowdrops in their thousands. Legend has it that snowdrops were created by an angel. Adam and Eve were driven from Paradise, so the story goes, into a bare snow-covered landscape. They were terrified, having never experienced winter's harshness before, so God took pity and sent an angel to reassure them that growth would return in the spring. As proof of this promise, the angel took a handful of snowflakes and threw them to the ground, whereupon they turned into snowdrops. The delicacy of snowdrops is combined with an exceptional toughness, their leaves and flower buds reinforced at the tips to pierce the frozen earth, and their fragile petals undamaged by the severest frosts. Going through most of their life cycle during the autumn and winter, they are indeed a reminder that growth does not come to an end when the autumn leaves - or the snowflakes - fall.

Snowdrops bloom in profusion at Dawyck on the banks of the Scrape Burn.

Fruits and nuts

Autumn fruits take on an almost infinite variety of shapes, colours and textures, from acorns in cups and colourful crab apples to maple keys and fir cones. A great range of these and others can be found at Dawyck. Even among the familiar there are surprises, such as the tiny cherry-like crab apples of *Malus hupehensis* or the pink winged fruits of *Acer erianthum*. Then there are the distinctly odd - the inflated pale green pods of the bladdernut (*Staphylea colchica*) and the massive globular cones of the monkey puzzle tree (*Araucaria araucana*).

Of deciduous trees, the beeches dominate Dawyck in autumn as in spring, their lettuce green now changed to a foxy red-brown. Among the fallen leaves are the four-lobed woody husks of the beech nuts which have a prickly outer layer and a velvety lining of greenish-gold hairs to protect the pair of triangular nuts. Beech mast is an important source of food for wild animals and birds whose activities at this time of year may easily be observed in the woods at Dawyck.

Everyone's favourites among autumn fruits are the conkers produced by the horse chestnut trees (*Aesculus hippocastanum*). The large hand-shaped leaves turn yellow and brown early in the season, drifting down to join the spiky fruits which fall heavily to earth in September. As has already been mentioned, the common horse

Left. Dawyck's collection of rowans includes *Sorbus commixta*, a red-fruited Japanese species which turns spectacular colours in autumn.

Below. The horse chestnut is a familar tree, especially in autumn when its conkers (*Top*) and yellow hand-shaped leaves (*Bottom*) begin to fall.

chestnut is not native to Britain but was introduced in the 1650s - Dawyck being the first estate in Scotland on which they were planted. Descendants of these pioneers can be seen near the entrance. Also grown at Dawyck is the Japanese horse chestnut (*A. turbinata*) which has larger leaves and flowers slightly later - in June rather than May - but otherwise looks similar. According to John Evelyn (1620-1706), author and diarist, the horse chestnut is so-called 'from its curing horses brokenwinded and other cattle of coughs'.

Whether poisonous or not, berries always look luscious, with their bright colours which are designed to attract birds and small mammals - who obviously find red, orange and yellow as appealing as we do. Brightest of all are the glossy red fruits of the fly honeysuckle (*Lonicera xylosteum*), an arching shrub which grows in profusion alongside the stream as it flows from Dynamo Pond. The berries are in fact its main attraction, the yellowish-white flowers being insignificant. This species is listed in British floras, as it apparently occurs wild in Sussex. However, it is mainly distributed across the European mainland into western Siberia. Dawyck's plants were collected as seed at Archangel in 1922 by Dr Balfour Gourlay, a relative of F R S Balfour, whilst a doctor with the British Expeditionary Force.

As a group, the rowans and whitebeams (*Sorbus*) are unfailingly attractive when in fruit. Dawyck has a very good collection of this genus, with some 45 species - a handful of which are not represented in the other three gardens. The rarities include *S. esserteauana* which occurs in a very small area of western China, and *S. sitchensis* from western North America. The former has small red fruits that are among the last to ripen; the latter produces pink berries which are soon gobbled up by the birds. Both have colourful autumn foliage too.

Most of the *Sorbus* collection is located south and west of the chapel. As well as the botanically interesting, it contains a good range of the most popular species in cultivation, including the blue-leaved pink-fruited *S. hupehensis*; 'Joseph Rock' with yellow berries and rich autumn colour; the white-fruited *S. cashmeriana*, *S. prattii* and *S. forrestii*; and *S. commixta* which has few rivals among red-fruited species for its vivid autumn colour. Also worth seeing is the specimen of *S. alnifolia* on Chapel Bank, which at over 45ft is one of the largest in Britain. This Japanese whitebeam has bright red egg-shaped fruits and ovate leaves that turn fiery colours in the autumn.

Fruits of the rare *Sorbus pseudofennica* from the Isle of Arran (*Top*), the Chinese crab apple (*Malus hupehensis*) (*Bottom right*) and cones of the monkey puzzle (*Araucaria araucana*) (*Bottom left*).

Curiosities of Scrape Glen

One of Dawyck's most attractive features is the view upstream to the Swiss Bridge which changes dramatically through the seasons. Overhanging Scrape Glen is a large Japanese katsura tree (*Cercidiphyllum japonicum*) which in early autumn fills the air with a caramel scent as its leaves turn a pale biscuit colour. As autumn advances, the Japanese maples (*Acer palmatum*) and spindles (*Euonymus*) stand out with their colourful foliage.

Scrape Glen has some very unusual trees and shrubs. Quite outstanding is *Kalopanax pictus* var. *maximowiczii*, the only species in a genus that belongs to the ivy family (Araliaceae). It has outsize ivy-like leaves, thorn-clad branches and, in autumn, heads of white flowers which measure up to 2ft across. Dawyck's specimen is the largest in Britain - over 60ft at the last count. Also little-known is *Euptelea polyandra*. This forms a large shrub or small tree with toothed leaves that turn lovely colours before they fall, and red-anthered petalless flowers along the bare branches in spring. Both *Kalopanax* and *Euptelea* are from Japan.

Above. Spindles (*Euonymus*) are hung with eye-catching fruits, consisting of brightly coloured seeds that dangle from a capsule to attract passing birds.

Left. Scrape Glen reveals a medley of autumn colours in the view upstream to the Swiss Bridge.

Birches

Birches (*Betula*) are characteristic of some of the coldest regions on earth, from exposed mountainsides and upland bogs in North America, Europe and Asia, to within the Arctic Circle in Alaska, Iceland and Greenland. There are over 40 species in the genus, ranging from small shrubs to trees over 100ft tall. In general, birch trees are light, graceful trees with slender twigs and small ovate leaves which turn yellow in autumn. All bear catkins in spring; the males being conspicuous and drooping; the females smaller and upright. The fruiting catkins take the form of soft scaly cones which contain minute winged seeds.

A dominant feature of birches is the bark which in many species is a silvery-white and peels away in horizontal strips. Though now valued largely for its ornamental appearance, for thousands of years birch bark has been of practical importance in many different cultures. Being tough and waterproof on account of the oil ('birch tar') content, yet easily split into fine layers, it is used to make paper, canoes, roofing tiles, gaiters, baskets and boxes, and in the tanning of leather. Indeed, the word 'birch' comes from the ancient Sanskrit bhurga, meaning 'a tree whose bark is used for writing upon'. Virtually all other parts of the tree have their uses too: the timber for utilitarian furniture, household articles, firewood and gunpowder charcoal; the twigs for thatching, brooms and flexible rods (as in 'the birch' for flogging offenders); the sap, drawn from the tree in spring, for medicinal purposes and for making beer, wine, spirits and vinegar; the leaves as a diuretic tea; and the oil for medicated soaps and insect repellants.

A collection of birches is being established at Dawyck on the grassy plateau to the south of the Chapel. One of the best birches for autumn colour is the yellow birch (*B. alleghaniensis*, formerly *B. lutea*) from eastern North America. It has larger leaves than most - over 4in long and 2in across - which turn bright yellow before falling and when fresh are aromatic, smelling like oil of wintergreen. The bark is a silvery-yellow to amber, peeling away to show new layers of golden-brown.

Among the less commonly seen species are two of the hardiest birches: *B. davurica* from Korea and northern Asia, a species with noticeably rugged bark; and *B. pubescens* subsp. *carpathica*, an exceedingly tough form of the common white or downy birch which grows wild from Iceland to the Carpathian Mountains of central and eastern Europe. *B. pubescens* is very similar in appearance to the silver birch

Above. The foliage of the Japanese katsura tree turns delightful colours in autumn.

Below. The fruiting bodies (toadstools) of the honey fungus (*Armillaria*) appear at the base of infected trees in autumn (*Left*), indicating that the tree's days are numbered. These were photographed on one of the ancient beeches in Dawyck's famous Beech Walk (*Right*).

(*B. pendula*) but can be told apart by its more upright twigs, whiter bark that lacks the black ridges, and rounder, more evenly toothed leaves on downy stalks. There are about 14 species of birch in the collection to date and further additions are planned as wild-origin material becomes available.

With most of the major restoration work now over, the emphasis at Dawyck in recent years has shifted toward the planting of scientific collections - though this in itself entails new clearing and landscaping. A great deal of importance is attached to planting in ways that enhance the landscape so that the garden develops simultaneously as an amenity and a resource for research and education. Thus there are birches and rowans on top of the hill, cotoneasters and barberries (*Berberis*) clinging to steep banks, and thickets of spiraeas beside the stream - plantings that can be appreciated by visitors and specialists alike.

Dawyck's great potential was obvious from the beginning, with its historic trees, incomparable setting and value as a site for growing the hardier trees and shrubs from montane and far-northern regions. Seeing that potential unfold in its new role as a botanic garden is as exciting for the staff today as it was for the Veitches, Naesmyths and Balfours as they shaped the estate.

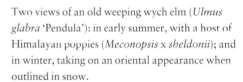
Two views of an old weeping wych elm (*Ulmus glabra* 'Pendula'): in early summer, with a host of Himalayan poppies (*Meconopsis* x *sheldonii*); and in winter, taking on an oriental appearance when outlined in snow.

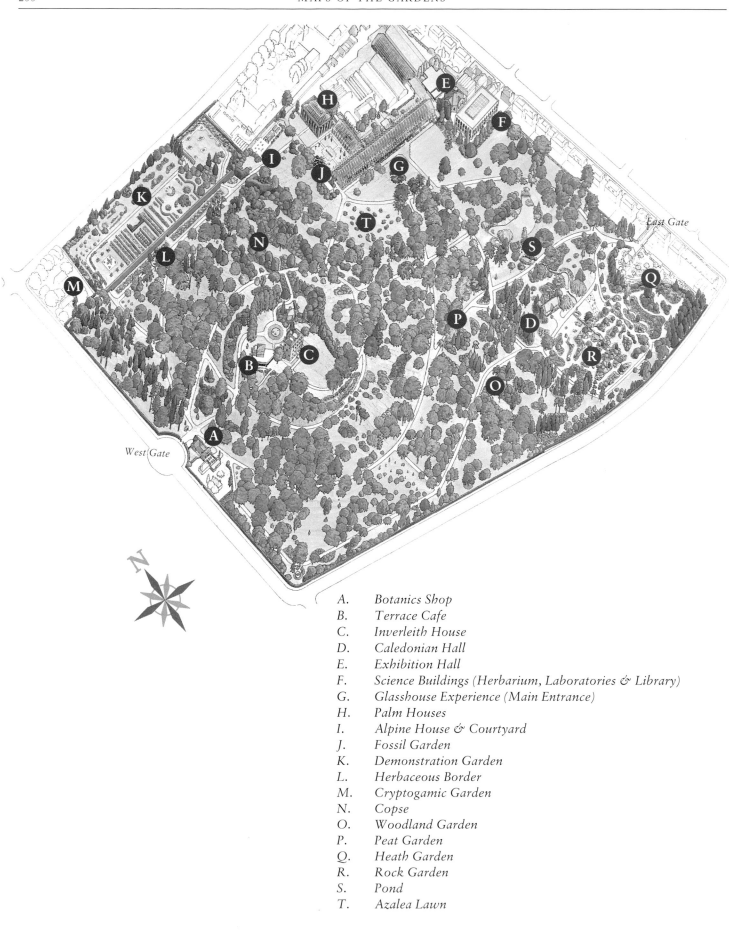

A.   Botanics Shop
B.   Terrace Cafe
C.   Inverleith House
D.   Caledonian Hall
E.   Exhibition Hall
F.   Science Buildings (Herbarium, Laboratories & Library)
G.   Glasshouse Experience (Main Entrance)
H.   Palm Houses
I.   Alpine House & Courtyard
J.   Fossil Garden
K.   Demonstration Garden
L.   Herbaceous Border
M.   Cryptogamic Garden
N.   Copse
O.   Woodland Garden
P.   Peat Garden
Q.   Heath Garden
R.   Rock Garden
S.   Pond
T.   Azalea Lawn

ROYAL BOTANIC GARDEN EDINBURGH
VISITOR INFORMATION

OPENING TIMES
The Garden is open every day except 25 December (Christmas Day) and 1 January (New Year's Day). The Garden opens at 10.00am. The Garden closes at 4pm November to February; 6pm March to April; 8pm May to August; 6pm September to October.
The Glasshouse Experience, Terrace Cafe and Exhibition Venues are open 10.00am to 5pm daily (close at 3.45pm November to February). The Botanics Shop is open daily 10am to 5pm with regular extensions.

ADMISSION
Admission to the Garden is free. Voluntary donations are invited, especially for the Glasshouse Experience. There is a charge for admission to selected exhibitions. A Garden Guide Service offers daily tours from April to September, and at all times to pre-booked groups. Adult, student and school groups are welcomed, but are asked to notify the Education Officer in advance. Special education services are available on request.

FACILITIES FOR THE DISABLED
All major buildings and areas of the Garden are accessible to disabled visitors, including the Shop, Terrace Cafe, Inverleith House, and Glasshouse Experience. Disabled toilets are available. Wheelchairs and an Electric Buggy are available on request from the West Gate.

PARKING
There is ample on-street parking near the West Gate in Arboretum Place.

REFRESHMENTS
The Terrace Cafe offers a full range of refreshments, with table licence, including morning coffee, luncheon and afternoon tea.

SHOP
The Botanics Shop beside the West Gate sells a wide variety of gifts, souvenirs, cards, books and gardening items as well as an exciting range of plants.

REGULATIONS
Animals : No animals except Guide Dogs should be brought in to the Garden.
Photography & Sketching : Are permitted for private use; equipment should not disrupt garden activities or other visitors.
Special permission and payment of fees is necessary for any commercial photography, filming or illustration.
Picnicking : Picnics are not allowed in the Garden.

LOCATION & ACCESS
The Garden is located in the Inverleith district of Edinburgh, about 1 mile north of the centre of the city. City bus services 8, 19, 23 & 27 stop at the East Gate on Inverleith Row. Access to the Garden Offices, the Science Buildings (including Herbarium and Library) as well as the Lecture Theatre and Teaching and Conference Rooms is at 20A Inverleith Row, about 150 metres north of the East Gate.

For further information please contact:
The Garden Secretary
Royal Botanic Garden
Inverleith Row
Edinburgh EH3 5LR
Tel: 031 552 7171
Fax: 031 552 0382

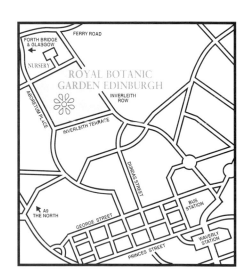

FRIENDS OF THE ROYAL BOTANIC GARDEN
Set up in 1991, the Friends aims are to support the Garden, encourage interest in its work and raise funds for future developments. To become a member or for further information please contact: The Honorary Secretary, The Friends of the Royal Botanic Garden, Royal Botanic Garden, Edinburgh EH3 5LR. Tel : 031 552 5339

THE BOTANICS TRADING COMPANY LIMITED
Set up in 1992 BTC is responsible for commercial operations at each of the Gardens and covenants its proceeds to the Royal Botanic Garden Edinburgh. Please contact: The Managing Director, The Botanics Trading Company, Royal Botanic Garden, Edinburgh EH3 5LR. Tel 031 552 7171

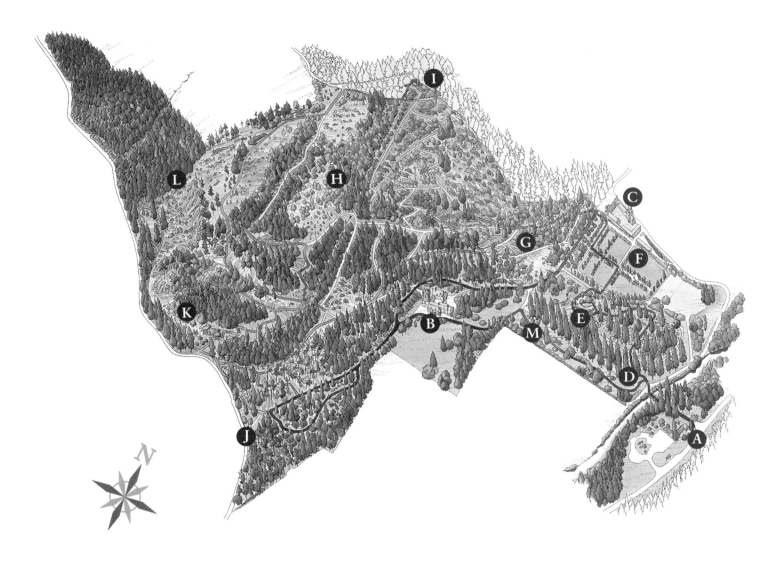

A.   Visitor Reception (including Tea Room & Shop)
B.   Benmore House (private)
C.   Benmore Courtyard (Botanic Garden Offices)
D.   Redwood Avenue
E.   Pond
F.   Formal Garden & Puck's Hut
G.   Rhododendron Bank
H.   Benmore Hill Arboretum
I.   Viewpoint & Wright Smith Memorial Shelter
J.   Golden Gates
K.   Glen Massan Arboretum
L.   Bhutanese Glade
M.   Younger Memorial Walk

YOUNGER BOTANIC GARDEN BENMORE
VISITOR INFORMATION

OPENING TIMES
The Garden is open daily, 15 March to 31 October 10.00am to 6.00pm and at other times by special arrangement.

ADMISSION
There is an admission charge, with concessionary rates for senior citizens, unemployed, disabled, full-time students, and school age children. Pre-school children are admitted free. Educational groups are also admitted free by prior arrangement. Party Vouchers offering a 10% discount on day admission prices are available for groups of 11 or more paying visitors. Season Tickets are available, which also admit the holder to the Botanic Gardens at Logan and Dawyck.

FACILITIES FOR THE DISABLED
The Tea Room and Shop are easily accessed, and there are disabled toilets. Wheelchairs are available on request. These are ideally suited to exploring the extensive lower areas of the Garden.

PARKING
Free parking is provided beside the Garden entrance, close to the Tea Room and Shop, for coaches, cars and other vehicles.

REFRESHMENTS
The Tea Room offers coffees, teas, snacks and light meals to Garden visitors daily throughout the season.

SHOP
The Garden Shop sells cards, books, and gifts as well as an exciting range of plants.

REGULATIONS:
A full set of regulations is displayed at the entrance to the Garden. *Please note:*
> Animals: Dogs are admitted but must be kept on a short leash. No other animals should be brought into the Garden.
> Photography & Sketching: Are permitted for private use; equipment should not disrupt garden activities or other visitors. Special permission and payment of fees is necessary for any commercial photography, filming or illustration.
> Picnicking: Picnics are permitted in the Garden, but not in the vicinity of the Tea Room; please avoid leaving any litter.

LOCATION & ACCESS
The Garden is situated on the Cowal peninsula in Argyllshire, 7 miles north of Dunoon, between the head of Holy Loch and the foot of Lock Eck. Situated beside the A815, it is readily approached from the north via Arrochar or Inveraray (no public transport), or via the regular car and passenger ferry services across the River Clyde from Gourock (which has rail links) to Dunoon. During the summer a bus service operates from Dunoon to the Garden.

For further information please contact:
The Assistant Curator
Younger Botanic Garden
Benmore
Dunoon
Argyll PA23 8QU
Tel: 0369 6261
Fax: 0369 6369

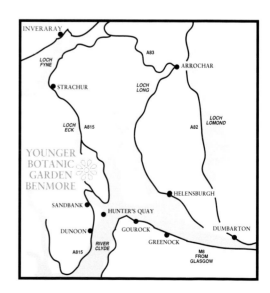

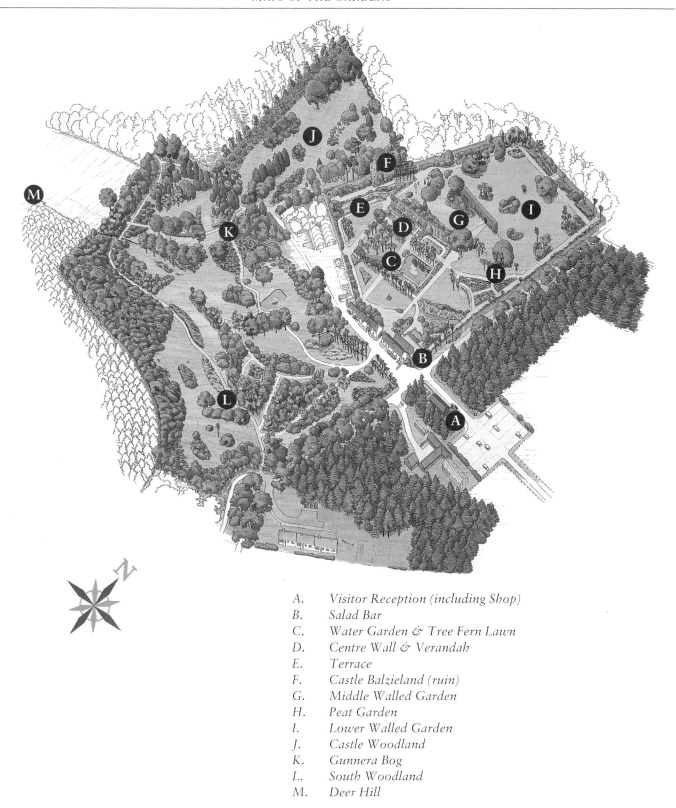

A.   *Visitor Reception (including Shop)*
B.   *Salad Bar*
C.   *Water Garden & Tree Fern Lawn*
D.   *Centre Wall & Verandah*
E.   *Terrace*
F.   *Castle Balzieland (ruin)*
G.   *Middle Walled Garden*
H.   *Peat Garden*
I.   *Lower Walled Garden*
J.   *Castle Woodland*
K.   *Gunnera Bog*
L.   *South Woodland*
M.   *Deer Hill*

LOGAN BOTANIC GARDEN
VISITOR INFORMATION

OPENING TIMES
The Garden is open daily, 15 March to 31 October 10.00am to 6.00pm and at other times by special arrangement.

ADMISSION
There is an admission charge, with concessionary rates for senior citizens, unemployed, disabled, full-time students, and school age children. Pre-school children are admitted free. Educational groups are also admitted free by prior arrangement. Party Vouchers offering a 10% discount on day admission prices are available for groups of 11 or more paying visitors. Season Tickets are available, which also admit the holder to the Botanic Gardens at Benmore and Dawyck.

FACILITIES FOR THE DISABLED
The Salad Bar and Shop are easily accessed, and there are disabled toilets. Wheelchairs are available on request. These are ideally suited to exploring the major parts of the Garden.

PARKING
Free parking is provided beside the Garden entrance, close to the Salad Bar and Shop, for coaches, cars and other vehicles.

REFRESHMENTS
The Salad Bar offers coffees, teas, snacks and hearty meals to Garden visitors daily throughout the season.

SHOP
There is a Shop beside the entrance selling cards, books, and gifts as well as an exciting range of plants.

REGULATIONS:
A full set of regulations is displayed at the entrance to the Garden. *Please note:*
    Animals: No animals except Guide Dogs should be brought into the Garden.
    Photography & Sketching: Are permitted for private use; equipment should not disrupt garden activities or other visitors.
    Special permission and payment of fees is necessary for any commercial photography, filming or illustration.
    Picnicking: Picnics are permitted in the Garden, but not in the vicinity of the Salad Bar; please avoid leaving any litter.

LOCATION & ACCESS
The Garden is situated in the Rhinns of Galloway, in Wigtownshire, 14 miles south of Stranraer. It is accessed from the B7065, about 1 mile outside Port Logan.

For further information please contact:
The Assistant Curator
Logan Botanic Garden
Port Logan
Stranraer
Wigtownshire DG9 9ND
Tel: 0776 86231
Fax: 0776 86333

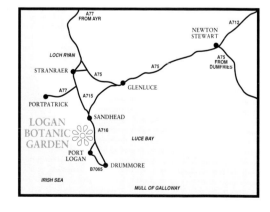

A.   Visitor Reception (including Shop & Cafe)
B.   Dawyck House (Private)
C.   Chapel
D.   Azalea Terrace
E.   Rhododendron Walk
F.   Scrape Glen & Swiss Bridge
G.   Chapel Bank
H.   Dynamo Pond
I.   Policy Bank
J.   Beech Walk
K.   Heron Wood
L.   Shaw Brae

DAWYCK BOTANIC GARDEN
VISITOR INFORMATION

OPENING TIMES
The Garden is open daily, 15 March to 22 October 10.00am to 6.00pm and at other times by special arrangement.

ADMISSION
There is an admission charge, with concessionary rates for senior citizens, unemployed, disabled, full-time students, and school age children. Pre-school children are admitted free. Educational groups are also admitted free by prior arrangement. Party Vouchers offering a 10% discount on day admission prices are available for groups of 11 or more paying visitors. Season Tickets are available, which also admit the holder to the Botanic Gardens at Logan and Benmore.

FACILITIES FOR THE DISABLED
The Conservatory and Shop are easily accessed, and there are disabled toilets. Wheelchairs are available on request. These are ideally suited for exploring the major tracks in the Garden.

PARKING
Free parking is provided beside the Garden entrance, close to the Conservatory and Shop, for coaches, cars and other vehicles.

REFRESHMENTS
The Conservatory offers a limited range of refreshments.

SHOP
There is a small Shop selling cards, books, gifts and plants.

REGULATIONS:
A full set of regulations is displayed at the entrance to the Garden. *Please note:*
    Animals: No animals except Guide Dogs should be brought into the Garden.
    Photography & Sketching: Are permitted for private use; equipment should not disrupt garden activities or other visitors.
    Special permission and payment of fees is necessary for any commercial photography, filming or illustration.
    Picnicking: Picnics are permitted in the Garden; please avoid leaving any litter.

LOCATION & ACCESS
The Garden is situated in Tweeddale, 8 miles southwest of Peebles on the B712, midway between Stobo and Drumelzier.

For further information please contact:
The Assistant Curator
Dawyck Botanic Garden
Stobo
Peeblesshire EH45 9JU
Tel: 0721 760254
Fax: 0721 760214

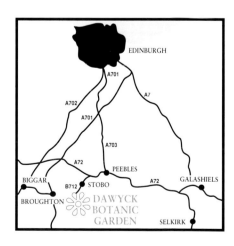

INDEX

Note: Page numbers in italics refer to illustrations.